ACADEMIA LUNARE

Spec Fic for Newbies
Vol 2

A Beginner's Guide to Writing More Subgenres of Science Fiction, Fantasy, and Horror

Tiffani Angus and Val Nolan

Cover Image © Francesca Barbini 2024

Text © Tiffani Angus and Val Nolan 2024

First published by Luna Press Publishing, Edinburgh, 2024

The right of Tiffani Angus and Val Nolan to be identified as the Authors of the Work has been asserted by each of them in accordance with the Copyright, Designs and Patents Act 1988.

Spec Fic for Newbies Vol 2 © 2024. All rights reserved. No part of this publication may be reproduced, stored in a retrieval system, or transmitted in any form or by any means, electronic, mechanical, photocopy, recording or otherwise, without prior written permission of the copyright owners. Nor can it be circulated in any form of binding or cover other than that in which it is published and without similar condition including this condition being imposed on a subsequent purchaser.

www.lunapresspublishing.com

ISBN-13: 978-1-915556-47-9

For all the cats who are lucky enough to 'own' a writer.

From Jones to Greebo to Spot to Churchill to Goose, SFF/H is cats all the way down.

The Internet was made for them, and our favourite genres wouldn't exist if not for them.

"In ancient times cats were worshipped as gods; they have not forgotten this."
Terry Pratchett

Contents

INTRODUCTION	1

CHAPTER ONE - SCIENCE FICTION — 5

SPACE OPERA	7
ASTRONAUTS	16
FIRST CONTACT	24
CLIMATE FICTION	32
PANDEMIC FICTION	40
UPLIFTED ANIMALS	48
SUBMARINE STORIES	56
MYSTERIOUS ISLANDS	64
BIOPUNK	72
THE MULTIVERSE	80

CHAPTER TWO - FANTASY — 89

MYTHIC (aka MYTHOLOGICAL) FANTASY	91
FAIRIES	99
THE GOBLIN MARKET	107
ENCHANTED CLOTHING	114
DRAGONS	122
CRYPTOZOOLOGY	130
BODY SWAPPING	138
PORTAL FANTASY	145
CARNIVALESQUE	152
COMEDIC FANTASY	160

CHAPTER THREE - HORROR 169
FOLK HORROR 171
GHOST STORIES 179
WEREWOLVES 187
POSSESSED, HAUNTED, AND CURSED ITEMS 195
ANIMALS THAT ATTACK 201
EVIL CHILDREN 208
ECOHORROR 215
GENDERCIDE 223
PLACES PEOPLE SHOULDN'T GO 232
LAST PERSON LEFT ALIVE 240

CONCLUDING THOUGHTS 247
SUBGENRES AND TROPES FROM VOLUME 1 248

REFERENCES 249

INTRODUCTION

Hailing Frequencies Open…

Some of the best times of our lives have been spent teaching Science Fiction, Fantasy, and Horror to students who want to write in some of the greatest toyboxes of literature. Some of our best experiences as teachers have been when a novice writer *gets it* and produces a work of Speculative Fiction that makes us go "*Wow*"! We have been fortunate enough to have experienced this, between us, for over two decades, delivering university lectures and workshops on writing and literature to bright-eyed undergraduates and determined postgrads at all levels. But, even so, we have barely reached a fraction of the people who want to write about, say, first contact with aliens or magical encounters with fairies or dubious exchanges with goblins. More than that, we're painfully aware that not everyone who wants to attend university gets a chance to do so, and not everyone who does so gets to study Speculative Fiction with sympathetic instructors who place it on the same tier as realist writing. In that lies the genesis of *Spec Fic for Newbies*. The project, of which this is the second volume, is our attempt to share our enthusiasm and our belief in the artistic validity of the speculative genres with as many novice writers as possible, and to do so beyond the physical, financial, and ideological walls of universities. It is our way of beaming you aboard your very own Science Fiction, Fantasy, and Horror classroom.

Of course, in this age of round-the-clock press releases from big companies promising "AI" that'll write your stories for you, some might wonder why they need a book like this at all? Can't you just get a generative algorithm to do it for you? Well, you could, but that's not writing. That's not creativity. That's not in any way *fulfilling*. Because, believe us, there's a special satisfaction in not just writing a story (or a novel or a film or a comic) but in figuring out how to write it. There's a sense of enormous gratification in challenging ourselves as creatives and, consequently, growing as people in response to that challenge. There's a special magic in being inspired. And you'll never achieve the same satisfaction from prompting an "AI" to spit out a story for you. How could you? Creation is, after all, part of what defines us. Imagination is part of who we are. And we have always told stories about characters that aren't human, about worlds that aren't ours, and about creatures that only exist in between the flickering of the campfire light. Delving into how various subgenres such as Biopunk, Mythic Fantasy, and Folk Horror came to be and then trying your hand at them is to become part of their history and evolution. And that's something a computer can never do.

How to Use *Spec Fic for Newbies* Volume 2

You may be asking yourself, "Can I use this book if I haven't read the first volume?" Well, the answer is yes, you absolutely can! This isn't the Marvel Cinematic Universe; you don't need to know everything that's come before in order to benefit. If the subgenres here appeal to you and you wish to know more about them then, yes, this book stands alone. Though we do have a way of cluing you in to what has come before; in terms of navigation, **Bolded** subgenre names here direct you to a separate section of this volume. Underlined subgenres indicate a relevant section in Volume 1 (do check out the full list at the back of the book if you're curious about what Volume 1 covered).

As with that first book, we've approached this instalment of *Spec Fic for Newbies* as though we're designing a series of writing workshops or lectures (indeed, many of the sections here are based on classes we delivered in the past). There are three main chapters—Science Fiction, Fantasy, and Horror—each containing ten sections, and each one of these sections focusing on a specific subgenre or recognisable genre trope (Dragons, for example, or Ecohorror). Our discussion of each begins with a brief history of that subject, including significant authors, texts, and stylistic developments. We then provide what we call a spotter's guide to the common manifestations of each subgenre (such as various types of ghosts or different kinds of submarines) and what sort of narrative options they offer a writer. This is followed in turn by a brief look at why it's fun to write that subgenre; by a list of additional aesthetic, historical, or intertextual approaches to consider when drafting your stories; and, finally, by a pair of activities to get you started writing. The idea is to give you a crash course in a broad variety of subgenres classified as Speculative Fiction. You can read each section individually and in any order that you like. You should also feel free to mix and match ideas *across* subgenres. That's part of the fun! Of course, as in Volume 1 we can't include *every* example from every medium. We try to be representative with our choices, but just because we didn't mention something doesn't mean we don't love it too (#TeamZardoz!).

It's our sincere hope that the ideas we discuss here will inspire you.

It's our intention that the activities we suggest (again, all based on approaches we've used in the classroom) will generate exciting new work for you.

It's our belief that your fiction will someday contribute to expanding the subgenre histories we recount here.

But, in the end, we just want you to write and to have a good time doing so!

CHAPTER ONE

SCIENCE FICTION

Make it Strange

Science Fiction is not just the literature of change and evolution; it is *itself* always changing and evolving. Venerable subgenres such as **Pandemic Fiction** that have existed for centuries are joined every day by more modern fields such as **Climate Fiction** in response to the challenges of the world around us. This evolution is directed by the writers of Science Fiction themselves using the tools of language, storytelling, and imagination to make strange all the assumptions, all the preconceptions, and all the rules that we unsee every day. Science Fiction *forces* such things back into our perception by setting them on an alien world or in the distant future. It smuggles radical ideas into our heads via rocket ship or an extraterrestrial organism's DNA. In short, it makes things weird so that we pay attention to them again, and this, known as cognitive estrangement (as theorised by academic Darko Suvin), has been the cornerstone of how Science Fiction has been read for decades.[1] Its glorious and wonderful challenges for writers thus lie in mastering the delivery of both exposition and description. We must learn the trick of conveying a (often literal) world of difference to our readers in as economical a fashion as possible.

The Science of Fiction

The sections that follow are a series of launching pads intended to get you thinking about just how these ideas of *difference* have been delivered in the past, and, crucially, how you might begin to approach the various socio-cultural, technological, and even psychological signifiers associated with each subgenre in your own work. They are designed to emphasise the permeability of subgenre barriers and how any one cluster of storytelling tropes usually overlaps with and influences those around it (**Submarine Stories**, for instance, blur into tales of **Mysterious Islands**; **Space Opera**, **Astronauts**, and **First Contact** stories exist together in a pleasing Venn

---

1. Suvin, 1972, p. 357.

diagram). They all present opportunities for experimentation; they all offer arenas for enjoyment. Practicing one subgenre will always help you improve your mastery of another. And on it goes, from the campfire tales of old to subgenres not yet conceived of!

Indeed, there's something quietly reassuring in the notion that, far from being siloed in different toolboxes, the various subgenres of Science Fiction—and, by extension, Fantasy, Horror, Romance, or whatever you want—continually draw on the same techniques to create radically different effects no matter how they're combined and recombined. Thus, the whole notion of what Science Fiction is, if we are still mad enough to be searching for a definition, becomes a description of how we use those tools. It reveals itself as a question of artistic intention and of craft. It becomes, in some respects, an issue of practice.

So go forth and practice some of the following!

Build the future one subgenre at a time!

Be Science Fiction writers!

SPACE OPERA

Beloved and scorned in equal measure—sometimes simultaneously—space opera is what most people think of when they think of Science Fiction (meaning *Star Wars*; it's *Star Wars*). Space opera is widescreen SF at its most, well… everything! Big battles, crazy Aliens, extravagant superweapons, and evil empires! It's your opportunity to empty out the toy box and smash all your action figures together! Pew, pew, pew!

A Short History of Space Opera

The term "Space Opera" was coined by Bob (Wilson) Tucker who, in 1941, wrote that "westerns are called 'horse operas', the morning housewife tear-jerkers are called 'soap operas'. For the hacky, grinding, stinking, outworn space-ship yarn, or world-saving for that matter, we offer 'space opera'".[1] Tucker intended this as a put down, but legions of readers and, later, film and television audiences embraced it as shorthand for glorious, impossible vistas and wise-cracking, seat-of-their-pants heroes and heroines. The critic David Pringle, who traces its linage through nautical adventure tales (what he brilliantly calls "Salt Opera"!), says it evokes "exuberant, adventuresome, more-than-a-little-naïve space-ship stories".[2] Meanwhile, academic Istvan Csicsery-Ronay, Jr., in one of the most comprehensive definitions, sees it as "spectacular romances set in vast, exotic outer spaces where larger-than-life protagonists encounter a variety of alien species, planetary cultures, futuristic technologies (especially weapons, spaceships and space stations), and sublime physical phenomena".[3] Yet what space opera ultimately provides, of course, is gigatonnes of fun for writers and readers alike.

Though some progenitors arguably exist (see William Cole's late-Victorian *The Struggle for Empire: A Story of the Year 2236*, 1900), space opera truly arrived in the late 1920s as a pulp-era artefact evolved from adolescent adventure fiction on the one hand and, on the other, Planetary Romances of the Edgar Rice Burroughs variety (think Sword and Sorcery set on Mars). It's Edmond Hamilton (whose penchant for destroying planets earned him the nickname "World Wrecker") who literary history records as the first significant space opera author. The prolific Hamilton's major contributions include the story 'Crashing Suns' (1928) and the Interstellar Patrol sequence that followed (1929–'30). Sweeping action-adventure meets space procedural, these tales follow galactic peacekeepers tasked

---

1. Tucker, 1941, n.p.
2. Pringle, 2000, pp. 37, 35.
3. Csicsery-Ronay, Jr., 2008, p. 218.

with resolving rogue stars, erratic nebulae, and nefarious alien threats. As Hamilton's wife Leigh Brackett—a crucial space opera creator in her own right; we'll get back to her—wrote in 1977: "Hamilton more than anybody opened up the horizons of science fiction, taking it out beyond Earth, out beyond the solar system, out to the farthest star, and still onward and onward to other galaxies".[4]

This energy would propel space opera to significant prominence in the decade that followed through writing from the likes of Jack Williamson, John W. Campbell, and others. However, as academic Lisa Yaszek points out, this early period of (mostly American) space opera was tinged with "the rhetoric of manifest destiny" and usually set in distant futures where (mostly White) humans "have colonized entire galaxies (often by engaging in war with other, usually humanoid, civilizations)".[5] Such work is laced with colonial and racist themes that are unpalatable today (and that's before one gets to the ugly strains of eugenic thought percolating through the early material). One example, first appearing the same month as 'Crashing Stars', is Philip Francis Nowlan's Buck Rogers (originally a World War I veteran named Anthony Rogers) who debuted in the hugely problematic 1928 novella *Armageddon 2419*. After 500 years in suspended animation, Rogers discovers that America has been conquered by "yellow peril" Asian caricatures. It's all quite unpleasant, and initially Earthbound, though the character—now renamed—would quickly be reinvented as the embodiment of space opera via the comic strip *Buck Rogers in the 25th Century A.D.* (1929). This in turn spawned a radio show (1932), a movie serial, and, much later, a campy 1980s television series. In the process of fighting space pirates and Martian Tiger-Men, Rogers also inspired the character Flash Gordon, created by Alex Raymond in 1934, and together these two figures went on to define space opera's zap-gun aesthetic for decades.

Most important of all, however, is surely the work of E.E. "Doc" Smith. In addition to *The Skylark of Space* (first serialised in 1928, surely *the* year for space opera), his Lensman sequence (1937–'48) proffered the ultimate foundational texts for generations of space opera readers and creators. Though academic Andy Sawyer describes the Lensman protagonists as "characters whose language and emotional development is barely advanced from the lowest level of sanitized, unchallenging children's fiction" (not atypical for the period), he's also keen to stress how it "encouraged its readers to look for big ideas".[6] In that way, the series elevated pulp offerings towards the vaster narrative possibilities presented by reaching across space *and* time.

---

4. Brackett, 1977, n.p.
5. Yaszek, 2009, p. 194.
6. Sawyer, 2009, p. 506.

This first era of space opera arguably culminates with the work of Leigh Brackett, who made a tantalising array of other worlds accessible to her readers. Brackett, sometimes called "the Queen of Space Opera" (and who would later write the first draft of the screenplay for *The Empire Strikes Back*, dir. Irvin Kershner, 1980), published her first SF story in 1940 and quickly became a pulp mainstay across the next three decades.[7] She was the first woman to be nominated for a Hugo Award, and her stylish writing displayed a talent for characterisation and dialogue as well as a vibrancy and cleverness that she injected into space opera (see 1952's *The Starmen* or 1953's *The Big Jump*). While most of her protagonists were male (a facet of the period also visible in the work of her near-contemporary Andre Norton), Brackett's writing nonetheless stood out for her refusal to sideline female characters as mere damsels in distress. Indeed, as critic Tom Milne put it, her "heroines never melt, simper, faint or whimper", something like the formidable author herself.[8]

The writers who followed Hamilton, Smith, and Brackett sought to reflect the complexities and ambiguities of the post-World War II world through "more sophisticated narratives than mere action/adventure plots with no wider consequence".[9] This new maturity is evident in challenging and influential works such as Samuel R. Delaney's proto-Cyberpunk *Nova* (1968), a tarot-toting virtuoso performance as much literary fiction as SF, and, later, in M. John Harrison's *The Centauri Device* (1974), a raw riposte to American genre writing that the author pitched as an anti-space opera. In comic books, the landmark French series *Valérian and Laureline* by Pierre Christin and Jean-Claude Mézières was first published in 1967, and its characteristic mix of space opera and Time Travel would continue until 2010. Television and filmmakers of the period also found inspiration in the subgenre, transforming it into a vehicle for melodramatic, effects-heavy crowd-pleasers. On the small screen, *Star Trek* (1966–'69) incorporated space opera's recognisable faster-than-light travel, galactic politicking, doomsday weapons, and so on into episodic adventures. Meanwhile, in cinemas, a young director named George Lucas, unable to secure the rights to Flash Gordon, set out to make his own space opera. The result was *Star Wars* (1977), a "bricolage of literary and visual sources ranging from 1930s chapter serials, to western and samurai films, and Frank Herbert's *Dune* (1965)" as well as taking heavy inspiration from *Valérian and Laureline*.[10] The film was a cultural behemoth, and in the wake of its success came Glen A. Larson's *Battlestar Galactica* (1978) and *Buck Rogers in the Twenty Fifth*

---

7. Liptak, 2015, n.p.
8. Francke, 1994, p. 83.
9. Reynolds, 2012, p. 13.
10. Wright, 2009, p. 92.

Century (1979–'81). Alongside these, the perpetually horny cult-classic *Flash Gordon* (dir. Mike Hodges, 1980) saw that hero reimagined as an all-American quarterback with an iconic soundtrack by rock band Queen. This suitably chaotic production evoked the trippy visuals of the comics and, somehow, became a fixture of Saturday-afternoon television.

The resulting clichés did not, of course, preclude creators from pursuing their own visions. The great C.J. Cherryh (multiple Hugo Awards *and* an actual asteroid named after her!) produced many distinctive space operas as part of her Alliance-Union and her Foreigner sequences during the 1980s and '90s (building on her Faded Sun trilogy, 1978–'79). Bruce Sterling's *Schismatrix* (1985) and his Hugo-winning Shaper/Mechanist stories took up the challenge of Delaney's writing with a typically hard-edged future history of polarised posthumans across a contested solar system under alien influence. Lois McMaster Bujold's signature Vorkosigan saga, particularly *Shards of Honour* (1986), utilised the vast canvas of space opera to energetic effect. Of further artistic and commercial significance are the Hugo-winning *Hyperion* (1989) and *The Fall of Hyperion* (1990) by Dan Simmons, which took *The Canterbury Tales* (c. 1387) as its model for a vast story of interstellar hegemony, AIs, and genetically modified humans. Further notable is Victor Vinge's innovative *A Fire Upon the Deep* (1992), which divided the galaxy into zones of different physical properties that in turn impacted biological and technological intelligence. Meanwhile, J. Michael Straczynski's epic *Babylon 5* (1993–'98) brought galactic tribulations and political skulduggery to television screens in perhaps the definitive space opera of the '90s, pre-empting the television-as-novel vogue of the twenty-first century with a storyline reaching thousands of years into both the past and the future.

Emerging around the same time, the field's next great innovation is known today as New Space Opera, a millennial variant that emphasises SF "as a work of art, an aesthetic construct to be enjoyed precisely because it's implausible, baroque, and surreal".[11] New Space Opera, which first developed in Britain, treats the subgenre seriously without abandoning the pulp tropes of galactic conflicts and giant spacecraft (if anything, the spacecraft became even *more* outlandish!). It's more overtly political than what came before, determined to interrogate questions of race, gender, and politics (particularly "the politics of empire"), which were left unaddressed by the "fantasies of imperialist expansion in the 1930s".[12] The most accessible example remains the landmark Culture series by Scottish writer Iain M. Banks. Gloriously unapologetic SF at its finest, the series follows various representatives and adversaries of The Culture, an immensely powerful post-scarcity interstellar

---

11. Caroti, 2015, p. 156.
12. Bould, Roberts, and Vint, 2009, p. xxi.

civilisation of multiple biological species and god-like artificial intelligences known as "minds". Banks presented The Culture as analogous to Anglo-American western hegemony, its smug superiority repeatedly undercut by stories of off-the-books interventions in the internal politics of potential competitors. Together with fellow travellers Ken MacLeod, Gwyneth Jones, Peter F. Hamilton, and, slightly later, Alastair Reynolds, Banks helped to confirm Delaney and Harrison's assertion that space opera could be a serious and undeniably literary undertaking.

Thus, once dismissed as childish (where have we heard that before?), space opera has long since become the beating heart of SF. It continues to enjoy huge success across media boundaries, with noteworthy efforts including the *Mass Effect* video games (2007–'17), the comic book *Saga* (2012–present) by Brian K. Vaughan and Fiona Staples, the film *The Guardians of the Galaxy* (dir. James Gunn, 2014), as well as a literal universe of authors putting their own distinct stamp on the subgenre. Among the most significant of these are *The Long Way to a Small, Angry Planet* (2014) by Becky Chambers, Nnedi Okorafor's wonderful Africanfuturist novella *Binti* (2015) and its sequels, Yoon Ha Lee's mind-bending *Ninefox Gambit* (2016), Kameron Hurley's powerhouse feminist novel *The Stars are Legion* (2017), Alex White's trope-revitalising *A Big Ship at the Edge of the Universe* (2018), Elizabeth Bear's barnstorming *Ancestral Night* (2019), Arkady Martine's Hugo-winning *A Memory Called Empire* (2019), and Kate Elliott's genderbent Alexander-the-Great-in-space novel *Unconquerable Sun* (2020). If such endless galaxies of imagination prove anything it is that, when it comes to space opera, the human adventure is only just beginning.

A Spotter's Guide: Strap Yourself Down!

- **Cosmic realms:** Space opera is told on *galactic* scales. These stories encompass vast distances, with the effects of that leveraged to create the feeling that anything can happen. Stories move from planet to planet without much fuss (and, as such, Spaceships are crucial). Dilapidated space stations (centres of commerce, piracy, or military power) provide frequent backdrops, as do terrifying cosmic phenomena such as nebulae or black holes. That said, more recent examples eschew the galaxy for terraformed solar systems that are made to feel vast and endless (see television's *Firefly*, 2002, or The Quiet War series by Paul McAuley, 2008–'13).
- **Deep time:** Space opera usually takes place in the far future or over impossible stretches of time, with characters often experiencing the effects of time dilation or longevity treatments (see **Biopunk**). Telling stories hundreds or even thousands of years from now frees

you from the constrains of contemporary politics, technology, social conventions, and so on. But don't forget about the deep *past* either, as the riddles of extinct alien races are reliable plot generators.
- **Empires:** Space opera is the subgenre of big—*really big*—government. Empires, Imperia, Federations, Alliances, Unions, Assemblies, and more present vast political and military entities tied together by impossible technology such as faster-than-light travel and communications. But their unwieldy nature makes them vulnerable to internal strife and rebellion, and we often find them on the verge of collapse. They'll frequently maintain a galactic repository of knowledge (see Isaac Asimov's *Foundation*, 1951) and are also known to engage in conflicts that regularly degenerate into literal wars of the worlds.
- **Superweapons:** Huge political entities have a love of equally huge symbols of power, usually weapons fuelled by imaginary super science and capable of destroying entire planets. The obvious point of reference is the Death Star from *Star Wars*, but dive into that franchise's extended universe (via *Wookieepedia*, of course!) for endless examples.
- **Crew manifest:** Any space opera is only as good as its characters. Wise-cracking scoundrels and rascals predominate here (think Han Solo and Chewbacca, or the cast of *Firefly*). Alien characters are commonplace, plus there's probably a Robot. Interpersonal conflict can offer an engaging mirror to the larger interstellar strife. Space operas make for perfect enemies-to-friends (or even enemies-to-lovers) tales and are frequently found-family narratives (Becky Chambers's books are a good example). Protagonists here have traditionally been morally straightforward, but the distinction between good and bad is less clear in New Space Opera, which is defined by its ambiguous characters.

Things That are Cool About Space Opera

Space opera serves as a narrative "stage" on which many recognizable SF elements—spaceships, aliens, Military SF, and Big Dumb Objects—"can be displayed and performed", usually as blistering tales of galactic derring-do by literally out-of-this-world characters![13] It's your chance to indulge in glorious, melodramatic, intergalactic nonsense. Do you need a cliffhanger? Then have a planet explode! Unsure of what happens next? Then drop a fleet of warships on top of your protagonists! Always remember, it's *supposed* to be over the top.

---

13. Csicsery-Ronay, Jr., 2008, p. 218.

Flying Blind on a Rocket Cycle

- **Style:** Space opera is great for writers of all levels and tastes. While early practitioners laid out a model of clean, straightforward prose, New Space Opera luxates in language and descriptive detail, but any style in between is totally valid, and many contemporary writers still succeed with efficient rather than artistic expression. We recommend you start with what you're most comfortable writing before experimenting with expanding your boundaries. Maybe you love baroque sentences and want to try something simpler? Maybe the opposite is true? Either way, space opera welcomes you with open tentacles.
- **Politics:** All stories are political (yes, *especially* the ones that aren't obviously political, as not being political is an authorial privilege). Think about who your heroes and villains represent. For example, the actions, aesthetics, and even language ("Stormtroopers") of the Empire in *Star Wars* are explicitly styled on the Nazis. The First Order of the sequel trilogy further evoke (down to the tantrums and haircuts) the neo-fascist Alt-Right of the 2010s and '20s. On the other hand, Banks's work is expressly left-leaning (like Harrison before him, this is largely in response to the conservatism of much American space opera). So, consider what you want to say with your fiction.
- **Goes with everything:** Any story can be space opera if you set it on a rickety spaceship or start things off in a disreputable alien cantina! The subgenre is infinitely customizable and readily dovetails not just with action-adventure, but with crime, mystery, romance, and any other number of genres. Consider how combining existing story types with the flavour of space opera can create something new and distinctive.
- **Hard SF:** It's not unusual to lump space opera and hard SF together, though, despite some overlap, this isn't technically correct. The main difference here is the approach to science: hard SF attempts to tell compelling stories beneath what Alastair Reynolds calls "chilly subservience to Einstein" (too much science, Reynolds goes on, "breaks Space Opera"!).[14] Space opera, by contrast, is a bit more, "Meh, here's a little faster-than-light travel as a treat". It's not beholden to physics and so is happy to reverse the polarity or slap the word "quantum" in front of basically everything. Though, at the end of the day, subgenre distinctions such as these will always collapse in the face of a good story.

---

14. Reynolds, 2012, pp. 16, 23.

- **Have fun with it:** In a lot of ways, space opera almost *invites* parody. And it's absolutely okay to have a laugh with the things that happen in your story! Consider Harry Harrison's *Star Smashers of the Galaxy Rangers* (1973) or how the 1930s *Flash Gordon* was, decades later, spoofed by *Star Trek: Voyager*'s holographic Captain Proton. Equally, space opera doesn't have anything to do with music, though some writers have made much of the possibility; for example, Catherynne M. Valente's *Space Opera* (2018) builds a delicious novel-length pun out of humanity having to sing for its survival in what is, essentially, an interstellar Eurovision Song Contest.

ACTIVITIES

The captain's table: Sitting in a dingy bar on a distant planet, your protagonist gets talking to a grizzled old space pilot. This character is full of tall tales about gigantic creatures in the depths of space, hidden caches of alien technology, and vast fleets clashing in the interstellar wastes. They are obviously exaggerating... or are they? Could these things possibly be real? Write the conversation that occurs when your protagonist challenges some of the captain's more outlandish claims.

Character selection: You're recruiting new crew members for your freighter in a spaceport at the edge of known space. Some will be humans looking to escape their past, some will be aliens with inscrutable agendas, and some may be artificial life forms fleeing enslavement. Some will be strong on engineering, others will have combat experience, and some may have linguistic or diplomatic knowledge that can aid your business. Design four characters with the potential to be a crew around whom you can build a series of space opera stories.

ASTRONAUTS

From Buzz Aldrin to Buzz Lightyear to MTV's silver Moon Person, the figure of the astronaut has firmly planted its flag on planet pop culture. These are stories about going higher, faster, and farther than ever before, with steely-eyed protagonists emphasising the science in Science Fiction. So, strap in and prepare for blast-off in 3... 2... 1...

A Short History of Astronauts

The Western term "Astronaut" derives from Greek words meaning "star" and "sailor", though the Russian version—"Cosmonaut" ("universe sailor")—is also in wide circulation. The word first came into usage at the end of the 1920s, initially derived from the French Astronomical Society's invention of "Astronautics" to describe "the problems of voyaging through space to other heavenly bodies".[1] Distinct from the galactic empires and faster-than-light travel of **Space Opera**, astronaut stories tend to have a more realistic tone (though occasionally astronauts wind up *in* space opera, such as John Crichton in *Farscape*, 1999–2003). Different from the crews of, say, *Star Trek*, astronauts typically conduct the type of missions that, with sufficient interest and training, you could conceivably see someone you know undertaking in contemporary times. This, of course, doesn't mean that they can't make for riveting drama (sometimes pivoting on actual rivets!).

The ancestors of modern astronaut stories include some of the first intentional, technological travellers to space in Jules Verne's *From the Earth to the Moon* (1865). That book and its sequel, *Around the Moon* (1869), in turn inspired the landmark silent film *Le Voyage dans la Lune* (dir. Georges Méliès, 1902). While the pulp stories that followed during the first half of the twentieth century offered a variety of fanciful Spaceships and larger-than-life heroes, it was only in the post-World War II era that "Astronaut" became a profession in its own right in both fiction and reality. 'Death of a Spaceman' (1954) by Walter M. Miller, Jr., offers offers a kind of transitional moment, portraying the life of "a spacer" as a blue-collar vocation of greasy engine rooms as redolent of battleships as anything else. More representative of the astronauts to come was the black-and-white television show *Men into Space* (1959), which sought to bring a realistic foretaste of America's space programme into people's homes (anticipating, among other things, women astronauts). The series dramatised real-world technical challenges such as orbital docking, the search for water on the Moon, and the construction of

---

[1]. *Science*, 1928, p. xiv/2.

space telescopes (but also found time for SF touches such as the discovery of an ancient extraterrestrial craft in Earth orbit). *Men Into Space* was produced in collaboration with the US Air Force's Ballistic Missile Office, and real-life footage of Atlas missile launches was used to bolster the special effects of miniature models. Indeed, astronaut fiction as we know it now would, like **Submarine Stories**, become a subgenre that evolved hand-in-hand with real-life developments. The shape of the contemporary field has thus been influenced by real space heroes such as Yuri Gagarin, the first person to successfully leave planet Earth; John Glenn, the first American to reach orbit; Valentina Tereshkova, the first woman in space; Neil Armstrong, the first person on the Moon; Sally Ride, the first known LGBTQIA+ astronaut; Mae Jemison, the first African-American woman in space; Scott Kelly, who spent almost a full year on the International Space Station; and many more.

The era of crewed spaceflight that these figures represent solidified the modern image of the astronaut in the public imagination and, in their heyday of the 1960s and '70s, astronauts were everywhere. Amid countless pulp tales, B-movies, and magazine features, an incomplete (!) but representative measure of the figure's footprint might include Jack Kirby and Stan Lee's comic book *The Fantastic Four* (1961), the protagonists of which gain superpowers from cosmic-ray exposure during spaceflight; Pierre Boulle's *La Planète des Singes*—translated as *Planet of the Apes*—and later adapted into a 1968 film (dir. Franklin J. Schaffner), which saw astronauts visiting a world where intelligent great apes are the dominant species (the film added the now famous twist ending); Martin Caidin's *Marooned* (1964), portraying an astronaut in a single-pilot capsule suffocating in space (a 1969 film version, dir. John Sturges and starring Gregory Peck, updated this to a three-person Apollo-era craft); a space-suited Barbie doll that debuted in 1965 four years before a man would walk on the Moon; Thomas M. Disch's 'Moondust, the Smell of Hay, and Dialectical Materialism' (1967), which considered the very real dangers of space as a cosmonaut awaits death after a malfunction on the lunar surface; David Bowie's song 'Space Oddity' (1969), partially inspired by the film *2001: A Space Odyssey* (dir. Stanley Kubrick, 1968), which tells the story of astronaut Major Tom stranded in space (the song was covered by, amongst others, real-life Canadian astronaut Chris Hadfield, who filmed the first music video in space aboard the International Space Station); Barry N. Malzberg's *The Falling Astronauts* (1971), which features a lunar psychological breakdown (one of several Malzberg works to express scepticism about government spaceflight); and *Capricorn One* (dir. Peter Hyams, 1977), which capitalised on post-Watergate conspiracy theorising for a story of how NASA fakes sending Elliott Gould and O.J. Simpson to the Red Planet. In that same year, legendary *Star Trek* actress Nichelle Nichols was tasked by NASA with recruiting a more diverse field of astronaut candidates, opening the door to women and minorities in particular (with the likes of Mae Jemison citing the campaign as what set her on the path to becoming an astronaut).

Arguably, some of the most artistically successful and impactful astronaut stories of this era are those of J.G. Ballard. They include 'A Question of Re-Entry' (1963), in which the first man on the Moon crashes in the jungle and is eaten by cannibals; 'My Dream of Flying to Wake Island' (1974), which features the fallout from a mental breakdown in space (this seems to happen *a lot* in fiction!); and 'News From the Sun' (1981), which typifies Ballard's notion of nostalgia for the lost possibilities of spaceflight and satellites. Of note, too, is Don DeLillo's story 'Human Moments in WWIII' (1983), which concerns a pair of astronauts observing a war-ravaged planet Earth and how their time in space transforms their perspectives. It's a neat bit of storytelling in which, appropriately, the imagined dissolution of national boundaries echoes the dissolution of genre barriers between SF and literary writing.

Throughout the 1990s and 2000s, the fictional astronaut would become even more successful in marrying drama to realistic technologies and procedures. The docudrama *Apollo 13* (dir. Ron Howard, 1995) brought that near-disastrous Moon mission to the big screen. So taken with the space race was the film's star Tom Hanks that he championed the magnificent companion television series *From the Earth to the Moon* (1998), which borrows its title from Verne to tell the story of the Apollo program from previously less-dramatised angles (such as the design and development of the Lunar Module, the struggles of the astronauts' partners, and the story of geologist Harrison Schmitt, the only professional scientist to have landed on the Moon). During the 2000s, Vaughan Stanger published a series of astronaut stories he framed as alternate Apollos, which were eventually collected in *Moondust Memories* (2014). Meanwhile, the widely successful novel *The Martian* (2011) by Andy Weir tells the story of an astronaut stranded on Mars who must survive by his wits and training (famously growing potatoes by using his own faeces as fertiliser). Such problem-solving astronauts were front and centre through the 2010s, not just in Ridley Scott's blockbuster adaptation of Weir's novel (2015), but also in the Sandra Bullock vehicle *Gravity* (dir. Alfonso Cuarón, 2013)—among the most visually stunning of space films—and *Interstellar* (dir. Christopher Nolan, 2014). Special notice, too, should be taken of 2016's *Hidden Figures* (dir. Theodore Melfi; based on the non-fiction book by Margot Lee Shetterly), which tells the real-life story of NASA's African-American women mathematicians who contributed greatly to America's earliest space missions despite the discriminations they faced. That film set the tone for the following decade of stories that sought to re-centre women and people of colour in the Space Race subgenre.

Among the more striking and celebrated examples of this trend is The Lady Astronaut series by Mary Robinette Kowal. Based on Kowal's Hugo-winning novelette 'The Lady Astronaut of Mars' (2012), this alternate history consists of the Hugo, Nebula, Locus, and Sideways-winning *The Calculating Stars* (2018), *The Fated Sky* (2018), and *The Relentless Moon* (2020). It begins in the 1950s with a meteorite destroying much of the American East Coast and triggering an extinction-level climate collapse (see **Climate Fiction**). In its aftermath, women are admitted to the astronaut ranks far earlier than in reality. Among them is the nuanced protagonist Dr Elma York who, as the series progresses, will be central to humanity's establishment of off-world colonies on the Moon and, eventually, Mars. Kowal wrenches her characters between personal responsibilities and professional ambitions via resonant stories of flawed human beings wrestling with thorny questions of prejudice (both misogyny and racism), religion, mental health, and politics.

Big love, too, for television's *For All Mankind* (2019–present). Like The Lady Astronaut series, *For All Mankind* brilliantly blurs the line between astronaut fiction and alternate history with, in this case, a compelling drama in which the Soviet Union beats the United States to land on the Moon and, consequently, the Space Race never ends. Beginning in an Apollo era transformed by the inclusion of women, characters of colour, and LGBTQIA+ protagonists both on the ground and in space, the series tells a generational tale spanning decades. It scrutinises how the foibles of individuals can make or break a whole civilisation's journey to the stars. Its powerful message is that the most mission-critical systems of all are human beings and their interpersonal relationships, which is an excellent lesson for storytellers to learn.

A Spotter's Guide: Rocket Science

- **Test pilots:** The stereotypical astronaut is the square-jawed American flyboy, a figured forged in the chauvinistic and patriarchal 1950s and '60s that lingers on in the popular imagination (a more feminist perspective is found in Carol Danvers's flashback scenes from 2019's *Captain Marvel*, dirs. Anna Boden and Ryan Fleck). The classic examples are Tom Wolfe's non-fiction book *The Right Stuff* (1979) and its spectacular big-screen adaptation by director Philip Kaufman in 1983. Astronauts of the test-pilot variety are born risktakers. They're all about pushing the envelope!
- **Scientists and explorers:** In the twenty-first century, these are who we most often think about when we think about astronauts. They tend to be team players with advanced degrees and significant experience—both practically and in terms of research—in both

aerospace and the hard sciences, with the goal of expanding human knowledge. Astronaut stories of this variety will usually offer what we call "competence porn", a term referring to "the very specific kind of satisfaction that we feel when watching folks competently handle complex situations using the kinds of specialized skills and expertise that we can all appreciate (even if we can't personally replicate them; see *The Martian* for a great example)".[2] Scientist astronauts also readily cross over with terraforming tales (see Kim Stanley Robinson's Mars Trilogy).

- **DIY astronauts:** Individuals with orbital aspirations building rockets in their backyards are often portrayed—occasionally even mocked—as tragic and misguided figures. Nevertheless, they can make for *fascinating* characters. Verne's "original" astronauts fall into this category but so, too, do more modern examples such as the Zambian Space Programme conceived of by Edward Makuka Nkoloso, a science teacher who hoped to beat the Americans and the Soviets to the Moon and Mars in the early 1960s. Nkoloso's training programme involved rolling recruits downhill in barrels to prepare them for re-entry and using a tyre swing to simulate weightlessness (often cutting the rope to give them experience of freefall!). The project's striking aspirational imagery is fondly remembered today and still asks us to question what we think an astronaut looks like and who gets to go into space. See Cristina De Middel's book *Afronauts* (2012) or Nuotama Bodomo's short film *Afronauts* (2014) for more.
- **Historical astronauts:** The Space Age began with the USSR's launch of Sputnik 1 in October 1957. But you're writing fiction! So, there's nothing stopping you if you want to extend it backwards to secret histories of Steampunk space travellers—riffs on Verne, for example—or to counterfactual extrapolations from the accidental invention of rockets by Chinese alchemists a thousand years ago (true story!).
- **Animal astronauts:** The first living things to leave Earth's atmosphere deserve to have their stories told. That said, a lot of the early real-life inspiration for animal astronauts have tragic endings, such the most famous space animal of all—and the first to orbit the Earth—Laika the dog, who unfortunately died aboard her capsule. Her tale has inspired many creative retellings, such as Brooke Bolander's 'Sun Dogs' (2012) and Laura Mauro's magnificent 'Looking for Laika' (2017). Many other animals did come back alive, though, including Han the chimpanzee. Sent into space in 1961, Han returned safely and lived until 1983. A variety of approaches to animal astronauts

---

2. Ayers, 2023, n.p.

are possible, with the animals themselves telling their tale or their human handlers recounting events. More fanciful instances may also involve **Uplifted Animals**.

Things That are Cool About Astronauts

At their most basic, astronaut stories are about humanity's drive for discovery. They're literally about finding out what's beyond the horizon and are a chance to write about the people who accept the very real risks and very great rewards that come with exploring an inhospitable universe. They provide unique opportunities for writers to mix fact and fiction, with cancelled missions and mothballed spacecraft designs providing avenues for tantalising stories of what might have been.

Sitting in a Tin Can Far Above the World

- **The overview effect:** Going to space changes how we think. Astronauts have long reported a kind of cognitive shift that occurs when they see planet Earth from space, one leading to "truly transformative experiences involving senses of wonder and awe, unity with nature, transcendence and universal brotherhood".[3] Consider how this might affect your astronaut characters. How might spaceflight transform their (literal) worldview? How might it effect their political, religious, or environmental beliefs? How might it change how they interact with those around them?
- **Three-dimensional spaces:** If you're writing about a traditional or near-contemporary astronaut, you're likely describing someone who works in microgravity. This means your character inhabits a truly three-dimensional environment: they probably sleep upright and keep things on the ceiling (Velcro being the most space-age material of all!) and if they let anything go it'll probably float away. Check out video fly-throughs of the International Space Station online for a good sense of what this is like. And, while it might not be glamorous, add a further realistic touch by considering space-sickness or the complicated process of using the bathroom in microgravity! See the book *Packing for Mars: The Curious Science of Life in the Void* (2010) by Mary Roach for more on the challenges of living in space (trust us, she has the gross stories).
- **Astrobiographies:** You've probably been advised to "Write about what you know", but this is perhaps better thought of as "Write what you know *emotionally* (love, loss, happiness, etc.) and research the

---

3. Vakoch, 2012, p. 29.

rest of the factual stuff"! When it comes to the latter, a great resource are the many books written by astronauts about their experiences. Ask your library to order some in (1974's *Carrying the Fire: An Astronaut's Journeys* by Apollo 11's Michael Collins is a solid example) and consult these for experiential detail and inspiration for your own stories. Also worth checking out are NASA's transcripts of actual space missions, which are available online. Aside from the technical jargon, they can provide writers with a strong feel for how astronauts and Mission Control behave.

- **For all humanity:** When we think of near-contemporary space travellers we typically think of the American or Russian variety, with the associated terminology a legacy of a time when only the USA and USSR were capable of transporting humans into orbit. Nowadays, however, a great many nations are reaching for the stars. China, for example, calls its space travellers "taikonauts" while India calls theirs "vyomanauts". Some publications, such as *The New Yorker*, have used Edward Makuka Nkoloso's term "Afronaut" to refer to space travellers from the African continent, but that's a huge swarth of territory and cultures, so maybe try to be more specific if you can (Congonauts? Pharaohnauts?). You should also have a go at making up your own terminology: think about Welsh "Cymronauts", Peruvian "Incanauts", and so on!

- **Astronauts on Earth:** Not everything an astronaut does is in space. In fact, while the space mission may initially seem the most dramatic option for storytelling, there is significant material to mine from astronauts' training and interpersonal relationships on the ground. In addition to *For All Mankind* and how it portrays family life on Earth, one might consider Douglas Coupland's *All Families are Psychotic* (2001), which follows an astronaut's dysfunctional siblings and parents. See, too, *The Wanderers* by Meg Howrey (2017). Of related interest is the question of how astronauts respond when they're grounded. The Sturgeon Award-nominated story 'The Irish Astronaut' (2013) by one of your present authors, Val Nolan, explores this territory.

ACTIVITIES

Isolation: Imagine a pair of astronauts orbiting the Earth. They've just concluded their mission when they lose communications with the ground. They have limited supplies of air, food, and water aboard their capsule. How do they react as the silent hours stretch on? What do they talk about? Will they begin to crack under the pressure? Will they disagree about attempting a dangerous landing without guidance from Mission Control?

***Mary Celeste* in space:** Your protagonist is one of a group of astronauts tasked with recovering an abandoned spacecraft in the inner solar system. Maybe it belongs to their own nation or to a competitor. What will they find aboard? Evidence of mutiny? Indications of abduction? This is an opportunity to experiment with tone by incorporating a Horror atmosphere into an SF tale.

FIRST CONTACT

Lots of SF takes place long after humanity's initial encounters with extraterrestrials, but there's something special in depicting our world's first meeting with aliens. Our protagonists often find meaning in being witnessed by an alien culture, in having the chance—as then-UN Secretary General Kurt Waldheim said on the Voyager probe's Golden Record—"to teach, if we are called upon; to be taught, if we are fortunate" (later paraphrased as a novella title by Becky Chambers). First-contact stories are thus an antidote to our existential loneliness and to the alarming notion that the universe might be known only to ourselves.

A Short History of First Contact

A subset of Aliens fiction, first-contact stories are about moments of recognition and change. The best—whether they take place in space or on Earth—offer "a meeting place between cultures or civilizations, a borderland or contact zone where there are always two sides to any story, and where exploring the radical differences between those two sides often becomes the heart of the adventure".[1] Indeed, the continued popularity of first contact as a trope betrays our "widespread fascination with, and anxiety about, the existence of other intelligent forms, and the prospect of meeting them".[2] Ancestors of the modern the modern first-contact story include well-known examples such as *The War of the Worlds* by H.G. Wells (1898), but also less remembered work such as Joseph Schlossel's 'A Message from Space' (1926), in which a ham-radio enthusiast builds his own television set and receives a transmission from an extraterrestrial who, upon realising they are being *witnessed* by another intelligent being, proceeds to tell their tale.

The trope's reliability as a story generator ensured that it continued to recur in recognisable form throughout the pulp era. Yet, it wasn't until 1945 that Murray Leinster (pseudonym of William Jenkins) introduced the term "First Contact" in his novelette of that name. Leinster's tale sees explorers from Earth encountering an alien craft in deep space. Each vessel's commander sees the obvious possibilities for trade and cultural exchange, but also the very real risk of their potentially hostile counterparts discovering their homeworld's location. While *The Encyclopedia of Science Fiction* considers the story's resolution "a gimmick" (the opposing sides essentially swap ships after removing any identifying information), it works

---

1. Rieder, 2015, p. 167.
2. Neal, 2014, p. 72.

as a Golden Age solution to a Golden Age problem.³ In its wake, the 1950s and '60s proved particularly fertile for first-contact narratives. The classic film *The Day the Earth Stood Still* (dir. Robert Wise, 1951; based on Harry Bates's 'Farewell to the Master') combined pulp energy with a post-atomic aesthetic of flying saucers and twitchy-fingered GIs for a story of an alien (and his giant Robot!) landing in Washington, D.C., as representatives of an interstellar community concerned with Earth's nuclear aggression. Arthur C. Clarke's *Childhood's End* (1953) begins with the much-imitated imagery of alien spacecraft arriving over the cities of Earth. The aliens impose peace, though in this case first contact heralds humanity's ultimate transformation. Andre Norton would profitably deploy the first-contact trope in her mid-'50s Free Traders series (sometimes known as the Solar Queen sequence). On the other hand, the masterful Argentinian comic *El Eternauta* (*The Eternaut*; 1957–'59) by Héctor Germán Oesterheld and Francisco Solano López sees a hostile first contact, with aliens invading Earth via a poisonous snowfall and a variety of surrogate beings before the story develops into a broader post-Apocalyptic narrative.

The metaphorical heft of *El Eternauta* (many read it as being about South American coups) prefigured the increased artistic and philosophical maturity of SF in the 1960s and '70s (see also **Space Opera**). Among the seminal works at the time were the novels *Solaris* (1961) and *His Master's Voice* (1967) by Polish author Stanisław Lem. Here Lem critiqued what he called the Myth of Cognitive Universality or, simply put, the optimistic idea that we could ever understand aliens. It's robust SF that resists the easy anthropomorphism found elsewhere in the genre; Lem dared to be sceptical of the human ability to comprehend the alien and to see first contact not as an optimistic answer to human longing but instead as a "radical failure".⁴ More light-hearted but equally dubious about humanity's readiness for contact is Fredric Brown's 'Puppet Show' (1962), which plays on the reader's preconceptions of what an alien "should" look like (and so has often been used in the classroom to prompt meaningful discussion of xenophobia). Ursula K. Le Guin's Hugo- and Nebula-winning *The Left Hand of Darkness* (1969) takes a long view of first contact, exploring it not as a singular event but—emphasised in its presentation as an anthropological report—as a years-long process of mutual discovery that transforms both the person doing the contacting and those who are contacted. In 1974, Larry Niven and Jerry Pournelle co-authored the self-described "*epitome* of first contact novels"⁵, *The Mote in God's Eye*, in which far-future humans unravel the dangerous secrets of a fascinating alien race. This period culminated in perhaps the most culturally significant

---

3. Langford and Nicholls, 2022, n.p.
4. Simons, 2021. p. 71.
5. Pournell and Niven, 1976, p. 100 (their emphasis).

first-contact narrative yet, Steven Spielberg's iconic *Close Encounters of the Third Kind* (1977) in which mysterious extraterrestrial activity leads to a quasi-spiritual "official" encounter between humans and aliens.

The transformative potential of first contact remained a core theme of SF throughout the late twentieth and early twenty-first centuries. Carl Sagan, the multitalented scientist responsible for sending humanity's first physical messages into space with the Pioneer plaque and the Voyager Golden Record, published the hugely influential *Contact* in 1985. The novel follows a radio astronomer (based on the real-life SETI researcher Jill Tarter) analysing a message from space containing plans for an interstellar transportation machine, one she eventually uses to meet an alien that takes the form of her deceased father. *Contact* thus unpacks potent themes around science and faith. Equally, *Dawn* (1987), the first book in the great Octavia Butler's Xenogenesis trilogy (the sequence was later renamed Lilith's Brood), explores "complex ethical dilemmas" at the "intersection of race, gender, and alien contact" as a young woman wakes from suspended animation to discover she's one of the few surviving humans rescued by aliens hundreds of years earlier.[6] The alien interest in hybridisation—genetic and otherwise—allows Butler to address a central anxiety of many first-contact stories with nuance and intelligence. Extraterrestrial interference in human affairs also forms the basis of *The State of the Art* (1989), part of Iain M. Banks's Culture series, in which a galactic superpower investigates Earth but, ultimately, decides *against* first contact so they can use humanity as a benchmark against which they can assess their interventions in other societies.

Le Guin's 'The First Contact with the Gorgonids' (1992) offers a satirical feminist tale of Americans abroad who mistake aliens for indigenous Australians. Mary Doria Russell's Arthur C. Clarke Award-winning *The Sparrow* (1996) makes overt connections between questionable Jesuit explorations of our world and humanity's first encounter with alien life. *Star Trek: First Contact* (dir. Jonathan Frakes, 1996) makes good on its title by dramatising how the humans of that franchise first officially encounter alien life (in the process, the film engendered an unsuccessful copyright infringement lawsuit from Murry Leinster's heirs, the court ruling that "First Contact" had long since become a generic term). Yet, for all of that, the defining first-contact story of the end of the century is doubtlessly Ted Chiang's *Story of Your Life* (1998; later adapted as the film *Arrival*, dir. Denis Villeneuve, 2016). In it, a linguist discovers that learning to think like aliens affects her own temporal perception. *The Three Body Problem* (2008) by Chinese writer Liu Cixin portrays first contact as a warning from extraterrestrials dissenters *not* to contact their planet further lest it leave Earth vulnerable to alien conquest (the astronomer who receives this message,

---

6. Harris-Fain, 2015, p. 41.

herself disillusioned with the Cultural Revolution, chooses to disregard the advice). Nnedi Okorafor's Africanfuturist *Lagoon* (2014) weaves together SF and folklore to explore the consequences of messy first contact via a sprawling cast of characters. *Valerian and the City of a Thousand Planets* (dir. Luc Besson, 2017; adapted from the French *Valérian and Laureline* comics by Pierre Christin and Jean-Claude Mézières) depicts multiple alien races making first contact with humanity. Meanwhile *Semiosis* (2018) by Sue Burke explores first contact with a sentient plant species on an alien planet. In the best tradition of SF, works like that from Burke, Okorafor, and Chiang ask us to think about the contact we already have with our own world and the people around us.

A Spotter's Guide: Take Me to Your Leader

- **Aliens arrive:** The most basic first-contact scenario, and the basis of any number of SF stories, is the arrival of extraterrestrials on Earth. Sometimes these are peaceful encounters, sometimes not, but in all cases they inject an unpredictable element into your narrative that forces your characters to confront the unimaginable. Such visitations can either be sanctioned contact (peaceful as in *Arrival*, or for the purposes of conquest as in *War of the Worlds*) or accidental (as in Spielberg's *ET*, 1982). Alien arrivals can be multi-domain events, taking place on land, in the air, or even at sea such as on television's *SeaQuest DSV* (1993–'96; see **Submarine Stories**). Classic variations include human interstellar travellers making contact with aliens in deep space, where the isolation often adds an element of sublime terror to the proceedings.
- **A signal received from space:** Many stories feature a message from extraterrestrial intelligence—via radio, neutrinos, gravitational waves, and more—being received on Earth. Examples include the warning from space constituting a proto-first contact in Camille Flammarion's Apocalyptic *La Fin du Monde* (1894), Lem's philosophical *His Master's Voice* (1968), Sagan's *Contact*, and the beings in *XX* by Rian Hughes (2020), who transmit themselves as digital constructs. Stories of this type are usually set in the present or, figuratively, five minutes in the future, with technology little changed from what we see around us used to decipher the alien signal. Add a little spice by playing with the timeline: maybe your alien signals are received by early-twentieth-century wireless operators, or perhaps by far-future humans who've long come to believe they're alone in the universe.
- **Too good to be true:** Some first contacts promise the world(s) but turn out to be deceitful at best and lies at worst. These Science

Fictional reflections of the deals-with-the-devil trope in Fantasy often see aliens arrive in friendship, offering to help humanity with its environmental, technological, or social ills as cover for their nefarious agenda. The classic example is the television miniseries *V* (1983; inspired by Sinclair Lewis's 1953 antifascist novel *It Can't Happen Here*); known as the Visitors, these aliens offer to share technology with humanity in exchange for valuable minerals. In actuality, they're intent on conquering the planet, softening up humanity for occupation by slowly turning people against science and scientists (wait, that sounds familiar…).

- **The aliens have no interest in us:** We imagine first contact as a two-way space-lane, but sometimes the contact is entirely on humanity's side. And the extraterrestrials? Well, sometimes they don't even notice us! Consider the enigmatic creators of the titular spacecraft in Clarke's 1973 novel *Rendezvous with Rama*. If aliens don't notice us then it denies our characters—and our fictional society—the moment of recognition we crave, something that challenges and changes humanity in a different way. Our characters may ask: are we not intelligent enough? Are we not what aliens consider worthwhile? Are we not… funny enough? Such crippling self-doubt is basically what a writer feels all the time, so put it to good use!
- **Last contact:** Occasionally a new beginning is actually the end, as in the case of contact with the last representative(s) of a dying race, who often has wisdom or knowledge to pass on (and competition for this knowledge can generate significant conflict). In the case of the heart-breaking *Star Trek: The Next Generation* episode 'The Inner Light' (dir. Peter Lauritson, 1992), an extinct race downloads the life of their representative into Captain Picard's mind. Meanwhile, Stephen Baxter's Hugo-nominated 'Last Contact' (2007) dramatises The End of the Universe and features a mysterious signal from space that just contains variations of the word "Goodbye".

Things That are Cool About First Contact

First-contact stories are about humanity's place in the universe. They're moments of Copernican de centring writ large. They ask us to imagine that we, as sentient, intelligent beings, are not alone. Indeed, many first-contact stories ask us to internalise the fact that humanity isn't even very special, and this—despite being wrapped up in funny foreheads and rubber ears—is big, profound stuff to think about. It's an opportunity to write about how our species might be changed by finding itself a part of a greater community. It's a chance to ask how coming to know the unknowable might better help us understand ourselves.

Close Encounters

- **The prime directive:** *Star Trek* fans will recognise the franchise's policy of non-interference in less technologically developed civilisations (basically, don't rock up to the Bronze Age Planet and say, "Hey, I'm from *space*!"). It's a conceit that's generated decades of drama when undercover anthropological missions go awry or a spacecraft crashes. Yet, while first contact in the *Trek* universe is carefully choreographed, many other franchises have no such compulsion. Consider *Stargate SG-1* (1997–2007), in which the US Air Force is happy to tell every mediaeval society it encounters that their gods aren't real and should be overthrown. That's a whole other kind of drama!
- **The wrong people are right for the job:** We sometimes think that the natural representatives of humanity to meet aliens for the first time are scientists or the military, but some of our best first-contact stories revolve around completely unexpected individuals. In *Close Encounters of the Third Kind*, the aliens are more interested in an electrical lineman played by Richard Dreyfuss than in the government's scientists. Equally, Lucy Kissick's *Plutoshine* (2022) grants a traumatised preteen girl the lead in humanity's first encounter with a sentient alien race.
- **Talk the talk:** First contact is all about communications. How do you say hello to an alien? How do you not offend a being you know nothing about? How do you discern their motivations? Some stories ignore the issue (*Childhood's End*, for example) but others make it their central concern. *The Story of Your Life* and *Arrival* unravel the practicalities of this conundrum in fantastic fashion and are essential reading/viewing. In Ann Leckie's Imperial Radch series, communicating with aliens is a risky proposition, with the alien Presger eating the first humans they encounter before eventually transforming dead people into dedicated translators. The difficulty of deciphering communications from alien intelligence is also a significant theme for Lem in *Solaris* and *His Master's Voice*, works that foreground the inherent unknowability or otherness of the alien. By contrast, many writers are happy to rely on universal translators, but those looking for a bit more realism might do well to think about the mechanics of alien/human chit-chat.
- **Lessons from history:** First-contact stories often provoke "questions about colonialism and racism" with our own tragic history offering examples of first contact between different peoples, often at different

technological levels.[7] First contact with Europeans had a devastating impact on the culturally sophisticated native populations of the Americas (not including the centuries-long social problems rooted in colonisation that continue to this day). Such horrific loss was caused not just by the removal of people from their ancestral lands, or by forced labour that attended the extractive colonial economies, but also by the sometimes accidental/sometimes intentional introduction of Old World diseases into populations lacking immunity. Such a viral scenario can all too readily be mapped onto almost any extraterrestrial contact narrative (see **Pandemic Fiction**) and, indeed, occurs in reverse fashion at the conclusion of *The War of the Worlds* when the Martian invaders are wiped out by terrestrial pathogens.

- **Impact on how we see ourselves:** First contact would, in many ways, be the most profound event in human history. As such, stories about it will benefit from at least tangentially addressing what Mark Neal calls the "socio-cultural and philosophical disjunction" it might provoke.[8] How would political movements on both the left and the right respond? How might the major religions react to proof of life beyond Earth, and how might that affect a particularly devout character? Or how would the environmental movement respond to an alien culture's criticism of how we've treated our planet (see **Climate Fiction**), and what kind of changes might this revelation demand of us? Beneath all this is a dilemma about "whether the exotic other can be understood in terms that are not merely a projection of what one already knows, and the risk that the contact zone might impose a redefinition on oneself".[9] That tension, more than anything else, lies at the heart of any good first-contact story.

---

7. Simons, 2021, p. 66.
8. Neal, 2014, p. 73.
9. Rieder, 2015, p. 175.

ACTIVITIES

Breaking news: Imagine you're a journalist reporting on the first summit between humans and aliens. Provide background covering how the initial contact was made, and add interviews with participants and comments from scientists or even people opposed to extraterrestrial contact. Tailor your report to the kind of newspaper you're writing for, either a respected broadsheet or a reactionary tabloid. Or perhaps go meta with a listicle of the best placards welcoming the visitors, a feature on celebrities' responses to alien life, or a survey of the best memes about the visitors' arrival!

Perspective shift: What is first contact with humans like from the perspective of the aliens? Tell this story from the point of view of the alien representative. How do they greet us? What first strikes them about human beings? What do they like or dislike about us? What do they make of our appearance or our voices? Are they suspicious, dismissive, or perhaps intimidated by us? This activity is slightly harder in that it requires you to avoid "the anthropomorphic pitfalls which appear during the process of imagining and conjuring up alien characters" to be contrasted with that of your chosen human culture.[10]

---

10. Živković, 2018, p.4.

CLIMATE FICTION

For a long time, the notion that human beings could change the Earth's climate was treated as Science Fiction... if not outright Fantasy! Yet Anthropocentric—that is human caused—climate change is now acknowledged as reality, and it's speculative writing rather than literary fiction that possesses the necessary tools to address it. This is, after all, a planetary emergency....

A Short History of Climate Fiction

As with SF more broadly, the origins of climate fiction are debated. Some scholars gesture as far back as the *Epic of Gilgamesh* (predating the Biblical flood by two millennia!) and frame climate fiction as "an ancient genre about beginnings and endings".[1] Much more recent precursors include a handful of climate-manipulation novels that appeared throughout the 1800s, such as Feddei Bulgarin's *Plausible Fantasies* (1824), in which twenty-ninth-century Russia warms its Arctic coast, or Byron Brooks's Utopian Earth Revisited (1893), which depicts a Sahara reclaimed as lakes and arable farmland. Yet, for contemporary readers, climate fiction is a modern phenomenon associated with "a growing awareness of the Anthropocene, and the scale of human impacts on planetary processes".[2] For writers, it's best thought of as work in which climate change is "central to the forces that propel the story".[3] The subgenre overlaps with Apocalyptic and Dystopian writing on the one hand, and with Solarpunk and utopian-based solutions on the other. So, too, with **Pandemic Fiction** (diseases released from thawing permafrost) and **Ecohorror** (where the Earth fights back).

Science Fiction, along with Fantasy and Horror, provides ideal responses to the climate crisis because, as academic Brent Ryan Bellamy puts it, "global warming unfolds at a spatial scale and temporal rhythm that exceed the capacities of even the most robust literary imagination".[4] Which is to say that the all-encompassing scope of climate change (philosopher Timothy Morton calls it a "hyperobject"[5]) presents representational challenges to any writer. Pondering this, the late novelist Christopher Priest described how writers of the fantastic have "three legitimate ways of dealing with climate change: (a) describing the consequences of it head-on, (b) ignoring

---

1. Dimock, 2017, n.p.
2. Sergeant, 2023, p. 1.
3. Woodbury, 2023, n.p.
4. Bellamy, 2018, p. 417.
5. Morton, 2013, p. 1.

it altogether"—which he deems "uninteresting"—"or (c) coming up with a possible solution. All three," he says, "are difficult creatively".[6] And yet, again and again, writers have risen to this task in work exhibiting a specific "sense of the environment as a process rather than as a constant or a given".[7] In this way, 1953's *The Kraken Wakes* by John Wyndham is "arguably the first work of climate fiction" as we understand it today.[8] Wyndham's novel is ostensibly an Alien-invasion narrative; however, "this escalating danger arrives in the form of disparate events across the globe over the course of years—even decades—and this, in many ways, reflects the unfolding of our current climate crisis".[9] Hiding underwater, the aliens begin to warm Earth's oceans and melt the ice caps, but the process is so slow that humanity wastes far too much time on denialism, infighting, and conspiracy-theory thinking. It is, as reviewer Matthew Seidel has astutely noted, the perfect metaphor for our contemporary climate crisis.[10]

Yet, despite a burgeoning environmental movement,[11] as well as foundational fiction including J.G. Ballard's *The Wind from Nowhere* (1961), *The Flood* (1962) and, especially, *The Burning World* (1964; expanded as *The Drought*, 1965), plus Anna Kavan's slipstream novel *Ice* (1967), "it wasn't until the late 1980s that climate change novels began to be written in significant numbers".[12] This journey paralleled mounting evidence of greenhouse gases causing global warming. One of the first works of fiction to respond to this, and one that retains its relevance, was Australian novelist George Turner's *The Sea and Summer* (1987), in which early-twenty-first-century Melbourne is drowning beneath rising seas that unequally affect the rich and poor. Nonetheless, this era's most defining work in this subgenre is Octavia E. Butler's *Parable of the Sower* (1993). A harrowing tale of social and environmental disintegration, it tells the apocalyptic story of an African-American teenager living in a parched, crime-ridden 2024 Los Angeles who escapes to Northern California where her environmental ideas expand into a new religion that will eventually lead humanity to the stars. Butler emphasises the interconnectivity of climate collapse with resource scarcity, wealth inequality, and authoritarian politics throughout (and in that way teaches us that the best climate fiction is often about more than *just* the climate).

A tsunami of work in the subgenre followed over the next three decades, with interest spiking at every "once in a lifetime" weather event or missed

---

6. Kincaid, 2023, pp. 135–136.
7. Buell, 1995, p. 6.
8. Seidel, 2022, n.p.
9. Seidel, 2022, n.p.
10. Seidel, 2022, n.p.
11. See the likes of Rachel Carson's hugely significant 1962 non-fiction book *Silent Spring*, which documented the growing harm caused by indiscriminate use of chemical pesticides.
12. Trexler, 2013, p. 8.

opportunity to arrest global temperatures. Ben Bova's *Empire Builders* (1993) presents the greenhouse effect as a cliff over which looms catastrophic ecosystem damage and sea-level rise. Gabrielle Lord's *Salt* (1998) follows its protagonists through an Australia decimated by rising salt levels, ozone-layer depletion, and infernal temperatures. Meanwhile, Maggie Gee's *The Flood* (2004) is a cutting British apocalyptic novel in which the rich live safely on high ground while the poor are left to drown in crime-ridden urban wastelands. Of particular note are two texts from the early 2010s: Paolo Bacigalupi's debut *The Windup Girl* (2010) mashes **Biopunk** with climate fiction in a novel in which "crops are regularly devastated by genetically engineered blights [and] cities threatened by risen sea levels"[13]; while trained biologist Barbara Kingsolver's *Flight Behaviour* (2012) portrays butterflies that have been throw off course by extreme weather, showing that climate change affects not just humans but our planet's wider natural community. Though the latter is a realist novel, its influence is such that it's recommended reading for spec-fic writers.

Elsewhere, the spectacle of climate collapse readily lends itself to cinema. The Mad Max franchise (1979–2024) takes place against a desolate backdrop increasingly degraded by war and pollution. The uneven *Waterworld* (dir. Kevin Reynolds, 1995) dives headfirst into postdiluvian spectacle, though its theme-park adaptation, the longest running show at Universal Studios (!), has perhaps a larger cultural footprint than the film itself. Disaster movie *The Day After Tomorrow* (dir. Roland Emmerich, 2004) offers viewers a sudden-onset Ice Age, while *Noah* (dir. Darren Aronofsky, 2014) updates the Biblical flood story for modern audiences with a distinctly SFF/H flavour as Maximus, Odin, Hermione, plus a group of Transformers, unite for a film about the effect of big-box pet stores on megafauna. Or about gun control. Or maybe about mineral rights. Honestly, it's hard to tell! More recently, the satirical *Don't Look Up* (dir. Adam McKay, 2021) uses a pending asteroid impact—that no one in government or the media wants to address—as a striking allegory for climate change. More nonsensical is the Sharknado franchise (2013–'18), though academic Mark Bould has convincingly argued that the series speaks to our Anthropocene Unconscious.[14]

Back on the page, the realist National Book Award-winning *Salvage the Bones* by Jesmyn Ward (2011) depicts working-class African Americans as they live through the Hurricane Katrina disaster. *Odds Against Tomorrow* (2013) by Nathaniel Rich (called "the first great climate-change novel" by *Rolling Stone*[15]) follows a worst-case scenario specialist whose life is turned upside down by the arrival of a superstorm. The Broken Earth Trilogy by the brilliant N.K. Jemisin (2015–'17) takes place on a fantasy

---

13. Roberts, 2010, n.p.
14. Bould, 2021, pp. 19–27.
15. Holmes, 2013, n.p

supercontinent that endures a period of catastrophic climate change every few centuries. *American War* (2017) by Canadian-Egyptian Omar El Akkad follows a climate refugee during a second American Civil War. The quietly urgent *Blackfish City* (2018) by Sam J. Miller mixes climate fiction with a welcome dash of Cyberpunk aboard a floating Arctic city after rising seas have led to huge geopolitical changes. Rita Indiana's slim but stunning *Tentacle* (2018) crosses timelines and genders for revelatory results. Kim Stanley Robinson's *The Ministry for the Future* (2020) explores how the capitalist infrastructure responsible for climate change might be dismantled. The Nebula-nominated '02 Arena' (2022) by Nigeria's Oghenechovwe Donald Ekpeki portends a future in which phytoplankton die-offs lead to an all-too-believable commodification of oxygen itself. Meanwhile Thomas Ha's 'On Planetary Palliative Care' (2023) delivers an affecting interstellar perspective on climate catastrophe.

A Spotter's Guide: Weather Report

- **Sea-level rise:** Academic Adam Trexler points out that floods have long been "the dominant literary strategy" for climate change.[16] Floods are, as he says, often used to show how climate change is typically experienced "as an estrangement from place".[17] In this way, fictional sea-level rise fulfils Darko Suvin's conception of SF as asking us to consider our world in a new and often unsettling fashion.[18] Writers in search of realistic flavour would do well to draw on accounts of how rising sea levels are threatening Pacific nations such as Tuvalu, or how New Orleans suffered devastating floods during 2005's Hurricane Katrina. Worth considering, too, are the logistical and infrastructural implications of flooding, such as how urban inundation will not just destroy homes but can spread disease among crowded populations or, more rurally, how salt water can pollute farmland leading to crop failure.
- **Extreme heat, droughts, and wildfires:** Familiar from cinema and, increasingly, from our real world, this kind of climate change is often shown to lead to resource conflict, famine, and societal collapse against a parched and dusty backdrop. Extreme heat in polar areas can lead to the melting of ice packs and have a catastrophic impact on the indigenous peoples who live there. Both Bacigalupi (in *The Water Knife*, 2015) and Claire Vaye Watkins (in *Gold Fame Citrus*, 2015) depict a drought-ravaged US filled with dusty echoes of the

---

16. Trexler, 2013, p. 24.
17. Trexler, 2013, p. 24.
18. Suvin, 1972, pp. 372–382.

American West's long history of environmental exploitation. Further notable is the brutal Indian heat wave that opens Robinson's *Ministry for the Future*. Indeed, with temperatures in the Middle East forecast to exceed human tolerance by the end of the century, there is also scope here for biopunk stories about human genetic adaptation.

- **Snowball Earth:** Science has long warned that melting ice caps may disrupt the ocean currents that distribute heat around the world and so lead, counterintuitively, to global cooling. SF, too, has found something evocative about imagining our cities covered in kilometres of ice with descriptive prose or visual imagery meshing accounts of Antarctic exploration with images of skyscrapers jutting out of the ice or tankers held firm on frozen oceans. The likes of Robert Silverberg's *Time of the Great Freeze* (1964) set the pattern for such stories with a group of climate-catastrophe survivors setting out to explore an icy North America and Atlantic Ocean. More recently, the comic *Snowpiercer* (first published in French in 1982 as *Le Transperceneige* by Jacques Lob, Benjamin Legrand, and Jean-Marc Rochette; later adapted for film, dir. Bong Joon-ho, 2013, and television, 2020–'22) finds social critique among the last survivors of humanity on a train that constantly circumnavigates a frozen Earth.

- **Biosphere collapse:** Human beings depend on the natural world, most obviously for food, but also for emotional connection to nature and even for animal companionship. Take that away and we're left with, at best, a slow slide into multigenerational despair (consider the mass die-offs of fish and birds, as well as the accelerated colony collapse of bees, which occur in James Bradley's *Clade*, 2015) or, at worst, sheer cannibalistic nihilism (as in the barren wasteland of Cormac McCarthy's *The Road*, 2006). Such collapses can factor into multiple climate-fiction scenarios. For those interested, Elizabeth Kolber's Pulitzer-winning *The Sixth Extinction* (2014) places our contemporary destruction of animal and plant species into valuable historical context.

- **Global weirding:** No, that's not a typo. This term, coined by Hunter Lovins of the Rocky Mountain Institute, but popularised by *New York Times* columnist Thomas Friedman, describes our increasingly post-normal climate conditions.[19] It acknowledges that climate change is neither equally distributed nor linear; it recognises that "the rise in average global temperature is going to lead to all sorts of crazy things—from hotter heat spells and droughts in some places, to colder cold spells and more violent storms, more intense flooding, forest fires and species loss".[20] It captures the messy, chaotic, near-

---

19. Friedman, 2007, n.p.
20. Friedman, 2007, n.p.

science-fictional aspects of climate change such as walruses in Wales or "Godzilla El Niños" in California. It prompts us to ask just how weird things can get.

Things That are Cool About Climate Fiction

Climate fiction is arguably one of the most important subgenres of literature today. Indeed, as novelist Ray Nayler puts it, "In a few generations, works of art from our time that are not engaged with concerns about the climate, the realities of human impact on our planetary environment, and our exploitative histories regarding other humans and other species will seem deeply anachronistic and naïve".[21] Climate fiction is thus a chance for you to actively address the defining challenge of our time. It is spec-fic as praxis (meaning the process by which theory is put into action), and it offers deeply human perspectives on critical issues of community, equity, political economy, vulnerability, and environmental justice.

A Storm is Coming

- **Gaia theory:** One prominent idea within environmentalism is the notion that the Earth and its organisms co-evolved, and so constitute a single synergistic and self-regulating whole. The concept was developed by chemist James Lovelock and microbiologist Lynn Margulis in the 1970s and is named for an ancient Greek personification of the Earth itself. Gaia theory maintains that planetary temperature, atmospheric composition, and even ocean salinity are all held in balance by a complex interaction of biological and geological influences. Dysregulation in one can have serious knock-on effects in another. Which is to say that you, as a writer, should consider the wider consequences of changes in your fictional biosphere.
- **Not "What if?" stories, but "if-then" stories**[22]: Academic Patrick D. Murphy makes the useful point that traditional "What if?" stories can be too easily divorced from the horrifying realities of the climate catastrophe around us; by contrast, "if-then" tales, which propose solutions (such as *The Ministry for the Future*), defy the fatalism of contemporary popular culture. This work is often "about the costs of inaction and about the efficacy and dangers of various actions".[23] Such stories are also an opportunity to foreground the vital participation of women and indigenous characters.

---

21. @raynayler, 2023, n.p.
22. Murphy, P.D., 2018, p. 426.
23. Murphy, P.D., 2018, p. 426.

- **Ecological grief:** Characters' emotional lives lie at the core of all great writing. Thus the climate fiction writer can greatly benefit from an awareness of what Ashlee Cunsolo and Neville Ellis term "the grief felt in relation to experienced or anticipated ecological losses".[24] It's an emotional dislocation that journalist Madeline Ostrander equates to the Welsh word *hiraeth*, meaning longing for a home one can no longer return to.[25] That is not to say that climate fiction should be entirely pessimistic, but instead that there's room for characters to experience and process—even mourn—the loss of the animals, plants, and landscapes (literature professor Stef Craps, for example, draws attention to the recent real-world practice of glacier funerals).[26] Paradoxically, much traditional SF is resistant to acknowledging and mourning our world's irreparable ecological damage, presumably because grief over anthropocentric environmental decline is "intermingled with feelings of guilt or shame".[27] Twenty-first-century climate fiction offers an arena in which these complicated feelings can be unravelled.
- **Geoengineered futures:** Filled with big tech and even bigger ideas, geoengineering is the most overtly science-fictional response to the climate crisis. It typically involves richly described infrastructure projects such as planetary sunshades or orbital mirrors, as in Lois McMaster Bujold's *Komarr* (1998). A more extreme example can be found in Liu Cixin's 'The Wandering Earth' (2000) in which giant "Earth engines" push the entire planet away from a predicted supernova. Writers should of course beware/rejoice (delete as appropriate!) that geoengineering can easily backfire, as it does in *Snowpiercer*, and so lead to even worse climate scenarios.
- **Climate-change denial:** One of the most frustrating aspects of contemporary environmental collapse is how many people are willing to ignore the available evidence and insist that climate change isn't real or is a conspiracy. The issue, for many, has become highly politicised. Yet it also offers a ready-made engine for conflict in your fiction. Introducing an antagonist who, for ideological or financial reasons, disputes the reality of what's happening presents your characters with an obstacle to overcome. Depending on the tone of your story, this can lend itself to moustache-twirling villains or complex and conflicted antagonists.

---

24. Cunsolo and Ellis, 2018, p. 275.
25. Ostrander, 2022, n.p.
26. Craps, 2023, p. 72.
27. Craps, 2023, pp. 71, 73.

ACTIVITIES

The water is rising: Imagine your neighbourhood fully or partially underwater. How would you describe these changes (try to use sensory language to convey the experience)? What might the government response be, or might your characters be forced to fend for themselves? Consider the origins of the flood (a cataclysmic event such as Hurricane Sandy's inundation of New York in 2012, or a slow rise over many years) as this will influence your protagonists' preparedness.

Climate refugees: An increasing aspect of real-world climate change is the phenomena of climate refugees displaced from their homes. Consider a story from the perspective of one such person, forced to travel (likely on foot) in a time of widespread disorder and crisis. Remember that this kind of climate fiction is a story about people, with the climate collapse occurring in the background. What kind of conflict—interpersonal, political, even military—might your character encounter? Will they find sanctuary at the end of their journey?

PANDEMIC FICTION

Pandemics are terrifying reminders of how vulnerable individuals and societies really are. Yet the most readily understood metaphors for pandemics are Science Fictional in nature: our bodies "are boarded by invaders like a vessel from *Star Trek* when its shields are down; we shed particles of a virus that erupts from our cells with less pizzazz than H.R. Giger's Xenomorph, perhaps, but with a similar desire to propagate".[1] Yet while there is no cure for stories about contagious or transformative diseases, there are imaginative inoculations....

A Short History of Pandemic Fiction

Science Fiction's interest in pandemics is traceable to the genre's Patient Zero, Mary Shelley, who reconnoitred the viral apocalypse subgenre in her dystopian 1826 novel *The Last Man,* a story of a plague that ravages the world. "The science of that novel," as academic Glyn Morgan points out, "is a product of its day, and Shelley's characters refer to the disease (which has attributes of various real diseases including plague, cholera, and scarlet fever) in terms of miasma rather than germ theory".[2] Nonetheless, *The Last Man* offered a tonal model for much of the pessimistic pandemic fiction to come. Classic examples include Edgar Allan Poe's much-adapted gothic tale 'The Masque of the Red Death' (1842), in which a thousand nobles take refuge in an abbey to party their way through a deadly disease outbreak outside. Little do they know, however, that they have sealed themselves in with the very illness they hoped to ignore. Poe's chilling tale would go on to influence another Red Death, this time Jack London's *The Scarlet Plague* (1912). Set in the late twenty-first century, years after most of humanity has been wiped out, London's novel is an early illustration of how comfortably pandemic fiction and post-Apocalyptic stories overlap.

While World War I (1914–'18) and the so-called Spanish Flu of 1918–'20 (it actually originated in the United States), along with the industrial level of death during World War II (1939–'45) predictably dampened enthusiasm for fiction about mass-causality events, pandemic fiction began to spread again in the second half of the twentieth century. George R. Stewart's *Earth Abides* (1949) echoes London's take on a post-plague America reverting to a more primitive existence, but it is techno-thriller *The Andromeda Strain* (1969) by Michael Crichton that best capitalised on space-age anxieties

---

1. Nolan, 2023, p. 345.
2. Morgan, 2021, p. 2.

with an extraterrestrial microbe bringing death and panic crashing down to Earth. Global disease (along with environmental collapse) again provides the backdrop for Kate Wilhelm's *Where Late the Sweet Birds Sang* (1976). Wilhelm, like London and Stewart, is as much interested in the aftermath of the pandemic as in how it immediately plays out, with a strong focus on how it affects human society across multiple generations. The biggie, of course, is Stephen King's epic *The Stand* (1978). King's book, arguably one of his best, depicts a weaponised superflu nicknamed "Captain Trips" that wipes out most of humanity and leaves the survivors in a tense battle between good and evil.

Another work of mutation that speaks to, and in some ways even anticipates, the early-twenty-first-century viral moment, is Irish writer Neil Jordan's phantasmagoric novella *The Dream of a Beast* (1983). The story follows an unnamed protagonist's transformation from suburban family man to animalistic being. In the process it prefigures the modern pandemic experience with a disquieting specificity: a "sense of lost time and future" prevails throughout the early portions of the book; the protagonist endures lockdown and social isolation—"You must keep him inside"!—as he undergoes his changes; getting a haircut or attending a dinner party become mere fantasies; and soldiers, not unlike those initially staffing COVID-19 vaccination centres, patrol the book's heretofore non-militarised spaces. In exaggerated fashion, the novella even foresaw how working from home during lockdown leads to physical and psychological transformations, our bodies becoming heavier and hairier even as our worldviews expand to question the many contradictions and absurdities of late-stage capitalism. All of which is to say that the novella portrays a now-recognisable rise of an existential biological challenge, depicts self-isolation in response to a widespread transformative event, and, perhaps most importantly, culminates in a desire for a profound reconsideration of how we live our lives.

In this way, pandemic fiction has continued to be a significant subgenre throughout the twenty-first century. One thinks immediately of the global pandemic that dominates Margaret Atwood's apocalyptic MaddAddam trilogy (2003–'13), or of Emily St. John Mandel's award-winning *Station Eleven* (2014), in which a fictional flu devastates the world. In the US, writers such as Colson Whitehead have critiqued not just the typical tropes of the Zombie narrative in his brilliant *Zone One* (2011) but have warned against any rush to normality before the pandemic is totally under control. Though *Zone One*'s protagonist exhibits what academic Svetlana Boym calls "Reflective Nostalgia"—he often recalls his childhood visits to New York but understands how that life is now gone forever—the government, "The American Phoenix", practises literal "Restorative Nostalgia" in their effort to control the end of the world. It's in fact darkly hilarious to see, from the perspective of the early 2020s, how Whitehead's satire of restorative government sloganeering ("We Make Tomorrow!"[3]) so accurately prefigured actual COVID-19 responses such as the British government's disastrous "Eat Out to Help Out" campaign. It is thus perhaps no surprise in such an atmosphere that SF in the UK has long taken a more cynical stance. Take, for instance, the post-plague responses of Alastair Reynolds's Revelation Space sequence (2000–'21), in which some humans resort to extreme self-isolation inside hermetically sealed palanquins to stay safe from infection and death. Or consider how Emma Newman's *Planetfall* series (2015–'19) presents invasive health-monitoring apps as a facet of everyday life in a germane depiction of crisis communication and the (re)construction of human interaction in our digitally dependent age.

Of course, television has also had its share of pandemics. Military action series *The Last Ship* (2014–'18) adapts the nuclear apocalypse of William Brinkley's 1988 novel for a genetically engineered flu pandemic and its impact on society and politics. More meditative is the television version of *Station Eleven* (2021–'22), which dropped at almost the exact right time for audiences during the COVID-19 pandemic. Meanwhile, on movie screens, pandemic stories lend themselves to large-scale scenes of panicked crowds and military-enforced quarantines. Terry Gilliam's *Twelve Monkeys* (1995) follows attempts by a plague-ravaged future to alter its own past by stopping the release of the disease before it happens. Wolfgang Petersen's *Outbreak* (1995; based on Richard Preston's 1994 book *The Hot Zone*) tackles a fictionalised version of the Ebola pandemic transplanted to California. Steven Soderbergh's *Contagion* (2011) is widely regarded as the gold standard of pandemic feature films, with real-life public health experts and epidemiologists praising its portrayal of the science involved in combating infectious diseases. Of note, too, is the South Korean disaster film *Flu* (dir. Kim Sung-su, 2013), though its portrayal of societal breakdown (looting, gun battles with the army, etc.) tends towards the sensationalist end of the spectrum.

More recently, it has been interesting to see works of SF teeter from imagination into the era of an actual pandemic. These include Ling Ma's timely *Severance* (2018), set in a "reimagined version of the recent past—specifically, autumn, 2011" in the aftermath of a global pandemic called Shen Fever believed to have originated in China.[4] The illness is "contracted through the inhalation of 'microscopic fungal spores'" and sends its victims "into a zombie-like cycle of repetition, endlessly performing familiar tasks unto death".[5] It's perhaps too obvious to see this as a metaphor for capitalism; better to read it, as Jiayang Fan in *The New Yorker* does, as a

---

3. Whitehead, 2011, p. 24.
4. Fan, 2018, n.p.
5. Fan, 2018, n.p.

withering disparagement of nostalgia. Elsewhere, the uncannily beautiful 'Alien Virus Love Disaster' (2018) by Abbey Mei Otis begins as "people in hospital masks come banging on our doors".[6] It quietly mutates into a thoughtful story of life transformed by external forces, an extraterrestrial agent or, perhaps, metaphorical gentrification. More interested in following the science is 'Martian Fever' by Czech author and evolutionary biologist Julie Nováková (2019). It concerns a team of scientists infected with a Martian organism and so potentially condemned to die on the Red Planet. In an interesting piece of authorial commentary, one that foreshadowed the then-imminent global hunger for scientific information, Nováková's story includes references to the scientific articles that inspired her story.

A Spotter's Guide: What Ails You?

For critic Andrew Milner, SF pandemics typically take "one of five main forms: post-apocalyptic survivalism, time-travel stories, political allegories, techno-thrillers, and, finally, scientifically plausible SF".[7] Writers, however, might also find it beneficial to think about the origins of the disease:

- **The spillover event:** A zoonotic disease is an infection transmitted between species. In situations in which there's close contact between the original host and people, such as in exotic-animal markets, there's the possibility of a disease jumping the species barrier from the existing animal reservoir into human hosts. Should such a novel virus overcome the new host species' immune response, it can very quickly begin to spread throughout the population. This, for instance, is the most likely origin of Ebola and COVID-19. The speed by which zoonotic diseases can appear lends them to stories of chaos and social panic. Moreover, their emergence is often a consequence of human environmental destruction.
- **The lab leak:** Closely tied to fears of genetic engineering and government shenanigans, a classic SF storyline is the bioweapon or experimental virus that escapes confinement (such as Justin Cronin's *The Passage*, 2006). Sometimes it infects the world; other times it's contained in a particular city or region by government intervention. Either way, these are stories that often privilege scientist-heroes bravely struggling against both the disease and human hubris. The release of the virus is almost always accidental, but some stories have disgruntled researchers or terrorists spreading the virus intentionally, as in *Twelve Monkeys*.

---

6. Otis, 2018, n.p.
7. Milner, 2022, p. 9.

- **The extraterrestrial contaminant:** Another classic SF trope is the contagious disease that falls to Earth (on a meteorite or a satellite) or is encountered by space travellers on a distant world and poses serious challenges to human medicine. The most obvious example is *The Andromeda Strain*, but one might also look to Alice Bradley Sheldon's pointed 1977 story 'The Screwfly Solution' (written as Raccoona Sheldon) in which aliens use a brain infection to cause men to murder all the women and so leave the planet empty for colonisation (see **Gendercide**). It is, as author Adam Roberts says, a story about the pandemic of "what we now call 'toxic masculinity'".[8]
- **The engineered weapon:** A reliable techno-thriller plot is the viral weapon, a particularly nasty piece of work that's sometimes designed to target a particular population or group. Releasing one is generally a war crime or the work of a totalitarian regime punishing those who stand against it (such as the *Star Trek: Deep Space Nine* episode 'The Quickening', dir. René Auberjonois, 1996). Combine this trope with the lab leak to generate stories critiquing the military-industrial complex.
- **The plague ship:** A spacecraft carrying an infectious agent looking to dock or make planetfall always presents challenges for our characters. These are stories in which "writing about disease becomes an easy metaphor for a fear of the external threat, of something different from outside".[9] Should such a vessel be allowed to dock so the crew can find treatment? Should they be warned off or even fired upon? Oh, the drama! *Plague Ship* (1956) by Andre Norton explores some of these issues. Another interesting example—a kind of plague ship within a plague ship—is found in Kim Stanley Robinson's *Aurora* (2015), which features a character presumed to be infected with an alien illness who must live their life confined to a shuttle interior.

Things That are Cool About Pandemic Fiction

People have always turned to stories in times of crisis. Yet it's SF—"itself a viral mutation, itself a literary strain that bred the Gothic and the Romantic in the moist bodies of the modern industrial-scientific age"—that's the creative industries' best contribution to modelling the directions available to both individuals and policymakers.[10] The genre speaks the rhetorical and visual language of viral times like no other. Terms like "cytokine storm" or

---

8. Roberts, 2020, n.p.
9. Morgan, 2021, p. 3.
10. Nolan, 2021, n.p.

"superspreader event" evoke "catastrophes straight out of a comic book".[11] Eerily designed mask-awareness posters seem to depict "aliens coming to devour you with a gaping mouthful of teeth".[12] Science Fiction is, in many respects, the natural "pandemic aesthetic".[13]

Pathology Report

- **Rising R numbers:** Any hugely contagious disease can burn through the global population. Its Reproduction Rate or R number (see *Contagion*) can be so high that it will overwhelm all responses. Your characters' reaction to this will be multifaceted, but remember that "fear is central to any portrayal of a pandemic".[14] How your characters respond to this will tell the reader a lot about them.
- **Vector from another subgenre:** Narratives of disease and infection offer a natural frame around which to construct stories one might think belong in entirely different subgenres. The most obvious examples are zombies and <u>Vampires,</u> for instance Richard Matheson's vampire novel *I am Legend* (1954) or M.R. Carey's zombie novel *The Girl with All the Gifts* (2014). In both cases, the authors reframe traditional Horror tropes as pandemics with scientifically explainable causes (viral and fungal respectively). This cross-genre exchange even extends to real-world public health promotion, with the United States Centres for Disease Control (CDC) using zombie metaphors and imagery "to talk about disease outbreaks and how we should respond to them".[15]
- **Exaggerating physical effects:** Some writers source their pandemic symptoms from recognisable but embellished conditions. *Blindness* (1995) by Portugal's Nobel Prize winner José Saramago depicts the social panic caused by an epidemic of sight loss; in Douglas Coupland's *Girlfriend in a Coma* (1998), a sleeping sickness leads to the end of the world, as it does again in the chilling *Nod* (2012) by Adrian Barnes; while in Octavia Butler's 'Speech Sounds' (1983), an illness deprives sufferers of the ability to read, write, and even speak. Familiar things are thus made strange by the auspices of pandemic fiction, and the results are all the more Science Fictional for it.
- **Techno-organic viruses:** We're all familiar with computer viruses but, in SF, these aren't strictly limited to our technology. Sometimes

---

11. Nolan, 2021, n.p.
12. @LibyaLiberty, 2020, n.p.
13. Nolan, 2023, p. 357.
14. Doherty and Giordano, 2020, n.p
15. Lynteris, 2019, p. 106.

they can blur the technological with the organic, such as the aptly named Techno-Organic Virus of the X-Men comics that converts people's bodies into technology. Equally, the Melding Plague of Reynolds's Revelation Space sequence combines this idea with the Extraterrestrial Contaminant for a pandemic that blends and binds (post)human organic material to the microscopic machinery inside their cells in grotesque fashion. This kind of pandemic fiction can (and frequently does) easily veer into Body Horror. As such, it also lends itself to fabulous opportunities for descriptive writing.

- **Permafrost pandemics:** Closely related to **Climate Fiction** is the notion of ancient Methuselah microbes frozen in the Arctic wastes being released by global warming. Loosely based on real-life science, these fictional pandemics are frequently framed as a direct consequence of the anthropocentric environmental damage we've inflicted on our planet. They're exciting tales in their own right, but they also serve as warnings that if we continue to abuse the Earth it'll likely cough up a dangerous reply.

ACTIVITIES

Alternate history: Pandemics are powerful drivers of historical change, so consider how a disease or illness might alter the course of human history. A great example is Robinson's *The Years of Rice and Salt* (2002), which begins with the arrival of the Black Death to Europe in the fourteenth century but, in this case, the plague kills almost everyone on the continent, opening up a radically different history in which Chinese and Islamic cultures spread across the world. Consider how *you* might change history. For example, how might Ebola have altered the European colonisation of Africa if it had arrived centuries earlier? Or how might an extraterrestrial amnesia virus have impacted the Russian Revolution?

"I haven't seen you since the plague": What happens in the years *after* your pandemic? How have your survivors started to rebuild society and, if so, have they been successful? This is Milner's "post-apocalyptic survivalism" mode and, indeed, there's much crossover here with dystopic material (see the video game *The Last of Us*, 2013) and **Last Person Left Alive** stories such as in *The Stand* or *Station Eleven*.[16] Tell the story of someone travelling from one settlement to another a decade after the end times. Has nature begun to reclaim the landscape? Are the people they meet friendly or suspicious? Do they uncover a dark secret related to the pandemic?

---

16. Milner, 2002, p. 9.

UPLIFTED ANIMALS

Do you talk to your dog? Do you converse with your cat? Sure you do! But wouldn't you love if they could talk *back*? If you could play board games together or build model spaceships with them? Well, Science Fiction has you covered! Only thing is, an intelligent beastie isn't just for the holidays… arguably they're not even an animal anymore. This is, for better or worse, the ultimate in anthropomorphism. These are uplifted animals.

A Short History of Uplifted Animals

Uplift, in SF, refers to an "assisted leap of Evolution" that transforms non-sentient beings "to a level of intelligence or technological capability comparable to or exceeding humanity's".[1] The use of the term derives from David Brin's fictional Uplift universe (1980–'98), but the concept has a long—though not completely unproblematic—history in speculative stories about our planet's animal citizens. The subgenre is an offshoot of mad-scientist stories, one fittingly hybridised with older talking-animal tales, but the key here is how the animal's increased intelligence is technologically induced (usually by humans, sometimes by <u>Aliens</u>). So, we're not talking about extraterrestrials who resemble Earth animals (looking at you, *Doctor Who* cat people) but, instead, at actual animals that have been altered by external interventions. You'll note, too, that we're not saying these animals have been "enhanced", though that's historically how the process is described, because to do so implies a hierarchy with humanity at the top.

The subgenre is usually traced to H.G. Wells's SF classic *The Island of Doctor Moreau* (1896). Moreau is a vivisectionist—a biologist who cuts open live animals for research—whose gruesome practices have led him to flee London for a **Mysterious Island**. Here he continues his agonising experiments, transforming animals into deformed human hybrids with the aim of imparting human-level intelligence to these creatures. Yet, despite some limited success, his creations eventually devolve back to their initial forms. Wells's book originates a crude distinction whereby authors associate "mental capacities—and specifically intelligence of any kind—with humanity", something we'll see again and again throughout the subgenre.[2] For example, Alexander Crawford's 1913 story 'The Experiment' presents readers with a dog that's granted human-level self-awareness and is driven mad and murderous by it. In Mikhail Bulgakov's satirical Russian novella

---

1. Langford, 2022, n.p.
2. Roy-Faderman, 2015, p. 81.

The Heart of a Dog (1925), a professor implants human testicles and a pituitary gland into a stray dog, accidentally turning the animal into an antagonistic human (called xenotransplantation, this is, bizarrely, something that "doctors" actually did in the early twentieth century with goat testicles; see 2008's non-fiction *Charlatan* by Pope Brock). The novel's intention was to lambaste Bolshevism's attempt to remake human beings, so it was quickly banned in the Soviet Union (though it circulated in dissident samizdat publications). Meanwhile, in 1938, L. Sprague de Camp began publishing his series of 'Johnny Black' stories featuring a black bear granted the intelligence of a human being, enough to save the world despite his clumsy claws and lack of human vocal cords.

The notion of uplifted animals continued to be popular throughout the following decades, with dogs and primates among the most prominent— though not the only— examples. Robert Heinlein gave the subgenre a whirl with 'Jerry Was a Man' (1941) and, while Jerry was in fact a chimpanzee, the story is notable as a civil-liberties allegory in which uplifted characters attempt to attain recognition of their human rights. Fredric Brown has aliens uplift 'The Star Mouse' (1942), with the story's protagonist proposing the creation of a new state called Mousetralia in exchange for wiping out the world's rat population. Of particular note is Olaf Stapledon's deeply moving *Sirius* (1944). Raised in a remote Welsh village, the canine Sirius is the result of an experiment in producing super-sheepdogs. In his case, he develops human-level consciousness but finds himself increasingly cut off from the world of his creators. Succumbing to loneliness and psychological trauma, Sirius eventually experiences a spiritual epiphany, finds and discards human religion, and eventually embraces his feral side in despair of human tyranny. It's a sad story, as many tales of uplifted animals are, but its sophistication has ensured its longevity among generations of readers. Elsewhere, Arthur C. Clarke depicts uplifted chimpanzees as menial workers in *Rendezvous with Rama* (1973) while, in *2001: A Space Odyssey*, his 1968 collaboration with Stanley Kubrick, he presents the tantalising notion that humans themselves are the result of animal uplift by alien forces. Throughout her Canopus in Argos series (1979–'83), Doris Lessing also tells several stories of forced evolution that explores both biological- and cultural-improvement projects conducted on humans by alien races. In 1980, Brian Aldiss visited *Moreau's Other Island* where a cyberised thalidomide victim has taken on the role of the vivisectionist in an update of the classic novel. Various characters from the *Teenage Mutant Ninja Turtles* franchise (1984–present), including its protagonists, gain intelligence and human-like anatomy via exposure to a mutagenetic substance (usually known as "the ooze"). The era's definitive take on the concept, however, has to be Brin's Uplift series, a half-dozen novels and various short stories throughout the 1980s and 1990s in which uplift is common practice in the universe, with patron races uplifting client species to sapience as a means of perpetuating civilisation and earning galactic status.

More recently, *Lives of the Monster Dogs* (1997) by Kirsten Bakis depicts a group of intelligent, elegant dogs—the upliftees of a mad Austrian in the early twentieth century—who arrive in New York City. The book is in many ways a Gothic descendent of *Doctor Moreau* and was widely hailed on publication. In Alastair Reynolds's Revelation Space universe (2000–'21), uplifted Hyperpigs serve as menial workers throughout human space having evolved accidentally from pigs cultivated for human-organ transplants. One of these characters, Scorpio, has a tremendous character arc across several books, growing from antagonistic crime-lord to trusted leader of the last human survivors in deep space. Meanwhile Carol Emschwiller's Philip K. Dick Award-winning *The Mount* (2002) flips the usual pattern with tiny invading aliens *down*lifting humans into, essentially, fancy horses. The heartbreaking comic book *We3* (2004) by Grant Morrison and Frank Quitely follows a squad of heavily armed, cybernetically enhanced animals—a dog, a cat, and a rabbit—who flee military captivity in search of a new home. Be warned: it's actually devastating. Further pulling at the heartstring are the modern *Planet of the Apes* movies, beginning with 2011's *Rise of the Planet of the Apes* (dir. Rupert Wyatt), which attribute increased primate intelligence to accidental uplift after the testing of an experimental Alzheimer's treatment on animal subjects. Nonetheless, one of the most thought-provoking contemporary takes on uplifted animals is the Adam Roberts novel *Bête* (2014) in which computer chips implanted into animal brains seem to grant the ability to communicate and even to think. The novel harkens back to Wells's original interrogation of intelligence as the defining difference between humans and animals. It initially toys with ambiguity—are the animals really speaking or are these pre-recorded messages?—but later sections clarify that the neurological transformation is genuine. This uplift permits the animals to "engage in logical thought, [and] organize into multispecies groups that engage in strategic planning", including "a takeover of rural England".[3] The animals' minds are even seen to persist in the brain chips after death, their experiences passing from one generation to the next, which is as good a metaphor for storytelling as anything else.

A Spotter's Guide: Tooth and Claw

- **They can talk!** One of the most exciting things about uplifted animals is how they can express themselves—their own thoughts, feelings, and sensory impressions of the world—in terms relatable to

---

3. Roy-Faderman, 2015, p. 86.

human characters. Because like humans, animals have inner lives… only now they can give literal voice to them through a variety of non-human narrative perspectives. Sometimes this will be broken speech (especially in the immediate aftermath of uplift); sometimes it'll have an exaggerated eloquence (often an old-timey style evoking the earliest eras of SF). Yet, in almost all cases, this ability to give voice to complicated thoughts is the key indicator that the animal has acquired human-level cognition (many critics have noted how, in these stories, human behaviour is generally characterised in mental or intellectual terms, while that of animals is defined by physical attributes; uplift is thus a means of hybridising them).

- **Experiments:** A typical uplifted-animal story begins in (or later flashes back to) the laboratory. It's a repeated beat, especially in terms of establishing sympathy for your animal protagonists. Lots of these stories were written in or set in our historical past, but contemporary variations tend to mine drama from circumventing modern scientific guardrails such as ethical oversight. Though this can be bypassed in your fiction via a mad scientist or, alternatively, by just setting your story off Earth (see *Guardians of the Galaxy Volume 3*, dir. James Gunn, 2023, which explores Rocket Racoon's backstory). Such experiments are often invasive and painful, so readers may appreciate a content warning. Note, too, that they might not be much fun to write (so don't think that you *have* to write them) but, if you do include such scenes, know that they are useful to convey the full weight of the transformation to your reader in visceral fashion.
- **Chip vs gene:** Primary routes to uplifted animals include "surgical intervention, genetic modification (including breeding programs or intervention of genetic technology), and/or techno-mechanical enhancements".[4] In practice, this boils down to neural prosthetics (as in *Bête*), tweaks to their genetic profile (sometimes accidental, as in the case of the Ninja Turtles), or a combination of both. In some cases, "uplifted animals can be regarded as Cyborgs".[5] Fantasy versions include uplift via a magical spell or a curse (often depicted as a science of sorts). Indeed, magical uplift occurs in Terry Pratchett's Discworld series; in *The Amazing Maurice and His Educated Rodents* (2001), rats gain intelligence by scavenging magic garbage and, in turn, pass this on to a cat who eats one of them. None of these approaches are narratively better or worse than the others, but they'll generally reflect the state of science and technology (often bleeding-edge research) in your story.

---

4. Roy-Faderman, 2015, p. 78.
5. Aalders, 2007, p. 3.

- **Military applications:** One of the most common depictions of uplifted animals is, sadly, their weaponisation by the military (see Military SF and **Animals That Attack**). These are often tragic stories in which animal protagonists are essentially abused. They offer metaphors for conscription or allegories for war's destructive nature and humanity's ability to turn anything into cannon fodder. The animals' traumatic experience in *We3* is the classic modern example. There are also military-adjacent stories; for instance, some uplifted animals might be **Astronauts** (a profession in which animals already have a long, albeit not voluntary, history of service. See, for example, the version of Laika the Russian space dog in *The Manhattan Projects*, 2012–'15, by Jonathan Hickman and Nick Pitarra).
- **They're still animals:** Your uplifted animals may have had their intelligence supercharged, but this isn't to say that they've been turned into humans (otherwise, wouldn't you just write about humans?). They'll usually retain at least some characteristics of their species: physical attributes (such as fur or tails); body language (such as gestures and postures); sensory traits (such as scents or specific vocalisations in addition to human dialogue); and even social conduct (such as pack behaviour or literal pecking orders). Watch and study animals, either in person if you can or via online videos, and use your descriptive prose to present a flavour of their nature.

Things That are Cool About Uplifted Animals

Talking animal stories have always been popular. They allow us to explore both the similarities and the differences between humans and animals. Uplift thus fulfil one of the core remits of SF in that, as Adam Roberts puts it, they're, "in a radical sense, about the encounter with otherness".[6] They allow animal characters to bear witness to their world and to ours. They may even prompt readers to wrestle with issues of environmental responsibility (see **Climate Fiction**) and species relations, as well as complex moral and ethical considerations. Woof!

Paws for Thought

- **Ethics:** Do our human characters have the right to uplift animals? Should they struggle with the implications of playing God and/or of potentially creating another servant caste to be abused by the worst among us? Because the basic concept of uplift raises thorny moral

---

6. Roberts, 2005, p. 138.

questions in that it assumes we're already better than animals, and, in the process—as the *Encyclopedia of Science Fiction* notes—leaves uplift rubbing shoulders with the ugly philosophy of eugenics.[7] Conversely, is there an ethical *imperative* to uplift animals? Such a discussion obviously gets dodgy in how it echoes the racism of historical White "improvement" schemes targeted at underprivileged social groups, but bioethicist George Dvorsky has argued that humans are "obligated to cognitively enhance animals if and when such technology becomes available".[8] By contrast, philosopher Michael Hauskeller deems this attitude "patronising".[9] A single paragraph in a writing guide book isn't going to resolve the issue, but maybe exploring big questions like this will grant additional moral and ethical heft to your fiction.

- **What they leave behind:** How do uplifted animals relate to others of their species who haven't been "improved"? Do they regard them as relatives or perhaps as inferiors (the reality of any story is that there'll likely be a spectrum of belief on display). What's it like to witness the abuse of their fellows? How do they feel about zoos or animal shelters? What do they think about animal skeletons in museums? Are some animals disdainful of those they've left behind, or do they see it as their responsibility to uplift others? As ever, asking ourselves questions about what our characters—animal or otherwise—believe is key to understanding them.

- **Psychology:** If our animals' intellect and cognition are raised to human levels then there's the possibility—maybe even the *inevitability*—that these creatures will be vulnerable to the same stresses and mental-health concerns that we are. Maybe a bomb-sniffing dog has PTSD? Maybe your animal experiences a learning difference or suffers from depression? Conducting some research here (reading about real experiences or even interviewing people) will ground your story and ensure it doesn't become exploitative or sensationalist. Consider, too, how mental health might shape your animal's relationships with others. How would it impact their day-to-day lives? Would they discover that diagnoses and help are difficult to come by? In this way, uplifted-animal stories are a useful means of taking allegorically about real-world challenges.

- **Animal art:** There's no reason why uplifted animals can't be as inspired as any human. After all, any number of animals already produce rudimentary "art" in real life; imagine what they might

---

7. Langford, 2022, n.p.
8. Xu, 2015, n.p.
9. Hauskeller, 2026, p. 103.

do if their abilities were boosted. Artistic expression might prove a fantastic way of sharing their experiences of the world. Alternatively, perhaps painting or writing poetry is just a hobby for your animal characters, which grants them a bit more three-dimensionality (you might include some examples of their verse in your story). Perhaps your animals are even more ambitious: maybe they're writing a *Science Fiction* novel! It is, after all, intriguing to wonder what animal spec-fic might be like....

- **How might uplifted animals change *humans*?** Like interactions with aliens or Robots, the way our human characters treat animals tells us a lot about them. Human nature being what it is, writers might consider how uplifted animals are vulnerable to persecution, prejudice, and inequality. Be sure to also consider how others might take a stand against this intolerance. While keeping in mind that it's not the responsibility of these creatures to make us better, we can ask what kind of social change their presence might engender. How would their existence in our lives transform society? Might there be a fight for legal recognition of uplifted animals as people? Could this result in "a potential future Earth civilization enlightened by diverse voices" of animals and humans alike?[10]

---

10. Roy-Faderman, 2015, p. 78.

ACTIVITIES

iFable: Select one of Aesop's fables and add cybernetic technology or genetic engineering to the mix. Perhaps an uplifted hare and tortoise compete not just with speed and persistence but with sophisticated tactical thinking. Maybe the goose that laid the golden eggs reflects on the injustices of being used for resource extraction. Perhaps the boy who cried wolf is really a story of a scorned researcher's ignored warnings about the ethical quandaries of animal uplift.

Labour is entitled to all that it creates: Write a story in which your uplifted animals form a union with the goal of improving their working conditions (see John Scalzi's *Starter Villain*, 2023, for an example). Maybe they're employees in a factory or on a dangerous construction project in outer space. Think about how, in *The Island of Doctor Moreau*, many uplifted beings are relegated to servitude. Or how Bakis's monster dogs were originally intended as soldiers. How might they wish to improve their lot? How might collective action help?

SUBMARINE STORIES

Arguably no other subject in this book has a better claim to be a sub-genre (#SorryNotSorry). But seriously, submarine stories have a long history within genre fiction, speaking directly to the exploratory, investigatory energies of classic Science Fiction as well as overlapping with mad-scientist fiction and Military SF. So, let's raise our periscope and see what's out there.

A Short History of Submarine Stories

The ocean is Earth's most unforgiving environment. There's no air for us to breathe. The sheer weight of water compresses our lungs and threatens to rupture our eardrums. Nitrogen narcosis causes us to hallucinate. Nonetheless—or perhaps *because* of such challenges—the notion of building craft for underwater travel has piqued the human imagination for thousands of years. Indeed, early real-life efforts to pursue this goal sound like sketches of Fantasy or alternate-history stories! They include how Alexander the Great was supposedly once lowered to the seabed in a glass diving bell[1]; how Dutch inventor Cornelius Van Drebbel demonstrated a kind of underwater rowboat sealed with greased leather in the 1620s[2]; and how, during the American Revolution, David Bushnell's Turtle, a kind of Steampunk submersible powered by a hand crank and foot treadle, was used in several unsuccessful attacks on British vessels.[3] Later again, the 1800s solidified a kind of reciprocal relationship between real and fictional undersea craft, starting with the *Nautilus*, designed by the American Robert Fulton for the French Navy and largely considered to be the first modern-day submarine (it featured ballast tanks and dive planes, but was still driven by hand cranks).[4] In 1863, another French vessel, this time named *Plongeur* (meaning "Diver"), was the first to be mechanically driven.[5] A model of this vessel was displayed at the Exposition Universelle in 1867 where it was studied by an inquisitive writer named Jules Verne.[6]

Inspired by *Plongeur*, Verne would produce the Ur-text of all contemporary submarine fiction and "the first book to imagine the planet as spanned by a holistic yet diverse undersea environment" with *Twenty*

---

1. Emley, 2017, n.p.
2. Editors of *Encyclopaedia Britannica*, 'Cornelis Drebbel', 2024, n.p..
3. Editors of *Encyclopaedia Britannica*, 'David Bushnell', 2024, n.p.
4. Whittet Thomson, 1942, n.p.
5. Wildenberg, 2022, n.p.
6. Wildenberg, 2022, n.p.

Thousand Leagues Under the Seas (1870).[7] This seminal novel tells of the sumptuous submarine *Nautilus* and the legendary Captain Nemo. An anti-imperialist contemptuous of the surface world and its politics, Nemo aligns himself with oppressed individuals, populations, and even sea creatures themselves. He is one-part political revolutionary (an edge largely dulled by translations) and one-part mad scientist; however, his particular love of the sea as a wondrous hidden world wouldn't often be reflected by the protagonists of contemporaneous submarine fiction. His anti-imperialism, in particular, would be tempered as Verne's immediate successors looked to the vast power of the *Nautilus* and prioritised the martial possibilities of submarine technology in their fiction.

Beginning in 1900, the pioneering Japanese SF writer Shunrō Oshikawa's *Kaitei Gunkan* ("Bottom of the Sea Military Ship") featured a ram-armed submarine in patriotic adventure tales of a future conflict between Japan and Russia. Anticipating the actual Russo-Japanese War (1904–'05), this six-volume series features much then-speculative technology and echoes the strong imperialist energies of the era. This image of the submarine as a weapon of war was solidified further by World Wars I and II. Those devastating conflicts brought much real-life experience with submarines, again primarily in military applications, especially with so-called Wolf Packs of German U-boats stalking the Atlantic and, on the Allied side, destroyers hunting their hidden adversaries. As sailors and submariners mustered-out into post-war civilian life, they brought submarine-technology terminology into wider usage (such as how submarines are typically known, regardless of size, as "boats" rather than "ships"). This interplay between real-life and fictional influences would continue to define the submarine genre for decades. Perhaps the most obvious example is yet another *Nautilus*, this time the USS *Nautilus*, designed by Captain (later Admiral) Hyman G. Rickover and commissioned in 1954. This vessel was the world's first operational nuclear-powered submarine and the first vessel to transit beneath the North Pole icecap ("Operation Sunshine").[8] In the same year, the fictional *Nautilus*—now also atomic-powered—returned in a well-received film adaptation of Verne's novel directed by Richard Fleischer. This slow leak of submarine fiction became a flood in the decade that followed. *Dune* author Frank Herbert's *A Dragon in the Sea* (1956) tells an action-packed spy story of underwater oil tugs engaged in a hazardous conflict between East and West. Hot on its heels was *The Deep Range* by Arthur C. Clarke (1957), which concerns a near-future **Astronaut** who takes an undersea job as a whale herder (readers may wish to note that the novel concerns the harvesting of whales for food as well as a campaign to bring this practice to an end).

---

7. Cohen, 2022, p. 5.
8. Hollingham, 2022, n.p.

In 1960, Swiss oceanographer Jacques Piccard (scion of a famous ballooning family) and US Navy lieutenant Don Walsh piloted a bathyscaphe (that's a fancy self-propelled submersible) named *Trieste* to the deepest part of the Earth's oceans in the Mariana Trench[9]; months later, the USS *Triton* made the first submerged circumnavigation of the globe.[10] Popular culture was quick to capitalise on interest in such achievements. Among the most inventive examples are the disaster film *Voyage to the Bottom of the Sea* (dir. Irwin Allen, 1961) and Ishirō Honda's *Atragon* (released in the US in 1965), the latter based on Shunrō Oshikawa's *Undersea Warship* and enlivening the source material with fantastical elements such as **Mysterious Islands**. It was followed by Gerry and Sylvia Anderson's fondly remembered 1964 children's television series *Stingray* ("Stand by for *action!*"), which features a team of "aquanauts" interacting with the ocean's various underwater civilisations (such as the "Aquaphibians") and facing off against mad scientists, pirates, and even the Loch Ness Monster (see **Cryptozoology**). A further wave of influential submarine and underwater fiction surfaced in the late 1980s. Michael Crichton's 1987 novel *Sphere* (later adapted into a poorly received 1998 film directed by Barry Levinson) melds SF with psychological-thriller elements for a story of a seemingly Alien spacecraft at the bottom of the Pacific (strongly referencing *Twenty Thousand Leagues Under the Sea* in the process). The award-winning manga series *The Silent Service* (1988–'96), written and illustrated by Kaiji Kawaguchi, wrestles with questions of militantism through the story of a Japanese nuclear submarine whose captain declares it an independent nation state. *The Abyss*, a 1989 film written and directed by James Cameron (and which began his interest in undersea exploration) stands out as one of the landmark underwater thrillers from the period, a typically impressive technical achievement in filmmaking from Cameron that again brings submariners and aliens into contact.

A cavalcade of pulp films followed in turn throughout the late 1980s/early 1990s. These include *Deep Star Six* (dir. Sean S. Cunningham, 1989), *Leviathan* (dir. Wayne Crawford, 1989), *Lords of the Deep* (dir. Mary Ann Fisher, 1989), and *The Rift* (dir. Juan Piquer Simón, 1990). Offering different flavours of dumb-but-fun entertainment, these movies besieged the claustrophobic settings of submarines and underwater bases with dodgily realised sea monsters, genetically engineered mutants, and all kinds of gelatinous alien entities. A bigger on-screen splash was created by cult-classic television series *SeaQuest DSV* (1993–'96). Best thought of as underwater *Star Trek: The Next Generation*, and created by *Farscape*'s Rockne S. O'Bannon, *SeaQuest DSV* offered viewers political, military, and environmental plotlines enhanced by an emphasis on realistic scientific

---

9. Anonymous, 2008, n.p.
10. Editors of *Encyclopaedia Britannica*, 2015, n.p.

details and themes (you know, as realistic as a show with a talking dolphin can be). The series distinguished itself from typical submarine fiction by presenting the oceans as wide-open spaces, a new frontier for exploration (and in this way was truer to Verne's legacy than others). This was further reflected in the generously sized sets of the hero submarine, a Deep Submergence Vehicle in the distant year 2018, described as a "thousand foot long Swiss Army Knife" that is tasked with a variety of research and peacekeeping missions in episodes that still look great and entertain today.[11] Though later seasons diluted the original educational energy of *SeaQuest* with aliens (Mark Hamill!), psychic powers, Greek gods, and killer plants, the show stands out as a genuine effort to excite a generation of SF fans about ocean exploration (and we'll admit it: the episode in which the submarine is tractor-beamed to an alien planet by a UFO is kind of gonzo amazing!).

In the twenty-first century, submarines and the underwater world continue to provide a fertile topic for SFF/H creators. The novel *Vorpal Blade* (2007) by John Ringo and Travis Taylor embraces pulpish energies for the story of a ballistic-missile submarine equipped with an alien hyperdrive that proceeds to explore interstellar space (in the process offering a good sense of the modifications necessary to transform a nuclear submarine into a starship). Video games, too, have explored the subject in a visually distinctive fashion, with the action-adventure game *Subnautica* (2018) allowing players to explore a dangerous alien waterworld, while the Horror-themed *Iron Lung* (2022) is a submarine simulator set in an ocean of human blood on a desolate moon. Two final works from this period circle back to Verne's influence on the subgenre in an interrogative manner. Alan Moore and Kevin O'Neill's *Nemo* trilogy (2013–'15) tells the fifty-year history of the pirate queen Janni Dakkar, daughter of Captain Nemo. Meanwhile, Adam Roberts's *Twenty Trillion Leagues Under the Sea* (2014, with illustrations by Mahendra Singh) revisits Verne's original with fantastical energy. The book follows a submarine sinking and sinking and sinking… beyond crush depth, beyond the presumed bottom of the ocean, and beyond what the human mind can sanely conceive. That, as they say, is deep.

A Spotter's Guide: Pressure Vessels

- **Military craft:** Submarines are often huge, complicated, and extremely expensive pieces of machinery. Such things tend to be the purview of nation states, so often have military applications. Historical and modern military submarines have both defensive and offensive functions (hunter/killers and ballistic-missile platforms respectively), as well as carrying out covert operations such as

---

11. Kershner, 1993, n.p.

tapping undersea communications links or smuggling operatives on or offshore. If you ever have the chance to visit one in a museum, you'll see the tight conditions their crews endure. Good examples of military submarines and their literal high-pressure environments can be found in Lothar-Günther Buchheim's 1973 novel *Das Boot* (adapted for film by Wolfgang Petersen, 1981) and the outstanding *Crimson Tide* (dir. Tony Scott, 1995).

- **Science and exploration vessels:** The other main use of submarines in fiction and film is as platforms for scientific research and exploration. Often such craft are deep-submergence vehicles or submersibles capable of reaching the most mysterious and dangerous parts of our planet. Such vessels are perfect for stories about spectacular natural phenomena, shipwrecks, crashed aliens, or even lost civilisations beneath the waves. Their crews often include mad scientists; their discoveries, occasionally touching on Cosmic Horror, have a knack for driving characters insane.
- **Shrunken submarines inside the body:** Believe it or not, this is a recurring use of submarines in SF. The classic example is *Fantastic Voyage* (dir. Richard Fleischer, 1966), a special-effects-heavy film in which a submarine carrying American scientists is shrunken to the size of a microbe and injected into the body of a Soviet defector to repair a blood clot. The material is largely played straight, though a comedic take on the same general idea is found in *Innerspace* (dir. Joe Dante, 1987) in which a naval aviator in a miniaturised pod is injected into the body of a hypochondriac grocery-store employee. Hijinks ensue.
- **Construction craft:** Assembling and maintaining crucial underwater infrastructure and colonies is a key part of worldbuilding for much submarine fiction. The specialist vehicles and trained operators involved in such tasks offer fresh narrative opportunities and intriguing perspectives on wider stories (see, for instance, Jeff Lemire's introspective graphic novel *The Underwater Welder*, 2012). Sensitive infrastructure such as internet cables, gas pipelines, aquaculture sites, undersea tunnels, and so on further provide flashpoints for conflict. Such scenarios also allow writers to interrogate the practice of extractive industries (intersecting with the concerns of **Climate Fiction**).
- **Pirates and smugglers:** An ocean's vast spaces can cloak whole worlds of criminality. Real-life drug-running submarines and smugglers' semi-submersibles offer Googleable examples, but consider the possibilities for underwater piracy in post-Apocalyptic or Cyberpunk futures. Perhaps these pirates have built their own

vessels Nemo-style; perhaps they've repurposed abandoned military craft (as have the antagonists of the second season of *The Last Ship*, 2014–'18). Another good example is the anime television series *Mars Daybreak* (2004) in which pirate submarines roam the oceans of a flooded future Mars.

Things That are Cool About Submarine Stories

Submarine stories grant us access to an alien world right on our shores! It is almost a cliché to say it, but we know less about the deep ocean than we do about the surface of the Moon. Sending characters forth to explore this mysterious realm speaks to our desire to discover more about the world we live on (and, sometimes, worlds beyond!). It's not for nothing that the original title for *SeaQuest DSV* was going to be *Deep Space*. Submarines and submersibles take us to the limits of what's possible on our planet (see **Places People Shouldn't Go**). Stories about them signify our technological might and, perhaps, our hubris.

Crush Depth

- **Oh captain, my captain:** More than surface vessels or even Spaceships, the captains of submarines tend to personify their boats. For example, Nemo is a cultured and educated leader whose vessel reflects this in its generously appointed library and galleries, yet Nemo's own quarters are spartan, containing just necessary navigation tools and texts, signifying his dedication. *SeaQuest*'s Nathan Bridger is a military officer who became a scientist (with actor Roy Scheider citing Nemo alongside the oceanographer Robert Ballard as part of his inspiration,[12] though Hyman Rickover is definitely also part of the character's DNA); in this way Bridger combines the two sides of his boat's mission. All that said, submarine fiction has long tended to have a quite masculine flavour (this is, after all, the genre of giant phallic tubes being sunk into wet spaces; the symbolism explains itself). It's perhaps time to mix that up!
- **Mayday, mayday:** Rescue missions are a mainstay of submarine fiction. They're high-stakes stories that come with a built-in ticking clock (usually on account of limited oxygen supplies). Often, they'll require quick thinking or improvisation from protagonists interacting with complex technology. Gerry and Sylvia Anderson's landmark television show *Thunderbirds* (1965–'66), made much of this with one of the titular rescue crafts being a Swinging-Sixties

---

12. Chunovic, 1994. pp. 48–50.

yellow submarine. Tonally, stories of this nature are tense affairs, with a submarine's claustrophobic nature in such instances readily veering into existential or Psychological Horror.

- **Marine life:** Much pulp fiction in the mid-twentieth century emphasised outlandish undersea monsters (what we'd nowadays call cryptids) as antagonistic presences (think of the stereotypical giant eyeball at a porthole). The giant squid of the 1954 version of *20,000 Leagues Under the Sea* is perhaps the classic example, but marine life continues to be an important aspect of the subgenre, such as the Megalodon in Steve Alten's *Meg: A Novel of Deep Terror* (1997; adapted for the screen by dir. Jon Turteltaub, 2018). These creatures' presence emphasises the alienness of the deep-sea environment and its hostility to human life. For solid inspiration about creating terrifying beasties, why not read up on prehistoric sea life?
- **Underwater aesthetics:** Visualising the undersea world is a challenge, especially given that "the aquatic atmosphere is cloudy instead of transparent, and when we look into the distance, particularly when the light is not directly overhead, objects rapidly fade into a fog".[13] In *The Underwater Eye* (2022), Margaret Cohen offers a fascinating history of underwater imagery in film and how it contributes to mood; this is true for prose writers, too, where our descriptions can conjure up awe (submarines "flying" past undersea mountain ranges) or fear (the same peaks looming out of dark and murky depths). In this way language, as ever, is *the* key writing tool.
- **Submarines on other planets:** Submarines, in many ways, are like spaceships in that they're sealed against a hostile exterior environment to which they allow humans access. Submarine stories thus readily extend to other worlds, such as the subsurface oceans theorised to exist on planets and moons in our solar system including Europa (see, for instance, Gary Gibson's *Europa Deep*, 2023) and even Pluto. Settings can include submarines on terraformed or partially terraformed worlds (as in *Mars Daybreak*) or even Sun-mersibles capable of being dropped into stars!

---

13. Cohen, 2022, p. 2.

ACTIVITIES

Create a captain: Who's your fictional craft's commander? Are they thoughtful or militant? Perhaps they've gone to sea to leave a personal tragedy behind or are a noble spirit driven to ecoterrorism by environmental destruction? Maybe they're a powerful woman in what, historically, is very much a man's world? Is their background one of engineering or the life sciences, and how might this inform their worldview? Once you've sketched your character, go back and see how this might cause you to reconsider your description of your submarine.

Blockade run: A coastal city state in the near future is at war with its neighbours. The city had been blockaded and so turns to a privateer submarine's rough-and-tumble crew to supply them with food and medicines. Tell the story of such a mission from the perspective of an idealistic young person who's recently joined the submarine. What's their experience of dodging depth charges or running silent to evade enemy hydrophones? How do they adapt to life in cramped quarters and to dealing with their anti-hero crewmates? How is their naivety and innocence challenged by the realities of war beneath the waves?

MYSTERIOUS ISLANDS

Whether accessible by boat or by magical **Portal**, by shipwreck or plane crash, lost, secret, and mysterious islands are an adaptable trope that, though rooted in Fantasy, has long been a familiar presence in Science Fiction and Horror. Their size makes our characters believe they can understand them, but in such hubris often lies downfall, for islands contain multitudes.

A Short History of Mysterious Islands

Islands, as geographer David Lowenthal has said, are "prime foci of legend and invention".[1] For writers, imaginary islands are infinitely versatile. They serve as microcosms of the world and offer petri dishes for social, scientific, or linguistic experiments. Long before spacecraft transported characters to other planets, ships traversed uncharted seas and encountered—or *claimed* to have encountered—mysterious islands populated by curious peoples and prowled by impossible monsters. Such tall tales inevitably made their way onto early maps, into oral and later written narratives, and, eventually, into Speculative Fiction where their elastic size, tailored topography, and variable geographic locations have allowed for centuries of storytelling.

The idea of mysterious islands reaches into humanity's deep past, to a time when post-glacial sea-level rise was reshaping coastal regions (especially in Europe) and was understood by our ancestors as the wrath of gods or as works of incomprehensible dark magic. The drowning of Doggerland, a vast plain that once connected the Island of Britain to Continental Europe, offers one early example.[2] A prehistoric instance of climate change (see **Climate Fiction**), this region's transformation into a series of low-lying islands and, eventually, into the North Sea, likely persisted for generations as folk memory of submergences and tales of vanishing islands (and, after literal millennia, would inspire Stephen Baxter's Northland Trilogy, 2010–'12). Leap ahead to literature in the modern sense and we find mysterious or lost islands are often of the enchanted variety, usually home to gods, goddesses, and frightening monsters. No more defining example exists than Homer's *Odyssey* (c. eighth century B.C.E.), in which the hero Odysseus wanders a fantastical Aegean Sea, encountering the islands of the Lotus-Eaters and their narcotic fruit, the island of the one-eyed giant Cyclops, the island of the bewitching Sirens, and many others (the 1981 Franco-Japanese series *Ulysses 31* would adapt this story into a cult-classic animated **Space Opera**). Some centuries later, the philosopher Plato introduced *the* mysterious island

---

1. Lowenthal, 2007, p. 202.
2. Freund, 2020, n.p.

(indeed *the* lost civilisation) with the story of Atlantis, a once prosperous island that was sunk to the bottom of the ocean by angry gods. Atlantis was probably based on folk memory of the destruction of the volcanic island of Santorini a thousand years earlier, which caused tsunamis that wiped out the Minoan civilisation on Crete; it would go on to inspire countless prequels, sequels, imitations, and pseudo-scientific explanations across Fantasy (J.R.R. Tolkien's Númenor, which we'll get to!) and SF (*Stargate: Atlantis*, 2004–'09).

Fast forward once more, this time to the early mediaeval period, and we find mysterious islands throughout the earliest **Mythic Fantasy**, with many iconic examples produced by the maritime cultures of the "peoples of Europe with westward-shores".[3] In Irish mythology, the fantastical island paradise Tír na nÓg is a bountiful realm, typically reached by boat, by riding magical horses across the water, or even by underground tunnels. It's the domain of ancient gods, a kind of Celtic otherworld said to grant immortality to those who reach it (though to return home and touch the ground, as the hero Oisín did, causes the years to instantly catch up with you). Another mythical island off the coast of Ireland, Hy-Brasil, is described as materialising once every seven years. This phantom "has appeared on maps and charts from as early as 1325 and up to the late 1800s", with many sailors and coastal-dwellers claiming to have seen it and even visited it (Margaret Elphinstone's 2002 novel *Hy Brasil* follows a writer sent to research the first travel book about this impossible place).[4] One island over, in west Wales, the mythological kingdom of Cantre'r Gwaelod is said to have drowned in what is now Cardigan Bay when a drunk prince neglected the protective sluice-gates and a flood washed the territory away. While technically not an island, it's notable for its connection to the real submerged forest at Ynyslas, near the village of Borth, which still emerges from the water at low tide, and for the drowned church bells said to ring out in times of danger. Further south is the sunken land of Lyonesse, a sort of Cornish Atlantis mentioned in Arthurian legend (and inspiration for a Jack Vance's Lyonesse trilogy, 1983–'89).

The early modern period brought a flood of mysterious islands as the European Age of Exploration made, for a while, the existence of such imaginary lands seem plausible. Both Thomas More's *Utopia* (1516) and Francis Bacon's *New Atlantis* (1626) used imaginary islands as laboratories to conceive ideal social structures. Shakespeare's play *The Tempest* (1611) is set on an enchanted island ruled by the sorcerer Prospero. Daniel Defoe's *Robinson Crusoe* (1719), which many regard as the first English-language novel in the modern sense, sees its protagonist reconstruct British culture on his desert island in what is nowadays read as a parable of colonialism. Hot

---

3. Tolkien, 2013b, p. 322.
4. Evans, 2019, n.p.

on Defoe's realistic heels, Jonathan Swift's satirical *Gulliver's Travels* (1726) skews to the fantastical with its flying island Laputa, which is propelled by magnetic levitation (and after which a region on the Martian moon Phobos is now named). In its wake, mysterious islands would supply sites for didactic manuals of self-reliance (*The Swiss Family Robinson* by Johann David Wyss, 1812), for adventure (Robert Louis Stevenson's pirate classic *Treasure Island*, 1882), and for outright SF, such as *The Island of Doctor Moreau* (1896) by H.G. Wells, in which a disgraced scientist uses his island's isolation to research **Uplifted Animals**. *Moreau*, like many of these books, "locates itself in the direct line of polemics concerning the right to colonize—and to 'civilize' by force—entire peoples on the pretext of their being (technologically) 'inferior'".[5] This use (intentional or otherwise) of mysterious islands to critique socio-political ills would continue well into the twentieth century (for example, William Golding's *The Lord of the Flies*, 1954).

One significant lost island in twentieth-century writing is Tolkien's Númenor, a key part of the Fantasy maestro's legendarium of Middle-earth. Númenor, Tolkien wrote, was his effort to get to grips with an "Atlantis complex" that had haunted him since childhood. As though he had inherited an echo of Doggerland, Tolkien claimed he was inspired by "the traditions of the North Sea" and the "dim memory of some ancient history [that] has always troubled me. In sleep I had the dreadful dream of the ineluctable Wave, either coming up out of a quiet sea, or coming in towering over the green islands. It still occurs occasionally" (he would bequeath this exact dream to Faramir in *The Lord of the Rings* itself).[6] Tolkien considered the Atlantis story to be "fundamental to mythical history".[7] As with Atlantis, the people of Númenor are brought low by divine punishment, in this case for allowing the great enemy Sauron to manipulate them into attacking the Undying Lands to the far west. Tolkien would later cement the connection by applying the Atlantis-like name "Atalantë", meaning "downfallen", to Númenor after it sinks beneath the ocean.

In the wake of Tolkien's great wave, mysterious islands continue to appear in contemporary fiction and on screen. *The Stone Raft* (1986) by Portugal's José Saramago sees a geological fissure separate the Iberian Peninsula from Europe and transform it into an island that drifts around the world. The hugely successful point-and-click game *Myst* (1993) transports players to a mysterious Steampunk island (through a magical book, which is a damn good metaphor for spec fic!). Umberto Eco's science fantasy *The Island of the Day Before* (1994) follows a seventeenth-century Italian nobleman slowly going insane after a shipwrecked near a Pacific island

---

5. Bozzetto, 1993, p. 34.
6. Tolkien, 1964, n.p.
7. Tolkien, 2013a, p. 212.

along the International Date Line and so, from his point of view, near an island that "will always be in the past".⁸ Disney's *Atlantis: The Lost Empire* (dirs. Gary Trousdale and Kirk Wise, 2001) revisits the original drowned city. Yet the modern era's preeminent mysterious island is undoubtedly that from television's *Lost* (2004–'10). With a series of bamboozling plots that probably weren't resolved to your satisfaction, the show follows the survivors of a transpacific airliner carrying an improbably high number of beautiful people that crashes on a seemingly deserted tropical island. While initially selling itself as *The Lord of the Flies* for the reality-television generation—Mismatched survivors! Paranoia! Love triangles! A monster that may or may not exist!—later seasons utilised the isolated setting as the ultimate SFF mystery box, with underground installations, mad scientists, **Ghosts**, telepathy, Time Travel, demonic smoke creatures, and magic. Meanwhile, in space, even *Star Wars* hero Luke Skywalker retires to a quasi-monastic life on a secret island (at least an island on a secret planet!) in 2017's *The Last Jedi* (dir. Rian Johnson), with scenes partially filmed on and inspired by the real monastic islands of The Skelligs in Ireland.

A Spotter's Guide: Nautical Charts

Academics such as Roger Bozzetto see islands in SFF/H as comprising "terrain of adventure", allegorical sites, mythic spaces, and "a calling into question of colonial myths".⁹ Others, such as Mark von Schlegell, break island narratives down into tales of "the Castaway, the Wild Man, the Pirates, the Treasure Map, the techno-Utopia, the natural wonder log, [and] the discovery".¹⁰ Writers constructing stories might benefit from integrating these notions with their islands' manifestation and purpose:

- **Sunken islands:** Atlantis is of course the ultimate and most influential example of islands that are no more… but that sometimes reappear. Searches for these lost civilisations tend to be big, exciting, globe-trotting narratives filled with adventurers and heroic archaeologists. Sunken islands tend to be depicted as sophisticated civilisations whose long-lost secrets and treasures are keenly sought after. Though be careful: lost-civilisation tales can easily slide into white-supremacist narratives of the kind favoured by the Nazis (boo!) who set up a special SS unit, the Bureau of Ancestral Heritage, to discover what became of the survivors of Atlantis.¹¹

---

8. Warner, 1995, n.p.
9. Bozzetto, 1993, pp. 34–44.
10. Von Schlegell, 2016, n.p.
11. McKie, 2022, n.p.

- **Hidden islands:** Often fulfilling the role of Bozzetto's allegorical sites on one hand and von Schlegell's techno-utopias on the other, some fictional islands are hidden by magic or cloaked by technological means. Our characters find them as much by accident as design. The (often advanced) island inhabitants don't wish to interact with the outside world, such as Themyscira in *Wonder Woman* (dir. Patty Jenkins, 2017). In some stories, "the existence of a perfect island in the middle of the ocean, which no one had seen" has also served as a metaphor for God (such a notion was particularly prominent in the mediaeval imagination).[12]
- **Out-of-phase islands:** Some islands are and are not hidden, they are and are not there (an effect no doubt inspired by how sea fog wreathes and camouflages real-life islands). These places phase in and out of our dimension and tend to exhibit cyclical appearances, such as Hy-Brasil. They're often depicted as prelapsarian fantasies and so a form of figurative time travel in which characters seem to leave behind decadent "modern" times. The island in *Lost*, which seems to move by magical means, also falls into this category.
- **Monster islands:** Remote and undisturbed places are often home to fantastical creatures that have evolved in curious and frequently frightening fashion (see **Cryptozoology**). The classic example is the literally named Monster Island that appears in various guises across the Godzilla franchise, home to not just the Big-G but also a plethora of legendary kaiju including Rodan and Mothra (Skull Island fulfils a similar purpose in the King Kong franchise; see *Kong: Skull Island*, dir. Jordan Vogt-Roberts, 2017). Equally, some islands *are* monsters or other living things. The Babylonian Talmud tells the story of a gigantic fish assumed to be an island by sailors who, upon landing and lighting a campfire, awaken a beast that throws them off. In *The X-Men* comics, Krakoa, known as "The Island That Walks Like a Man", is a sentient island in the Pacific.
- **Artificial islands:** The most Science Fictional of all islands are those deliberately created by human hands (or, at least, by human dredging machines). The Chinese construction of artificial islands to project military power in the South China Sea is one example. So, too, is the ancient city of Atlantis—a gigantic spacecraft floating on an alien ocean—in the Stargate franchise. Less obvious, and something that sounds like SF but isn't, is the Principality of Sealand, a self-proclaimed micronation on a decommissioned World War II defensive platform off the coast of England that declared independence and produced a constitution, a national flag, a national

---

12. Pinet, 2003, p. 180.

anthem, passports, coins, and stamps. The tiny Sealand eventually faced mercenary attacks (!) and a brief civil war (!!), spawned a rebel "government in exile" (!!!) and, ultimately, found itself at the centre of a drug-trafficking and money laundering ring (!!!!). It still exists today.

Things That are Cool About Mysterious Islands

There's something romantic about the notion that there are still secret and peculiar places in our increasingly "known" world. As such, islands are useful for writers looking to create a mysterious and ethereal atmosphere in Fantasy or a setting for unsafe or even immoral undertakings in Science Fiction or Horror. They allow us to separate our protagonists from their support networks—and sometimes their sanity—and to tell stories about characters operating beyond the legal, moral, and ethical frameworks that define our lives.

Here There Be Dragons

- **Disputed islands:** Some islands are metaphorically "lost" because of jurisdictional disagreement and, consequently, can give rise to curious stories. Hans Island, for example, is a tiny island between Greenland and the Canadian Arctic Archipelago. For many years it was contested between Canada and Denmark, who conducted a light-hearted "Whisky War" whereby each would remove the other's flag and leave a bottle of either Canadian Whisky or Danish Schnapps behind. Such islands are liminal spaces—neither one place nor another—and so the usual narrative rules and certainties can be suspended there. This makes them ideal settings for Fantasy or Horror stories!
- **Secret bases:** Mysterious islands make fantastic locations for mad scientists, villains, or even superheroes to use as bases of operation out of sight of the authorities. Captain Nemo's **Submarine** *Nautilus* is home-ported on just such a secret island (see Jules Verne's *The Mysterious Island*, 1875), as were the various Thunderbirds craft of that television show (1965–'66). Drawing on the military tradition of fortress islands, any number of spy-fi characters, including several James Bond antagonists, also take advantage of secret islands to further their evil schemes. Need a hidden base? There's no better place than somewhere literally not on any map!
- **Intentionally preserved cultures:** Just because an island is mysterious to your protagonist/The West doesn't mean there isn't

already someone living there. Access to some islands is restricted to preserve indigenous cultures from contamination. On North Sentinel Island, in the Andaman Islands, the Indian government protects the privacy of the indigenous people by both legal and military means to shield them from outside interference and infectious mainland diseases. Similar fictional islands offer the potential for interesting **First Contact** tales, but, as ever, please be respectful when depicting someone else's culture in your writing.

- **Phantom islands:** A great source of inspiration can be the imaginary islands that once appeared on historical maps. Cartographers call these Phantom Islands. In centuries past they were believed to be real but have been disproven via modern knowledge. Examples include the (supposedly haunted) Isle of Demons off Newfoundland and the purportedly magnetic Rupes Nigra ("Black Rock") believed to lie in a whirlpool at the North Pole (this island still featured on maps as late as the seventeenth century, including those of the pioneering cartographer Gerardus Mercator[13]). Maybe you can rediscover one of these "un-discovered" places?
- **Lost geology:** There are many stories to be found in the endless cataclysms etched into our world by volcanoes, tsunamis, and sea-level rise. Alongside lost islands are entire lost continents, such as Zeelandia (known as Te Riu-a-Māui in Māori), a submerged mass of billion-year-old continental crust surrounding New Zealand. What if one of these areas was to suddenly re-emerge? Or if it was to be raised by scientific means. What would it be like to explore such a place?

---

13. Kelechava, 2016, n.p.

ACTIVITIES

Cartography: Let's design an island setting for a story. Start with a basic circle and add detail: a craggy, irregular coastline; a mountainous and maybe volcanic interior; bays, caves, and other sheltered places; perhaps satellite islands and shipwrecks. Map out where people and/or animals might live. Is there a settlement? Or even a city? Are there loners living in the wilderness? Think about this island as an engine for generating story ideas.

Shipwreck: Your protagonist has washed up on a mysterious island, perhaps even the one you designed above. How will they survive? They'll need to find water and shelter. Possibly they'll need to light a signal fire. But are they alone? Is there something or someone already living on the island? Are these people welcoming or do they hide a terrible secret? Will your protagonist want to stay or want to leave?

BIOPUNK

What if you could hack your body the same way you can hack a computer? What if you could rewrite your DNA the way you rewrite a paragraph of text? Well, here's a subgenre in which your characters can do all this and more. It exists in the gooey Venn-space between Cyberpunk and Body Horror but, ultimately, it's evolved its own distinct identity. It's where hard science meets a DIY attitude. It's about characters improving themselves and, just maybe, society to boot. So, forget outer space, this is all about inner space! This is biopunk.

A Short History of Biopunk

Biopunk has a spine. It has a nervous system. Its themes and imagery run from what's arguably the first SF novel, Mary Shelley's *Frankenstein: The Modern Prometheus* (1818), through H.G. Wells's *The Island of Doctor Moreau* (1896; see **Uplifted Animals**), via Karel Čapek's *R.U.R.* in 1920 (for some, "the first Biopunk text"[1]) and Julian Huxley's 'The Tissue-Culture King' (1927), down through the work of Octavia E. Butler and Michael Crichton in the 1980s and '90s, all the way to satires of agribusiness and pharmaceutical giants dominating the contemporary stock exchange. Such stories exist at the intersection of the technologically possible ("Wouldn't it be interesting if we..."') and the aesthetically satisfying ("Wouldn't it be cool if we..."). They consider the social implications of both (and the more unforeseen, the better!). The subgenre is often framed as a descendent of cyberpunk and, while there's some overlap—a shared anti-authority energy personified by outsider figures, as well as an interest in transcending seemingly immutable physical limitations—biopunk has mostly been doing its own thing since the 1990s, eschewing the cerebral virtual spaces of information science for the messy, complex, mysterious realms of the body. Which is to say, as sociologist Nikolas Rose does, that Biopunk's "molecular enhancement technologies do not attempt to hybridise the body with mechanical equipment but to transform it at the organic level, to reshape vitality from the inside: in the process the human becomes, not less biological, but all the more biological".[2] Thus, gestures towards cyberpunk's cool "deviancy and provocation" suggest merely, in the view of theorists such as Lars Schmeink, "a connection made by clever authors and publishers"—and, just maybe, by writing-guide authors—"in order to market yet another

---

1. McQueen, 2016, p. 15.
2. Rose, N., 2007, p. 20.

subgenre".³ Nonetheless biopunk does legitimately reflect a shift in culture, science, and fiction, one beginning with the 1953 discovery of the DNA double helix by James Watson and Francis Crick—based on data and work by Rosalind Franklin—and culminating in how "biotechnology acquired cultural and economic relevance in the late 1970s and early 1980s".⁴

Bruce Sterling's *Schismatrix* (1985) is as good a marker as any of the point at which biopunk and cyberpunk went their separate ways, depicting a "conflict between Shapers, who use biotechnology, and Mechanists, who use software and cyberpunk technology to alter their bodies".⁵ Highly influential, too, is Greg Bear's *Blood Music* (1985), in which a renegade scientist's creation of biological computers leads to the emergence of a self-aware nanoscale civilisation that begins to assimilate and transform the world. Most important of all is arguably Octavia E. Butler's Lilith's Brood trilogy (1987–'89; previously known as Xenogenesis). Beginning with *Dawn* (1987), the series follows humanity's last survivors awakened by an Alien species who propagate by mutating other races. Lilith, Butler's protagonist, must convince the human characters of the value in a gene trade with this three-sexed alien race to produce a new hybrid species to populate the Earth. Butler's work offers an incisive perspective on key biopunk themes such as bodily autonomy, hybridity, and "how a closer look at gender and race reveals the seemingly biological determinants to be less 'scientific' than culturally constructed".⁶ It remains an essential work of SF.

The 1990s brought with it a period of thematic consolidation and popularisation, particularly in American writing. Biological plot devices and the use of speculative technologies burst onto the mainstream with Michael Crichton's epic *Jurassic Park* (1990), along with Stephen Spielberg's big-screen adaptation (1993), in which a biotech billionaire resurrects extinct dinosaurs from DNA retrieved from amber-encased mosquito blood. The Sleepless series from Nancy Kress (beginning with 1993's *Beggars in Spain*) explores a future in which genetic modification eliminates the need for sleep, allowing some to capitalise on their time and productivity in a way sleepers (ordinary people) cannot. This inevitably leads to a two-tier society, with Kress exploring classic biopunk concerns via the impact of unevenly distributed biotech. In 1996, author Paul Di Filippo attempted the ambitious project of simultaneously defining biopunk, severing its ties to cyberpunk, *and* redirecting its energies into something genuinely new and urgent in *Ribofunk*, one part fiction project, one part manifesto. Ribofunk, explains Di Filippo, draws its name from ribonucleic acid (RNA) and funk music (rather

---

3. Schmeink, 2016, p. 24.
4. McQueen, 2016, p. 7.
5. McQueen, 2016, p. 14.
6. Blumtritt, 2017, n.p.

than punk). He envisioned it as more optimistic and life-affirming than the majority of biopunk (especially those examples that still retain a strain of cyberpunk within them). According to him, ribofunk "must be as sensual as sex, as unsparing in sweat, cum, bile and lymph as the body is prolific in these substances".[7] Yet his emphasis on bodily imagery was perhaps embraced more than his plea for optimism or his dismissal of cybernetics as a "dead science".[8] A good example of this is David Cronenberg's 1999 film *Existenz*, which straddles the biopunk/body horror/cyberpunk divide with organic pistols to circumvent security procedures as well as biotech game-pods accessed via umbilical cords that allow people to enter virtual realities. Somewhat overshadowed by *The Matrix* (dirs. The Wachowskis, 1999), which itself tapped a strain of biopunk in its gooey and Dystopian human-battery farms, *Existenz* is still a wild ride even today.

In the early twenty-first century, biopunk has become an almost ubiquitous part of the SF ecology. The backstory of Margaret Atwood's terrific dystopian novel *Oryx and Crake* (2003) involves genetic engineering gone bad in a world dominated by biotech conglomerates. In 2008's *Starfish*, Peter Watts tells the story of human convicts genetically modified for the exploration and exploitation of deep-ocean resources who discover a deadly microorganism that threatens the surface world. Paolo Bacigalupi's Hugo and Nebula-winning debut *The Windup Girl* (2009), one of the definitive biopunk novels, is set in a post-climate-collapse world essentially ruled by generic engineering corporations, a twenty-third century defined by bioterrorism, plagues, famines, and gene-hacked seeds. Vincenzo Natali's unsettling Horror film *Splice* (2009) updates Doctor Moreau's animal-human hybrids for a new generation. Meanwhile, television's brilliant *Orphan Black* (2013–'17) depicts the full gamut of biopunk tropes and themes, all anchored by Tatiana Maslany's truly phenomenal performance as a series of clones. A necessary binge watch, the series considers the ramifications of illegal cloning, unregulated scientific experimentation, copyrighted DNA, body modification (one character gives themselves a tail!), and issues of consent and physical autonomy, as well as touching on biopunk as a fashion statement/cool aesthetic with visits to biopunk clubs and subcultures. It stands as one of the most accessible pieces of SF to address the contemporary ascendency of biopunk as a fiction subgenre.

A Spotter's Guide: Body Plans

- **Biohacking:** Rather than mechanistic or cybernetic augmentations, biopunk stories privilege genetic or biological enhancements. This

---

7. Di Filippo, 1996, n.p.
8. Di Filippo, 1996, n.p.

is especially true in near-future stories in which easy-to-use gene-editing tech escapes laboratories for the basement or backstreet bloodcutters. "Wild" genetic engineering in biopunk stories allows characters to build or change living things as though they were playing with Lego. Maybe they're trying to better the world by curing cancer at their kitchen table. Maybe they're trying to stick it to capitalism by giving themselves glands that secrete patented pharmaceuticals. Such biohacking, a route around traditional surgical or cosmetic interventions, offers writers a versatile means of addressing one of the hot-button issues of our times: your right to control your body as you wish.

- **Clones:** An easily understood form of genetic manipulation, cloning—creating an identical copy of a person, animal, or even plant—has long been a staple of SF in general. Cloning finds a ready home in biopunk, where it intersects with anxieties about identity, questions of biological determinism, and suspicions about the commodification of genetic information. On the page, Kazuo Ishiguro's *Never Let Me Go* (2005) provides an emotionally engaging take on the idea; however, a captivating television example of cloning in SF is *Orphan Black*, which wrestles with the trope from numerous intriguing perspectives.
- **Posthumanism:** Biopunk opens the possibilities of genuinely transformative experiences for our characters, ones that radically reconceive what we today consider as human. In "posthuman traditions, bodies are composite entities, at once biological, technological, and political," and, in biopunk stories, all aspects of these can be tweaked and modified.[9] It's about giving forms to different identities and, at its most speculative, depicts what academic Sean McQueen calls "new forms of embodiment," that being characters whose abilities are almost unrecognisable as human in the baseline sense.[10] Posthumanism is about critiquing, even rejecting, the one-size-fits-all image of the human and queering—in the broadest sense of the word—our seemingly predetermined biological limitations. Posthumanism says that our physical form is not our destiny; posthumanists would argue that it can and should be changed. In the process, and in the best traditions of SF, human perspectives themselves are likely to undergo radical expansion.
- **New living creatures:** Biopunk has long had an "affinity with the maker movement".[11] What this means in today's "era of garage biology", let alone in near-future stories with even more advanced

---

9. Braun, 2007, p. 7.
10. McQueen, 2016, p. 10.
11. Keulartz and van den Belt, 2016, p. 2.

technology, is the possibility of homebrew lifeforms being created.[12] This might be as simple as dogs or cats with tweaked genes, or as revolutionary as the creation of a whole new species. No less than Freeman Dyson—yes, he of the sphere fame—foresaw it as an "explosion of diversity of new living creatures," but such a rise in DIY biotechnology has obvious ethical implications for writers and their characters to wrestle with.[13] Is it morally right to create a new living being? Considerable potential for conflict exists here in the tension between biopunk's anti-regulation ethos and the moral requirements for oversight found in laboratory science.

- **Biocapitalism:** Biopunk stories frequently feature industries that "discover and commercialise new products based on biological resources".[14] These are often depicted as antagonistic capitalist entities to be subverted or exposed for their crimes (maybe for exploiting customers and their genetics, or perhaps, as in **Pandemic Fiction**, for accidentally or otherwise producing infectious diseases). Protagonists will sometimes be employees or ex-employees of such companies, positions that imply the advanced education that's characteristic of the subgenre and, in many cases, grant characters access to the sophisticated technology necessary to pursue their goals. Yet, unlike cyberpunk, this subgenre's anti-capitalist energies are largely directed towards righting intersectional inequalities associated with gender and race. Against this pessimistic—occasionally even dystopian—backdrop, amateur biopunks operating out of their garage can make for compelling characters, especially if they're out to change the world with fresh science and old-fashioned determination.

Things That are Cool About Biopunk

Biopunk allows your characters to rewrite their stories by rewriting their bodies. Such self-directed enhancement can be as simple as swapping shortsighted eyes for replacements grown for 20/20 vision, or as complex as resequencing a genome to better tolerate hostile environments (gills to breathe underwater, say, or heat-resistant skin for foundry workers). Biopunk thus grants characters routes towards greater agency but, for writers, it allows Science Fictional spins on be-careful-what-you-wish-for wisdom. Because down in the backstreet bloodcutters, body mods often come with a price beyond the monetary. Characters may be surprised by what they need to leave behind, by who they might become, or even by what might stay the same.

---

12. Carlson, 2005, n.p.
13. Dyson, 2007, n.p.
14. Ghosn and Jazairy, 2018, p. 436.

Splice Up Your Life

- **Biopolitics:** Biopolitics is the "aggregate of governmental, political, institutional and economic techniques" that administer things such as "hygiene, birth rate and life expectancy".[15] Everyday stuff, in many respects, but they're subject to a largely invisible framework of regulation and review. Biopunk stories tend to disrupt these structures (such as the sterilisation pill in *Oryx and Crake*, or the Zombie plague of Colson Whitehead's 2011 novel *Zone One*). What this means in practice is that robust biopunk won't just be about cool gee-whiz gene therapy or the like; it'll make points and it'll take positions on social, cultural, and even political issues. It might be a fiction subgenre, but biopunk's intimate connection with the biopolitics that govern our lives allows it to—perhaps even demands it to—critique the establishment (and in this the subgenre nods to the roots of punk sensibilities).
- **Body farming:** In the real world, scientists use so-called body farms to study decomposition. But they also have a long history in fiction and popular culture. Many early Vampire panics were caused by how medical schools and perverts-of-the-week used to steal bodies from graveyards. Meanwhile, Shelley's Doctor Frankenstein famously used salvaged corpses to create his creature. In biopunk, the notion of "farming" bodies is reborn (sorry) as a means of supplying a market for replacement limbs or organs. They can even be used to cultivate viruses or diseases (as in *Doctor Who*'s 'New Earth', dir. James Hawes, 2006). Depending on your story's tone, these can be shady operations or as open as supermarkets. Need a new set of ears? Off to the body farm! They also offer the possibility of addressing ethical questions with your writing, such as the rights and wrongs of cultivating bodies for the sole purpose of harvesting them (see again Ishiguro's *Never Let Me Go*).
- **DNA data storage:** DNA—the very stuff that you and I are made of—is a very stable, very high-density information-storage medium. So high density, in fact, that all the information in the US Library of Congress "could be crammed into a DNA archive the size of a poppy seed".[16] That's kind of amazing! And, in biopunk, it's also a great way of smuggling valuable information. Here the message and the medium become the same thing as characters literally use their own bodies to circumvent commercial, industrial, or private security procedures (it's not DNA, but something similar happens in *Blood*

---

15. McQueen, 2016, p. 9.
16. Ionkov and Settlemyer, 2021, n.p.

Music). Here, too, are shades of criminality, because stolen data will often be encrypted, and breaking the codes stored in a character's DNA brings a whole new meaning to the term "cracking heads".

- **Planned obsolescence:** An irksome facet of our contemporary world is the way so much of our technology seems—by accident or design—to have a built-in break-down date. Bad enough when it's just your cell phone, but now imagine that the genetic technology your health relies on needs a regular update (or, even worse, is sold on a subscription model!). A real-world example might be the intrauterine copper coil (IUD) for contraception, which needs to be replaced after a few years, but a great fictional example can be found in *Parasite* (2013) by Mira Grant, which features genetically engineered tapeworms that maintain people's immune systems. Consider how such planned obsolescence (and the financial, even psychological strain) might affect your biopunk characters; might they be forced into dangerous black-market alternatives just to get the medical care they require?
- **Who wants to live forever?** Biopunk often rubs up against typical SF tropes of longevity treatments, life extension, and even immortality. Can genetic engineering make your characters young again? And, if so, is that technology evenly distributed or is it restricted to an economic or political elite? What are the social consequences for life extension in your story-world? Consider what stories could be generated by longevity treatments going wrong. For example, can blackmailers use the therapy as a Trojan horse to smuggle in more malevolent manipulation? Indeed, genetic life extension is the perfect time to reflect upon the observation usually attributed to Frederik Pohl (though Isaac Asimov likely said it first) that "a good science fiction story should be able to predict not the automobile but the traffic jam".[17]

---

17. Pohl, 1968, p. 6.

ACTIVITIES

Journalling: You're a character who's given the opportunity to change something about your body. Maybe it's as simple as your height or eye colour. Perhaps it's more radical, such as changing your gender via gene therapy. Keep a journal of the process. Record not just the physical changes but also the psychological/emotional impact of the transformation (how does it make you *feel*?). Try to create the effect of honesty and vulnerability throughout. Attempt to cover the whole period of this procedure and, at the end, reflect on what you've learnt.

Feature article: Imagine you're a near-future journalist covering the debate about "wild" genetic engineering. Write an article in which you investigate different aspects of this world. Incorporate interviews with kitchen-table geneticists and backstreet biopunk enthusiasts. Get the views of people who have engineered themselves, say, night vision or other body modifications. Talk to doctors who fear prosecution for helping people become who they want to be. Also consider the dangers of unregulated biotech. Try to convey a broad sense of the transformative biopunk community and its internal contradictions and anxieties.

THE MULTIVERSE

Dimensions, realms, discrete domains, alternate histories, and parallel worlds: the terminology varies, but, in this reality at least, we're going to refer to a collection of alternative universes as the multiverse, a vast and versatile setting in which anything that can happen does happen. Somewhere out there, you're already writing about it....

A Short History of the Multiverse

Hollywood blockbusters would like you to think that the multiverse has just happened, but mythology and religion offer a long history of parallel realms that foreshadow later developments in Speculative Fiction. In the broadest sense these encompass any alternative spiritual or godly dominion. Obvious examples include the Christian multiverse of Heaven, Purgatory, and Hell; the alternate domains of the Norse Asgard; or the afterlife of Egyptian theology. The earliest examples from speculative writing utilised variations on Time Travel as either the mechanism by which the parallel world was accessed or, indeed, how it was created (the latter continues to be a popular plot device). Notorious time traveller H.G. Wells played with this notion in *Men Like Gods* (1923), while Murray Leinster's hugely influential pulp tale 'Sidewise in Time' (1934) showed alternate timelines—manifesting as recognisable historical periods—bleeding into our reality. Nonetheless, in terms of the multiverse as readers and viewers understand it today, the foundational text must surely be the Jorge Luis Borges story 'The Garden of Forking Paths' (1941). At the heart of this tale is the discussion of a book that attempts to tell all the stories infinitely branching out from the characters' decisions: "in some you exist, and not I; in others I, and not you; in others, both of us".[1] All these stories, these timelines, exist concurrently, and so raise the question of how much individual choice actually matters. Building on this, as well as Leinster's example, H. Beam Piper's intricately thought-through Paratime stories and short novels (1948–'65, later continued by John F. Carr) feature an interdimensional civilisation that exists across an infinite number of alternate histories. Travel and commerce occur across the many levels (determined by their removal from the home timeline) of what is a multiverse in all but name.

Borges and Piper anticipated what we now call the Many-Worlds Interpretation (MWI) of quantum mechanics as developed in 1957 by physicist Hugh Everett III. The MWI, which has by now been woven whole

---

1. Borges, 1964, pp. 19–29.

cloth into modern Speculative Fiction, rejects the idea of wavefunction collapse, which is the elimination of alternative choices once a decision is made. Put more straightforwardly, if you had tea rather than coffee this morning, there's another universe out there where you chose the opposite. Or where you chose orange juice. Or Bovril (#DarkestTimeline). In the MWI, all possibilities exist Borges-style as a series of branching paths (a good example is found in the *Star Trek: The Next Generation* episode 'Parallels', dir. Robert Wiemer, 1993). It implies an infinite number of universes resulting in a frighteningly large canvas for storytelling. Yet while the concept of the multiverse was clearly circulating in the mid-twentieth century, the use of the term in discussions of fiction wouldn't appear until Fantasy novelist Michael Moorcock named it in 1963's *The Sundered Worlds*. Moorcock's multiverse is of the recognisably modern narrative variety, a multi-level structure of reality that his protagonists (like Piper's) navigate via technological means. Moorcock would eventually expand his multiverse to metafictionally encompass much of his output (Stephen King would later do similar with his Dark Tower series, 1982–2004).

Concurrent with Moorcock, one of the defining innovations in multiverse storytelling came not from prose but from comic books, the popular appeal of which helped cement the concept in the public imagination. Attempting to reconcile the Golden Age (1938–'56) and Silver Age (1956–'70) continuity of its superheroes, DC Comics published 'The Flash of Two Worlds' in 1961 (written by Gardner Fox, illustrated by Carmine Infantino). This hugely influential story sees the then contemporary Flash Barry Allen vibrate across realities and encounter the Golden Age Flash Jay Garrick in a parallel world that came to be known as Earth Two. This notion allowed DC to reconcile vastly different variants of its intellectual properties, as well as to easily fold the characters from publishers they acquired into their own stable. DC's main rival Marvel Comics later adopted a similar idea, though Marvel intentionally eschewed DC's exceptionalism for a "main" reality known as Earth 616. The multiverse would provide considerable story material for both companies for decades to come, with DC in particular generating so many alternate realities that they would be forced to streamline their multiverse with 1985's seminal *Crisis on Infinite Earths* (written by Marv Wolfman with art by George Pérez), which left only one composite Earth in existence (don't worry, multiverse fans, this *really* didn't last!).

While all this was happening, the multiverse continued to expand on the page and screen. Roger Zelazny's Chronicles of Amber series (1970–'91) saw its characters visit and manipulate a dizzying series of "shadow" worlds—of which our Earth is one—between the ordered Amber and the reality of Chaos. Joanna Russ's landmark feminist novel *The Female Man* (1975) introduces four versions of the same character existing in four different realities through which Russ explores how women's social status could vary if their power dynamic with men was different (see **Gendercide**). On television, the multiverse was a mainstay of 1990s SF offerings. The most obvious example is *Sliders* (1995–2000), which sees a motley group of lost multi-universal travellers searching for their home universe. The series drew on many obvious alternate realities (the American War of Independence failed! Dinosaurs never died out!) but, at its most ambitious, interrogated Russ-esque notions of gender inequality, satirised the demeaning of intellectualism in society, and posited genuinely intriguing SF ideas such as a militaristic race of sentient primates bent on the destruction of homo sapiens across parallel worlds.

Subsequently, stories about the multiverse have become one of the defining subgenres of the twenty-first century. Interesting contemporary examples include 'Tiger, Burning' (2006) by Alastair Reynolds, which features a detective converted into information and transmitted across the local multiverse (this being the only way people can cross the barriers between realities), as well as *Cowboy Angels* by Paul McAuley (2007), a spy-fi novel taking place across the many "sheafs" of a pan-dimensional American empire. The whimsically genre-hopping *How to Live Safely in a Science Fictional Universe* (2010) by Charles Yu follows a time-machine repairman in the alternate realities that his employers maintain as, essentially, theme parks. The film *Coherence* (dir. James Ward Byrkit, 2013) is a twisty-turny multiverse drama set mostly in a single room where alternate realities are differentiated by only the tiniest changes. Television show *Rick and Morty* (2013–present) offers a whole education on the multiverse, irreverently riffing on many classic characteristics such as doppelgangers, multi-universal wars and councils, and big paradoxical ideas such as the Central Finite Curve that walls off one infinite portion of the multiverse from another. Meanwhile, *A Thousand Pieces of You* by Claudia Gray (2014) makes great use of the notion of inhabiting the lives of your alternate selves. The Long Earth series (2012–'16) by genre heavyweights Terry Pratchett and Stephen Baxter is a mostly delightful romp through the stimulating notion of infinite unpopulated alternate Earths to the multiversal "east" and "west". The series begins as a light satire of Manifest Destiny but quickly evolves into an engrossing narrative conversant with decades of SFF.

Crossing genres and media as easily as dimensional barriers, the multiverse has, by the late 2010s/early 2020s, achieved pre-eminence in speculative writing. *A Darker Shade of Magic* (2015) by V.E. Schwab is a carefully constructed Fantasy novel taking place across four alternate Londons where the practice of magic is either ascendent or in crisis. The story 'And Then There Were (N-One)' is a 2017 SF/murder mystery by

Sarah Pinsker set, rather brilliantly, at a convention of Sarah Pinskers from across the multiverse. The animated film *Spider-Man: Into the Spider-Verse* (dirs. Bob Persichetti, Peter Ramsey, and Rodney Rothman, 2018) packages a tremendously dynamic representation of the multiverse into probably the best superhero film of the decade. Even social media is getting in on the game, with Blue Neustifter's Twitter narrative 'Unknown Number' (2021)—the first social-media content nominated for a Hugo award!—seeing its trans protagonist Gaby receiving a message from a pre-transition variant of herself elsewhere in the multiverse. Gaby is thus able to act as the guide and the mentor she always wanted in this sympathetic and compassionate tale. Finally, the crowning achievement of multiverse storytelling is surely the Oscar-winning *Everything Everywhere all at Once* (dirs. Daniel Kwan and Daniel Scheinert, 2022), an absurdist and visually blistering story of a middle-aged Chinese immigrant dissatisfied with her job and marriage who discovers she's the saviour of the multiverse. The film's success has led to widespread discourse about contemporary storytelling's fascination with the conceit. SF scholar Jake Casella Brookins has wondered if this "explosion of multiverse narratives" is a consequence of the essentially nihilist times in which we live, asking whether it's a trend "betraying an essentially foreclosed, emptied futurity, escapable only in fantasy".[2] This is perhaps something worth interrogating by any writers interested in the subgenre.

A Spotter's Guide: Parallel Worlds

- **Lost in the multiverse:** A staple of this subgenre are stories about characters trying to find their way home through an infinity of worlds, which allow the writer to experiment with a rotating series of other genres—now we're in the Western world, say, or now we're in the underwater world—without necessarily abandoning their original protagonists. Such tales go back to the early 1940s, in work such as L. Sprague de Camp's 'The Wheels of If' (1940); the protagonist is reluctantly thrust through a series of alternate universes and eventually chooses to remain in a parallel world. Characters lost in the multiverse offer a good spine for ongoing narratives such as comics or television shows.
- **Life in the multiverse:** Ask yourself who your characters might be if things were different. Because the best multiverse stories are about what it's like to *be* something or someone different. They're about interrogating how the multiverse "upends not only the idea of linear narrative but also concepts like identity, purpose, 'success,' or

---
2. @jakecasella, 2023, n.p.

'failure'".[3] *Sliders* offers a good template here, with the main cast often interacting with variants of themselves who have different jobs, different families, very different motivations/priorities, and, occasionally, different genders. Though do try to avoid the tired trope of a gay variant also being the only evil variant. We're beyond that by now.

- **Exploring and exploiting the multiverse:** Whereas lost characters enter the multiverse accidentally, many others deliberately embark on pan-dimensional expeditions (paging the Fantastic Four) or even engage in extractive industries. Piper's Paratime stories, for example, depict a bustling trade across parallel Earths, with environmentally ravaged worlds being prime consumers. And, of course, demand for resources can easily spawn conflict, even in an infinity of worlds.
- **The multiverse war:** In some respects, multiverse wars aren't that different from traditional conflict. You have strategy, combatants, armies, and spies, but what is different is the scale: they often see the destruction—and restoration—of entire universes. They're fought with weapons that are existential as much as anything else and occur beyond what's ordinarily perceptible (consider the brilliant 2019 novella *This Is How You Lose the Time War* by Amal El-Mohtar and Max Gladstone). Note, too, that these kinds of conflicts can often destabilise the structure of existence itself, leading to…
- **The collapsing multiverse:** Favoured by comic books and related media, the collapsing multiverse spells the end of literally everything, as in Jonathan Hickman's *Avengers/New Avengers* (2013–'15) and *Secret Wars* (2016). Often, the collapse is a metaphor for present-day environmental catastrophe (see **Climate Fiction**) or offers a means for writers to critique aspects of their own creative industry. Such stories typically see a group of heroes/variants from across different realities band together to restore their universes. Go team!

Things That are Cool About the Multiverse

Everything. Everything is cool about the multiverse *somewhere* in the multiverse. That's the point. Everything is a spectrum in the multiverse. As Ted Chiang observed, this is momentous because "for much of human history, stories reinforced the idea of fate. They told us that events unfolded the way they did because of destiny or the will of God".[4] Now, however, the concept of the multiverse grants writers the chance to explore "What if?" scenarios writ large (see, for instance, Harry Turtledove's many alternate

---

3. de León, 2023, n.p.
4. Quoted in Klein, 2022, n.p.

histories). From a cultural-criticism perspective, the multiverse speaks to "the fragmentation of our postmodern identities".[5] It's a way for writers to imaginatively address the challenges of the present.

Worlds Without End

- **If everything is possible, then nothing is interesting:** The best multiverse stories set limits on what is and isn't possible. If they don't, then even huge events such as the death of characters can become blasé or, for that matter, even choice itself can lose meaning as 'The Garden of Forking Paths' warns us. So, consider what kind of constraints exist in your multiverse and how that might generate narrative peril. In *Stargate SG-1*, for example, visitors from nearby realities are vulnerable to cellular breakdown caused by the increased entropy of sharing a universe with their variant. Woopsie!
- **Moments of transition:** While the subgenre obviously bumps up against alternate history, multiverse stories distinguish themselves by privileging contact (implied or actual) between different realities. Thus, writers should consider how the passage between universes occurs. Technological or magical explanations are equally valid depending on your story's tone. Is it via a wormhole or machine of some description? Or does one simply wake up in an alternate reality every time one goes to sleep, as in *Doors of Sleep* (2021) by Tim Pratt (admit it, we've all worried about that!)? Consider, too, how the notion of transition is obviously a potent one to many people nowadays, an opportunity for them to achieve a sense of identity heretofore denied.
- **Steps, paratimes, and hypertimes, oh my!** There's a lot to be gained by a writer conceiving of the *shape* of their multiverse and how its various worlds interact. For Pratchett and Baxter, it's as easy as stepping from one world to the next, with distances measured from ours as the datum. For Piper in the Paratime series, the closer they are to each other the more similar the worlds are. For comics writers Mark Waid and Grant Morrison, the multiverse became "Hypertime", a crisscrossing series of branches to explain away continuity errors.
- **Travel beyond the obvious:** A lot—and we do mean *a lot*—of stories have been told about realities in which the Nazis won World War II or the Confederacy won the American Civil War or the Roman Empire never fell. So how about a world where Native Americans colonised Europe? Or where an Angolan space programme landed

---
5. Burt, 2022, n.p.

women on the Moon? The possibilities of the multiverse are infinite, so be sure to take full advantage of that!
- **Follow the science:** Physicist Brian Greene has speculated that there are nine different types of multiverses.[6] Not all will apply to every story, of course, but each offers an interesting starting point for fiction. Greene's list comprises (deep breath, everybody):
  - The Quilted Multiverse: an infinite space in which every part of the universe repeats infinitely (essentially leading to parallel worlds).
  - The Inflationary Multiverse: a series of bubbles, of which our universe is one.
  - The Brane Multiverse: parallel universes float above and below our dimension.
  - The Cyclic Multiverse: a series of sequential big bangs creating parallel realities in sequence.
  - The Landscape Multiverse: an esoteric reading of inflationary cosmology and string theory.
  - The Quantum Multiverse or Many Worlds Interpretation: each choice creates a new universe (you'll recognise this one from television/film).
  - The Holographic Multiverse: the reality of regions is a reflection of the surface area of those spaces.
  - The Simulated Multiverse: we're all just a computer program (à la *Agents of SHIELD*'s fourth season)
  - The so-called Ultimate Multiverse: every possible universe is a real universe, thus making irrelevant the question of which is genuine or if ours is special.

---

6. Greene, 2011.

ACTIVITIES

Let's get metafictional: Drafts of your stories are like alternate versions of your final result. Radically different incarnations of your characters inhabit these alternate worlds. So, pick a story you've worked on and redrafted several times, and consider whether there's a way to bring different versions of your protagonists into contact and conflict with one another. Perhaps they have different motivations and goals. Perhaps their differing backstories have imparted them with opposing ideological perspectives. Maybe they are even jealous of their counterparts' worlds?

Make it weird: For a subgenre of infinite possibilities, multiverse stories are often, well, surprisingly ordinary! Even *Doctor Strange in the Multiverse of Madness* (dir. Sam Raimi, 2022) presented worlds that, except for the briefly seen universe where everyone is made of paint, are just reskins of conventional reality. For this activity, try to stray further from what we see around us. Imagine a character transported to a world with *radically* different social structures or a plane of existence with different physical laws (see Stephen Baxter's *Raft*, 1992). How will they get home? Will they find local allies to help them (even other versions of themselves)? Perhaps they even want to stay in this new reality.

CHAPTER TWO

FANTASY

Where Do New Subgenres Come From?

Genres are wiggly things. They don't stand still. They spill over whatever edges we set up around them. That's because they're living, breathing, *growing* things that multiply and mutate more quickly than we can catalogue them. These new subgenres are constantly overtaking us even as we rush to name them with cool new portmanteaux (those being blendings of existing words, terms like "spork" or "mocumentary")! So don't blink, or, like the Weeping Angels of *Doctor Who*, all these new subgenres will be up in your face before you know it!

We can easily illustrate the concept of subgenre proliferation with an example such as Romantasy—or Romance/Fantasy—which has lately graduated from social media to the bestseller lists. Romantasy is the perfect instance of subgenre hybridity in how effortlessly it combines two existing sets of reader expectations into something that resonates with a new generation. Romance, for instance, is often predicated on everything ending happily ever after. It has typically focused on contemporary or historical settings. By blending this with Fantasy, however, contemporary Romance authors have unlocked a toybox of phenomenal depth and imagination: **Dragons**! Sword-wielding sorceresses! Magical **Portals**! And more! Fantasy authors, in turn, suddenly have access to the tropes and conventions (and readers) of Romance writing. New subgenres like this are a win for everyone.

The Question of Definition

One issue that new subgenres bring up is the question of how we define them in relation to what's come before. So, in this case, you're maybe asking yourself if Romantasy isn't just <u>Paranormal Romance</u> in a fancy new cloak. As academics and critics, and indeed as writers, we examine the identifying characteristics and look for where they diverge. Paranormal romance, for example, hit it big in the 1980s and '90s with stories about humans (typically women) and creatures (usually male <u>Vampires</u>, **Werewolves**, **Ghosts**, etc.), and often in a contemporary setting (so is itself a branch of <u>Urban Fantasy</u>). Romantasy differentiates itself in that it's usually set in a more traditional Fantasy setting (castles, knights, magicians, and so on). The protagonists are usually residents of those secondary worlds rather than, say, individuals existing in a slightly modified version of our here and now. Moreover, Romantasy allows writers and readers to revisit chaste fairytales or classic stories/films in a more "adult" fashion.

The lesson here is that SFF/H is *fun*. It allows you the space and freedom to mix 'n' match elements that you like from all the (sub)genres to create something new.

So, what are you gonna try mixing together next? Perhaps some of the following....

MYTHIC (aka MYTHOLOGICAL) FANTASY

Raise your hand if you have ever said—or wanted to say—in your deepest voice, "Release the Kraken!" <counts hands...> Yep, that's everybody, then! Even if you aren't old enough to have seen *The Clash of the Titans* the first time around in 1981, and you think Ray Harryhausen is a member of the newest boy band, you've heard of the Kraken. So, you're on the right track. Now, in your best epic voice, repeat after us: RELEASE THE MYTHIC FANTASY!

A Short History of Mythic Fantasy

Pretty much all our Fantasy stories (such as <u>Folktales and Fairy Tales</u>) can be traced back to mythology, so a history of mythic fantasy is a history of our oldest tales. One way to describe this subgenre is to look at what mythology is and what it *does* for us. A mythology is a collection of stories that explain a culture's origin and even religion. In many cases it tells how the world (or natural phenomenon) works. For example, in Greco-Roman mythology the sun's movement across the sky is explained as a god—Apollo or Helios depending on your time frame and location—driving his chariot across the sky. What we now call myths weren't fictional stories at the time but beliefs; they *became* myths because they were so culturally significant that they were remembered. On top of which, some mythologies overlapped with religion, such as the ancient Norse tales of gods and goddesses (#TeamLoki). Furthermore, some mythologies are still significant and influential today even though the culture has changed and no longer follows the mythology as a religion.

Mythology has spawned countless studies and analysis, but looking at how one of our more revered SFF/H writers engaged with myth as a writer and thinker can give us more insight into how this subgenre works. Multi-award winner (a description that barely scratches the surface of her accolades!) Ursula K. Le Guin didn't just write fiction, she also left us numerous essays and non-fiction titles. Essays such as 'The Child and the Shadow' and 'Myth and Archetype in Science Fiction' are especially relevant here. In the former, she argues that we need Fantasy because of how it describes things that we have a difficult time describing without it:

> The great fantasies, myths and tales are indeed like dreams: they speak *from* the unconscious *to* the unconscious in the *language* of the unconscious—symbol and archetype. Though they use words, they work the way music does: they short-circuit verbal reasoning, and go straight to the thoughts

that lie too deep to utter. ... They are profoundly meaningful, and usable—practical—in terms of ethics; of insight; of growth.[1]

Because of the darkness inside all of us (and we don't necessarily mean a lack of morals or ethics, but a true connection to what it means to be a messy human), and because of the light we carry that defies description, we use Fantasy—and, in extension, myths—to tell the story of ourselves.

Myths also contain archetypes and symbolism that help us better point at something nearly indescribable as a whole and say, "Oh, this is *that*," whether it's love or capriciousness or revenge or any number of other human behaviours. We use it to tap into our own deepest selves and share with others. In 'Myth and Archetype in Science Fiction', Le Guin uses SF (in the loosest sense; this also applies to Fantasy) to investigate how we as a modern society still engage with mythology. She sees it as a way of writing stories that readers will relate to on the deepest level, but only if we as authors engage with the truth of what we are: "The only way to the truly collective, to the image that is alive and meaningful in all of us, seems to be through the truly personal."[2] (This seems counterproductive but stick with us here!) Le Guin says that connecting to the things that myth represents—via the "language of the unconscious"—helps to better connect to each other and readers:

> The writer who draws not only upon the works and thoughts of others, but upon his own thoughts and his own deep being, will inevitably hit upon common material. The more original his work, the more imperiously *recognizable* it will be. ... The characters, figures, images, motifs, plots, events of the story may be obvious parallels, even seemingly reproductions, of the material of myth and legend. There will be—openly in fantasy, covertly in naturalism—dragons, heroes, quests, objects of power, voyages at night and under sea, and so forth. In narrative, as in painting, certain familiar patterns will become visible. ... It means that we can communicate, that alienation isn't the final human condition, since there is a vast common ground on which we can meet, not only rationally, but aesthetically, intuitively, emotionally.[3]

What this means is that we can look at a writer's use of myth, whether as a small element or in a whole revisitation, as a way for them to look more deeply within themselves and our common humanity to tell a story that readers will engage with.

Every culture's mythology and folklore started as oral tales, but because of variations in how cultures evolved—including the negative influences of

---
1. Le Guin, 'The Child and the Shadow', 1979, p. 62 (her emphasis).
2. Le Guin, 'Myth and Archetype in Science Fiction', 1979, p. 78.
3. Le Guin, 'Myth and Archetype in Science Fiction', 1979, p. 79 (her emphasis).

colonisation, land grabs, and enslavement—only some mythologies exist as early written manuscripts. Other mythologies, especially from parts of Africa, the Americas (South, Central, and North), and Australia and New Zealand existed mainly as oral tales specific to individual groups or tribes (from the Incas to the Sioux to the Māori, and so many more). The loss or violent movement of their people, as well as systemic disenfranchisement (such as the removal of Native American children from their tribal lands to force them into Christian schools), means that there often isn't an easily accessed collected written source of a culture's mythology from which to find inspiration for new stories. In some cases, anthropologists and others have worked to collect these stories, but even this discipline isn't safe from biases, such as Aboriginal Australian studies (whose oral mythology is known as the Dreamtime) where even anthropologists can't agree on the definition of their subject.[4] An early example of someone studying their own culture and its oral tradition is author and anthropologist Zora Neale Hurston's *Mules and Men* (1935), a collection of materials including folklore and even Vodou tales from African Americans in the American South, with many of the tales displaying the clear influence of Christianity on the subject's lives, which isn't a surprise considering many are tales about enslaved people or from those whose very recent ancestors would have been enslaved.

Some of our earliest written mythologies are our earliest written Fantasy and, those, in turn, have inspired *modern* mythic fantasy. One example is ancient Greek mythology. Homer's *Iliad* (c. 800 B.C.E.; about the Trojan War) and *Odyssey* (c. 800 B.C.E.; about Odysseus's long voyage home after the war) contain all manner of gods and goddesses and their interference in the lives of humans, as well as fantastical beings and sorcery. This has been reimagined in the likes of *Clash of the Titans* (dir. Desmond Davis, 1981) and its remake (dir. Louis Leterrier, 2010) in which the gods squabble on an epic scale, as if they're in a "Big Brother, Greek Gods" house; though the 1981 version's stop-motion special effects by film legend Ray Harryhausen were a bit old-fashioned at the time, they give the film serious nostalgia vibes. In *Lore* (2021) by Alexandra Bracken, the gods are brought to modern New York City when they fight it out as mortals once every seven years. And Miles Cameron's Age of Bronze trilogy (2022–'24) is set in an alternate Bronze age and features capricious and terrible gods, humans, and monsters in a power struggle.

From India we have manuscripts including the epic poems the *Ramayana* (c. 500 B.C.E.) and the *Mahabharata* (c. 400 B.C.E.), which contain history as well as folklore and stories that have inspired mythic fantasy. In one example, the middle-grade *Aru Shah and the End of Time* (2018) by Roshani Chokshi, elements from these Hindu texts are included in the story about

---

4. Cowlishaw, 1988, n.p.

how Aru Shah accidentally releases a demon from a lamp, and to save the world she must go on a quest into the Kingdom of Death. *Kaikeyi* (2022) by Vaishnavi Patel, inspired by the *Ramayana*, is about Kaikeyi, Rama's mother, telling her own story. And from the Middle East we have the folklore collection *One Thousand and One Nights*, in which Shahrazad (often known as Scheherazade) tells a story each night, ending on a cliffhanger, to avoid her husband's murderous wrath. Though not published in Arabic until the mid-nineteenth century, "the first known reference to the *Nights* is a 9th-century fragment" and it was named "A Thousand Tales" in the mid-tenth century.[5] This has inspired *The Wrath and the Dawn* (2015), a YA retelling by Renée Ahdieh.

China, which also has an extremely long written history, contains an extensive and elaborate mythology recorded in myriad sources from plays to inscriptions on pottery to the recently discovered Dunhuang manuscripts. However, there exists a sixteenth-century Fantasy novel, *Investiture of the Gods* by Xu Zhonglin, that's set during the overthrow of the Shang dynasty (c. 1000 B.C.E.) and the subsequent Zhou dynasty, featuring gods, spirits, demons, magic, and humans. It's been adapted as television shows, video games, and films, the most recent being *Creation of the Gods I: Kingdom of Storms* (dir. Wuershan, 2023), with two more films due to complete the trilogy. Another recent series that's taken inspiration from these tales, as well as Chinese history more broadly, is R.F. Kuang's award-winning Poppy War trilogy (2018–'20).

Early sources of Norse mythology include the *Prose Edda* and the *Poetic Edda*—from which comes the Codex Regius, or the "King's Book", which contains poems about various Norse deities—all collected and recorded during the thirteenth century. Scandinavian myths have had a bit of a heyday recently due to the popularity of the television series *Vikings* (2013–'20) and *The Last Kingdom* (2015–'22) as well as the various Asgardians of the Marvel Cinematic Universe. Joanne M. Harris has written two sets of Norse-inspired novels: *Runemarks* (2007) and *Runelight* (2011) are for children, about a young girl caught between the people who follow the old gods and those who've turned their backs on the old ways; *The Gospel of Loki* (2014) and *The Testament of Loki* (2018) are for adults, with the trickster god telling his own story in ancient Asgard and then in the modern world. Meanwhile, in Britain, mythology and legends have inspired no end of mythic fantasy. Welsh mythology is most accessible via a collection of four tales (known as branches) called the *Mabinogion* (see the 2018 translation by Matthew Francis simply titled *The Mabinogi*). Arthurian fantasy is probably the easiest to identify, from Sir Thomas Malory's *Le Morte d'Arthur* (1485), a compilation and translation of Old French and Middle English tales. Finally,

---

5. Editors of *Encyclopaedia Britannica*, 'The Thousand and One Nights', 2023, n.p.

we can't talk about mythic fantasy without mentioning the granddaddy of the modern Fantasy epics, J.R.R. Tolkien. His *Lord of the Rings* trilogy, as well as much of his other writing, was heavily inspired by Nordic sagas, Celtic myth, Old and Middle English tales (such as *Beowulf*; see **Dragons**), and Arthurian fare, among others.[6]

A Spotter's Guide: Around the World in 80 Myths

Mythic fantasy uses myths, legends, and folktales in various ways. Of special note here is how authors from cultures that don't have access to a long history of written mythology have employed their folktales and myths in pursuit of expressing their rich cultural heritage (you may see this described as Own Voices writing but, in many cases, that term has been dropped in favour of more specific self-descriptions).[7]

- **The springboard approach:** Taking an element from a myth and weaving it into a larger mythic tale is something we see a lot of in middle-grade or Young Adult fiction, especially in stories with wider representation. In *Akata Witch* (2011; titled *What Sunny Saw in the Flames* in the UK and Nigeria) by Nnedi Okorafor, Sunny, a young Nigerian-American girl whose parents moved back to Africa when she was nine, discovers she has magic; she's one of the Leopard People, and she must help defeat Black Hat Otokoto, who's killing children. In *The Serpent's Secret* (2018) by Satantani Dasgupta, twelve-year-old Kiranmala's parents disappear and a demon shows up in her kitchen, starting an adventure via interdimensional travel to the Kingdom Beyond, all of which is inspired by Bengali folklore.
- **Let me re-tell you a story:** Some contemporary mythic fantasy straight-up retells myths either in our present world or in their original place and (sort of) time. In many cases, this is an opportunity to tell the story from the point of view of someone who hasn't had a voice before (often that of female characters), and in many cases, these are marketed not as SFF but as contemporary fiction or even more "literary" historical fiction. One example is *Circe* (2018) by Madeline Miller, with the story told from the sorceress's point of view. A more spec-fic example is T.L. Morganfield's *Bone Flower* series (2013–'16), a retelling of a Toltec myth from what is now Mexico, following a female protagonist in the story of a war among the gods.

---

6. Anderson, 2022, n.p.
7. Lapointe, 2022, n.p.

- **Switcheroo:** An interesting way to create mythic fantasy and use it to engage with the deeper themes of humanity is to take one culture's myth and retell it in another culture's context (such as the author's own culture). *Taduno's Song* (2017) by Odafe Atogun is a contemporary retelling of the Greek Orpheus and Eurydice myth set in Nigeria in which a musician tries to rebuild his life torn apart by a repressive regime. Another retelling of the same myth, this time set in New York City, more magical realism than full-on Fantasy, is *Never Look Back* (2020) by Lilliam Rivera featuring Afro-Latinx characters. Finally, a famous example that mixes several myths but brings them into the present is Neil Gaiman's *American Gods* (2001), about the old gods from various mythologies trying to become relevant again in the modern world that's turned to the new gods of television, drugs, and so on.
- **A new creation:** Finally, we have stories in which the author has created their own mythologies. An early example is *The Gods of Pegāna* (1905) by Lord Dunsany, in which he tells a series of linked stories about an original pantheon. Later, Richard Adams did this in *Watership Down* (1972), in which the rabbits share tales about archetypal bunnies that have adventures out in the world. Finally, we can't forget Tolkien's *The Simarillion* (published posthumously in 1977), which details the history of Middle-earth in the thousands of years before *The Hobbit*. To say that Tolkien took mythic fantasy to its extreme is an understatement, but his influence on Fantasy can't be ignored.

Things That are Cool About Mythic Fantasy

Mythic fantasy lets us play in a sandbox full of the best and worst of human behaviour acted out by gods and monsters. It takes place on a stage where magic is taken for granted, so prepare to get weird. Whether you decide to bring the story of Apollo chasing Daphne, whose father turns her into a tree, into a story about eco-warriors trying to save a forest, or set the tale of Gawain and the Green Knight in an African-American community in a 1960s housing project, there's a plethora of stories out there from which to find inspiration.

Now is the Time of Our Telling

Mythology and Fantasy are both topics that people can take quite seriously, so don't get too caught up in older genre expectations that mythic fantasy must depict a story with a scope of a thousand years or be complex and multilayered with a long list of characters. Sure, some mythic fantasy does work to depict myths and folklore on an epic scale, but not every mythic fantasy is going to be a doorstop. Because the mythologies can be multifaceted, authors will find inspiration at times in the "smaller" stories or lesser-known characters. And, as usual, do be careful when depicting a culture that isn't your own; do your research!

ACTIVITIES

In your own back yard: Bring your mythic fantasy into your own town or city, much like Suyi Davies Okungbowa has done in *David Mogo, Godhunter* (2019; sometimes termed "godpunk" because it brings gods into our world via an Urban Fantasy twist[8]). Consider something happening in your locale that's troubling or making news and then introduce a mythological deity into the situation. What will this being think about what matters to humanity? How will their appearance positively or negatively affect the situation? Consider how wanting to get rid of the deity—or even keep it there!—will complicate matters.

Mythic scale: Take a mythology (one noted in this section or one of the hundreds more in the world) and list the main gods, goddesses, demi-gods, spirits, etc. Then, play casting director and cast celebrities, politicians, authors, musicians, or sports stars, etc., as the deities according to how the personalities and characteristics match. For example, who would be the Zeus equivalent in your pantheon? (Remember, the gods and goddesses have positive *and* negative traits, so while you might not like a certain celeb, they might be the right fit for your pantheon!) Then, use your list to cast something as mundane as a family dinner or surreal as a reality-television show. How will their personalities clash? What will the main arguments be about? And how can you use this activity to explore deeper themes relating to how humans engage with one another and the world?

---

8. A term simultaneously coined by *Age of Godpunk* author James Lovegrove and editors David Moore and Jared Shurin. In *SFX*, 2013, n.p.

FAIRIES

Graceful pixies frolicking in the undergrowth or menacing supernatural tricksters looking for their next victim, the fairy is a mutable figure in Fantasy and folklore (see <u>Folktales and Fairy Tales</u>). It has had a considerable history, and our popular understanding of it has frequently shifted throughout the centuries. These days, there are probably as many takes on fairies as there are writers and readers. Now that's real magic!

A Short History of Fairies

First off, and for our purposes, we're going to distinguish between fairies and elves. Is this distinction arbitrary? Well, yes and no; in terms of popular conception, these beings are often discussed together and are frequently portrayed with similar characteristics (shout-out to Santa's famous fairyesque elves). Yet when it comes to literary history, we find that depictions of these beings represent two different narrative clusters that have developed alongside two different cultural traditions. Elves derive from a Northern European cultural context and originally connoted a powerful and malignant supernatural entity. But the fairies—or the fae as they're often known in Fantasy fiction—stem from a mediaeval softening of this terrifying creature into a more diminutive and often more mischievous figure. A good example of fairies from this era is William Shakespeare's *A Midsummer Night's Dream* (1595–'96), though their divergence from elves would continue to widen as time moved on (one strand of fictional fairy, for example, developed wings in seventeenth-century children's stories). At some point between the mediaeval and early modern periods (probably on a Thursday; these things tend to happen on a Thursday) the literary fairy solidified its now characteristic identification with the folklore and cultural traditions of Celtic nations and communities such as Ireland, Wales, Scotland, and Cornwall. This led to fairies becoming a topic of fascination for popular writers and readers in England and, in the process, they completed their transition into "little people" unrecognisable as the elves enjoyed by earlier audiences. Yet while Victorian writers perpetuated an image of the fairy as an almost gentrified supernatural representative—all pretty dresses and sparkling lights at the bottom of well-tended gardens—this entity's tempestuous nature and narrative independence would not be so easily restrained.

Many significant literary figures sought to claim association with fairies at this time, among them future Nobel Prize-winning poet W.B. Yeats. Yeats saw an opportunity in Irish folklore to craft a distinct literary identity separate from that which the colonising English sought to impose (though, crucially, the ever-contradictory Yeats was himself of Anglo-Irish descent, lived in

London for much of his life, and absolutely profited from his reputation and notoriety in English circles). He was to utilise the fairy as a tool of national distinctiveness to great effect during his early period, especially in books such as 1888's *Irish Fairy and Folktales*, which sought to preserve many vernacular stories lest they were lost to time, and in poems such as 'The Stolen Child' (1889), which recounts the fairies' efforts to enchant a child to come away with them. In his 1890 essay 'Irish Fairies', Yeats recounts stories of fairy paths and mountain gateways to the otherworld and how "brides and new-born children are especially in danger. Peasant mothers, too, are sometimes carried off to nurse the children of the fairies" (or "'the gentry', as the fairies are called for politeness").[1] His work defined the image of fairies in the public imagination as a vital and irrepressible supernatural presence in the world. Also influential at this time were Lang's Fairy Books, a series of brightly liveried children's texts that popularised dozens of now famous fairy stories (many appearing in English for the first time). The series is often attributed to literary critic Andrew Lang, but in actuality (and in his own words), "the fairy books have been almost wholly the work of Mrs. Lang, who has translated and adapted them from the French, German, Portuguese, Italian, Spanish, Catalan, and other languages".[2] Thus, Leonora Blanche Lang (née Alleyne), known as Nora, takes her place as a significant figure in the development of fairy stories as a subgenre. Elsewhere, Scottish author J.M. Barrie debuted the well-known fairy Tinker Bell in his 1904 play *Peter Pan*, where she was presented as a dart of light and represented on stage by a lamp reflecting off a mirror. The character, a fairy in the lithe, tiny, winged, and whimsical mould, subsequently appeared as the hero's mischievous best friend in multiple sequels and adaptations. She could be jealous and vindictive, but also incredibly loyal. Further notable are the so-called Cottingley Fairies, a series of photographs taken in 1917 and 1920 by two young cousins in Yorkshire that appeared to show fairies of the winged and gentrified variety dancing in bushes in their garden. They caught the attention of Sherlock Holmes creator Arthur Conan Doyle—like Yeats, a spiritualist—who published them in a 1920 article about fairies. Doyle hoped that evidence of fairies would point to, and ultimately generate serious research into, the existence of a world beyond our material reality. With such backing, the Cottingley Fairies attracted widespread public interest, yet while Doyle made efforts to have the photographs authenticated by experts, they would eventually (though not until the *1980s!*) be revealed as a simple hoax. Said Frances Griffiths, one of the perpetrators: "I can't understand to this day why people were taken in. They wanted to be taken in".[3]

---

1. Yeats, 2015, n.p.
2. Quoted in Harrington, n.d., n.p.
3. *BBC News*, 2020, n.p.

Of perhaps more consequence to modern Fantasy writers is the later intervention of J.R.R. Tolkien in his much-studied essay 'On Fairy-Stories' (1947). Tolkien was very particular in how he separated what he considered weighty literary undertakings from the kitsch and literally garden-variety Victorian fairies. He dismissed the diminutive size of fairies in those stories, as well as "that long line of flower-fairies and fluttering sprites", as "largely a sophisticated product of literary fancy".[4] In his own stories (modelled on the great Germanic/Northern European story cycles) Tolkien favoured elves; nevertheless, his thinking about fairies was to be influential. It arguably contributed to the return of human-sized fairies to fiction and film in the latter half of the twentieth century. Certainly, today's depictions continue to eschew the cutesy and diminutive Victorian versions in favour of life-sized and morally ambivalent characters. On the one hand, this speaks to the fitting malleability of the literary fairy in adapting to changing storytelling tastes. On the other, and in more practical terms, the return of human-sized fairies enables their cost-effective depiction on the screen and their easy incorporation into modern Urban Fantasy milieus. Interesting examples from the post-Tolkien decades include Sylvia Townsend Warner's *Kingdoms of Elfin* (1977), a collection of satirical stories about European fairy courts; Emma Bull's *War for the Oaks* (1987), in which rival groups of fairies vie for control of Minneapolis with a human musician caught between them; Steven Spielberg's *Peter Pan* adaptation *Hook* (1991), which brought Tinker Bell to the big screen; *Mortal Love* by Elizabeth Hand (2004), a treatise on art that warns of the dangers of too much contact with the fairies (featuring one fairy addicted to sex with humans); Seanan McGuire's bestselling October Daye series (2009–present) in which a half-fae private investigator tackles cases in modern San Francisco (and Fairyland!); Mishell Baker's Nebula-nominated *Borderline* (2016), the protagonist of which polices the thin boundary between Hollywood and Fairyland; Neil Jordan's *Carnivalesque* (2017), which features the withered remains of fairy society hiding as circus performers where their magical abilities can be passed off as acrobatic feats; and Heather Fawcett's novel *Emily Wilde's Encyclopaedia of Faeries* (2023), which offers readers a painfully realistic portrait of an academic who prioritises her research into fairies above everything else!

A Spotter's Guide: Come Away, Oh Human Child…

Fairy categorisation is a kind of a hodgepodge of folkloric types, literary classes, and pop-cultural understandings. Yet any good starter pack for novice writers might include the following (though, as ever, mix, match, or straight up do the opposite as appropriate!):

---

4. Tolkien, 2008, p. 29.

- **Seelie courts:** This is the term generally used to refer to "good" fairies. The word derives from Scottish folklore and, with its connotations of "happy" or "blessed", may have been a measure of appeasement towards these potentially dangerous entities. They can and will indulge in mischief as much as the next fae but, overall, the Seelie are depicted as understanding of human foibles. They're often grateful for human kindness and willing to tolerate offence to a degree, especially if it's accidental and an apology is issued. Despite their generally peaceful nature, they're capable of marshalling powerful supernatural and even military force, and in many stories stand as allies of humanity against more malevolent magical beings.
- **Unseelie courts:** By contrast, these are "bad" fairies and actively hostile to humans. The wickedness of Unseelie fairies is not to be underestimated, and stories will frequently portray them as tormenting humans for sport. They are the Seelie fairies' adversaries, and many tales portray the courts in a state of cold war (the engine of many a modern tale being the threat of this conflict turning hot). Unpredictable and malicious, Unseelie fairies are practitioners of dark magics. As adversaries, they often bring human and Seelie together in a common cause.
- **Solitary fairies:** These beings are generally depicted as having an unfriendly disposition. The term comes from Yeats, who considers them "nearly all gloomy and terrible".[5] They tend to be tricksters or bringers of evil dreams with little agenda beyond their own amusement (the imp-like Rumpelstiltskin is a good example). They've often been expelled from their court or troop (frequently for excessive interference in human affairs). Somewhat related to solitary fairies are leprechauns. Yeats pictured the archetypical leprechaun as a "miser of great wealth" often "seen sitting under a hedge mending a shoe, and one who catches him can make him deliver up his crocks of gold" (or his breakfast cereal if you're American).[6] The Leprechaun series of horror-comedy films (1993–2018) offers a dubious take on this figure.
- **Trooping fairies:** Another Yeats term. Some fairies live on the move in communal groups. These fairies are friendly—arguably *too* friendly!—and their behaviour is characterised by singing, dancing, and majestic processions through the countryside as they pass from one underground kingdom to another in a semi-permanent state of **Carnivalesque**. They dress in fine clothes, keep beautiful horses, and are often presented as enchanting those who stumble across

---

5. Healey, 2018, n.p.
6. Healey, 2018, n.p.

them. They might be on your side, or they might regard you as a plaything, who knows?!
- **Changelings:** A common trope of fairy stories is the idea of the child who is stolen and/or surreptitiously replaced by the fairies. Yeats made much of this "one most malicious habit: They steal children and leave a withered fairy, a thousand or maybe two thousand years old, instead".[7] In the real world, in times past, changelings were frequently used as an explanation for a sickly child or, more cruelly, as a means of rationalising a learning difference or intellectual disability. Of course, in McGuire's October Daye books, changeling is the term for mortal/fairy hybrids such as her protagonist, who comes to earn the respect of human and fae alike.

Things That are Cool About Fairies

There is something enchanting and intoxicating about a magical, and potentially very dangerous, society existing just out of everyday sight. Because fairies don't play by human rules, their intervention in our characters' lives introduces risk and unpredictability. Their enchantments lead our protagonists down paths—literal and figurative—they may not ever have considered. Their palace intrigues threaten to wreak havoc on mere mortals. They're something ancient that feels right at home in contemporary times.

Heed the Warnings

- **Curses:** In much folklore, and in fact in some current beliefs, fairies will *mess you up* if you cross them. Their supernatural retribution can be mischievous, limited to mere annoyances, or as drastic as serious illness or even death. In fiction, a fairy curse can be a powerful story engine, motivating your protagonist to investigate and rectify the situation (and, in the process, how they deal with misfortune can tell us a lot about who they are). Perhaps they retain the services of a mortal or magical intermediary to argue their case. Maybe lifting the curse requires righting their initial action or becoming indentured to the fae for a period of time (though your characters should be wary of tricksy small print in any arrangement they sign with the fairies! See **Goblin Markets** for more about magical deals).
- **Fairy forts/trees:** Fairies are often depicted as possessing an innate connection to nature. They're said to congregate at ruined and overgrown forts or beneath magical trees, and to have done so for

---
7. Healey, 2018, n.p.

hundreds of years. It's all very atmospheric and magical! However, interfering with these sites is considered a major wrongdoing with serious consequences. Even today, a wariness of interfering with fairy forts or trees remains embedded in the cultures of Europe's western flanks. It is not uncommon in Ireland, for example, to hear stories of misfortune attributed to someone clearing away a fairy fort on their land. Persistence of this belief is so strong that there are several instances of major road projects being rerouted due to local protestations that the fairies would be displeased.

- **The underworld/otherworld:** In his essay on 'Irish Fairies', Yeats wrote that "there is no more inaccessible place in existence" than the entrance to Fairyland.[8] So give some thought to how you portray your character's journey (often accidental) to this remarkable realm. These otherworlds are said to exist deep in the forest or hidden under hillsides, often ruled by royalty (as in *A Midsummer's Night Dream*), and are spaces in which time passes at a different rate. Typical otherworlds can look old-fashioned to contemporary eyes, but that's as much because of the era in which fairy stories were originally codified as anything else. So don't feel locked into, say, nineteenth-century aesthetics if you don't want to. What about a technological otherworld? What's fairy Silicon Valley like? Indeed, sometimes these fairy realms intersect with our modern cities, hence urban fantasy, which often leads to…

- **Conflicts with modernity:** Many fairy stories revolve around a clash of the traditional and the modern. Obviously, this is a powerful metaphor for how change is resisted and processed in the real world, but, in stories of the fae, it can also supply writers with a compelling central conflict. Thinking through the relationship between fairies and the modern world can help us fashion captivating narratives. Sometimes fairies are completely concealed from human eyes (unless or until an inciting story event threatens this seclusion). Sometimes they're hiding in plain sight, such as in Jordan's *Carnivalesque* and in many magical realism texts. Sometimes they're open about who they are, participating in human society as lawyers, doctors, or media figures in stories with the magical and mortal existing side-by-side. There's no wrong way of approaching this. It all depends on the story you wish to tell.

- **The truth is out there:** There are many interesting stories to be told about those who search for the fairies or evidence (photographs, etc.) of their existence. Perhaps your character is a lone researcher whose obsessive crusade for the truth is scorned by their peers, or

---

8. Yeats, 2015, n.p.

an academic, as in Fawcett's *Encyclopaedia of Faeries*, or part of a wider organisation, potentially even a government department openly responsible for supernatural affairs (imagine them having to partner with a fairy to solve a crime that concerns both worlds). In all cases, of course, you can imagine the notoriously publicity-shy fairies might not necessarily savour the attention.

ACTIVITIES

Zoned land: An engineer is sent to survey land for a new development on the edge of a village. At the centre of this land is a fairy fort. Locals caution the engineer not to interfere with this sacred gathering place, but the engineer is initially dismissive of their warnings. When the project begins to run into problems (mechanical breakdowns, injuries, financial issues, etc.), the engineer must reluctantly engage with the local and the supernatural communities. Will they be able to appease the fairies? Will they be able to negotiate a compromise acceptable to all? Consider your story's tone, which could be anything from comedic to straight-up Horror.

Pub crawl: Your protagonist is a student on a night out who falls in with group of strangers on a raucous pub crawl. These strangers—exuberant, chaotic, and seductive—drink, sing, and are the life of every establishment they enter. Over time, little instances of magic lead your character to realise that these are fairies following an ancient trooping route from long before the town existed. Is your character intrigued? Are they scared? Will they be carried away to the otherworld at the end of the night or can they escape back to their everyday life?

THE GOBLIN MARKET

You've just nipped down to the corner shop, a trip you make dozens of times a year. Only tonight, under the full moon, the shop's walls glow with a strange luminescence. Inside, when you open the glass door to the refrigerated section, you find.... What's this? A doorway?! And through that doorway is a row of tents decked out in colourful spangles and bells. You hear a voice offering you all manner of magical things. You have, without quite understanding how, found yourself in a goblin market.

A Short History of the Goblin Market

The goblin market (sometimes a fairy market, sometimes a bazaar of the bizarre) is where the mundane meets the strange and where you can buy anything your heart desires *if* you're willing to pay the price. Writers fill these tents and tables, stalls, and shops with all manner of miraculous, enchanting things, and *we are here for it*. However, when you peel away the layers of the trope, sometimes you'll find that it's often made of cardboard with some paste and glitter rather than fully realised because characters might go to the market—a place of great opportunity—but they won't make a purchase or trade and leave empty-handed. And this feels like a missed opportunity.

    A magical market—or, rather, a magical exchange—is part of many stories, but the name for the trope is only as old as Christina Rossetti's famous poem 'Goblin Market' (1862) and so younger than Fairy Tales (though there's no actual market in the poem, but rather a collection of fae creatures with strange fruit to trade when they encounter the narrator and her sister; one sister eats the fruit and wastes away, nearly dying as a result). Prior to Rossetti, however, we find **Fairies**, an integral part of folklore, often appearing alongside magical markets, or involved with magic in connection with markets. In his 1684 book on demonology, Richard Bovet conveys stories he has heard "of Fairies, or Spirits" who would at times "keep a great Fair or Market".[1] In one story recounted to him, a man sees "a great company of People, that seemed to him like Country Folks, Assembled, as at a Fair" and decides to ride amongst them, but as he passes through the crowd he cannot see anything of the fair and only sees it again after he is at a distance from it.[2] Wirt Sikes in his *British Goblins: Welsh Folk-lore, Fairy Mythology, Legends and Traditions* (1880), relays the stories sailors tell about going to **Mysterious Islands** of fairy folk west of Penbrokeshire and of humans who

---

1. Bovet, 1684, p. 207.
2. Bovet, 1684, pp. 208–209.

claimed that fairies "regularly attended the markets at Milford Haven and Laugharne. They made their purchases without speaking, laid down their money and departed, always leaving the exact sum required, which they seemed to know, without asking the price of anything. Sometimes they were invisible, but they were often seen, by sharp-eyed persons".[3] So the fairies hold their markets but don't let humans in, or they visit the human markets only to buy mundane items. The magic is the fairies themselves and not the wares for sale.

Nonetheless, in fairy tales we do begin to see trades or exchanges that contain fairy magic. In 'Rumpelstiltskin' a girl makes a deal with the mysterious trickster so she can spin straw into gold. A smith makes a deal with the Devil or a demon for power and then tricks the demon in 'The Smith and the Devil'. And in 'Jack and the Beanstalk' our hero trades the cow he's meant to take to market for magic beans, much to his mother's chagrin; but he's amazed when the beans grow into a huge beanstalk that he climbs into the sky. The closest any of these get to an actual market is 'Jack and the Beanstalk', but the idea of a place where magical items can be bought began to emerge via stories that followed.

This trope pops up, in a morphed form, throughout SFF stories of the late nineteenth and early twentieth centuries. In H.G. Wells's 'The Crystal Egg' (1897), a shopkeeper ends up with the titular McGuffin through which he can view what's happening on Mars, but, later, the egg ends up sold to an anonymous someone and can't be traced. In another story that Wells wrote only six years later, 'The Magic Shop' (1903), a man takes his son to a shop full of miraculous items, but the shop later seems to vanish. In Lord Dunsany's 1916 take on the idea, 'The Bureau d'Echange de Maux' (or 'The Evil Exchange Office'), the magical shop is where people go to exchange their evil for someone else's, and, once they make the exchange, they cannot find the shop again. Fritz Leiber placed one of his Sword and Sorcery Fafhrd and the Grey Mouser tales in a magical market that disappears; called 'The Bazaar of the Bizarre' (1963), the story bequeaths the subgenre its alternative name.

Contemporary Fantasy stories and games have expanded on this trope, often allowing humans to venture into the market. Bruce Coville's *Magic Shop* series for kids (1989–2003) features an establishment run by S.H. Elives that carries amazing items from a dragon egg to a ring that can turn a child into a monster and back. In Neil Gaiman's **Portal Fantasy** *Stardust* (1999) a fairy market near the village of Wall appears only once every nine years, on May Day, and Dunstan Thorne visits to find a gift for a girl; he exchanges a kiss, and then much more, for a glass flower and ends up fathering a half-fairy child, Tristran. One setting of the role-playing game *Changeling: The Lost* (2007–'22) is a goblin market; there's even a digital

---

3. Sikes, 1880, n.p.

sourcebook, *Goblin Markets* (2009), as well as information on the market law, risks, and rewards. In Jeannette Ng's *Under the Pendulum Sun* (2017), the narrator goes to a goblin market and another character buys a brooch for her that's uncannily like one she had pinned to a corpse's dress at the funeral. Even some contemporary SF stories play with the trope. The 2013 *Doctor Who* episode 'The Rings of Akhaten' (dir. Farren Blackburn) finds Clara and the Doctor in an alien market where all the items traded are of sentimental value, and Clara can only get to the market because an Alien has escorted her there. The market in *Valerian and the City of a Thousand Planets* (dir. Luc Besson, 2017), based on the comic book series *Valérian and Laureline* (written by Pierre Christin, illustrated by Jean-Claude Mézières), is equally inspired by the outlandishness of goblin or fairy markets. Industrial Light & Magic (of *Star Wars* fame) was tasked with creating that universe's biggest shopping bazaar: "The Big Market consists of five million stores that line a cross-shaped canyon extending 500 floors deep. But shoppers in the 28th century needn't walk through 500 floors of stores to find what they want. Instead, they stand within a large desert arena, in a helmet and gloves, and shop virtually".[4] Finally, everyone's favourite television series about Vampires, *What We Do in the Shadows* (2019–present), aired the episode 'The Night Market' (dir. Yana Gorskaya, 2022) in which various supernatural creatures shop at the market, though the majority of the episode focuses on the "familiar fight" during which vampire familiars battle to the death.

So, despite many stories using the trope, very few really lean in and take advantage of the various complications that can arise from magical beings making magical deals. Examples do exist. In *Not for Good Maidens* (2022) by Tori Bovalino, a girl's aunt delves into the goblin market beneath York but doesn't return, sending her family to find her in a place where there are very tricky rules and the main item for sale is human body parts. *A Market of Dreams and Destiny* (2023) by Trip Galey is set fully in the *Untermarkt* beneath an alternate Victorian London; Deri, a human raised by a goblin merchant, uses his market knowledge to try to set himself—and other indentured children—free of their contracts while falling in love with Owain. The book is full of trades and exchanges, keeping track of contracts and loopholes galore.

A Spotter's Guide: Read the T&Cs

The uneven use of the goblin-market trope inspired one academic, Powder Thompson, to analyse how it's been used in Fantasy fiction, narrowing down the definition for this particular trope to elements that should be present, which we think is a good starting point if you're considering writing a goblin

---

4. Industrial Light & Magic, n.d., n.p.

market! Using all five elements helps you create a fully realised fantastical market, one that characters *use* rather than skirt around on their way to somewhere else. Furthermore, the market and the trade or exchange itself is a good way to enhance conflict and roadblocks: you want your character to have to pay a price for what they want, and goblins are nothing if not canny to tricks. Thompson's list of goblin-market trope elements[5] is composed of five specifics:

- **Inhuman or alien merchants:** Rossetti's original 'Goblin Market' banked on this, with the goblins described as little men with animal faces or other body parts. A human dealing with a non-human entity immediately puts our character on the back foot, which enhances narrative and plot complications.
- **Capitalising on the potential for exchange:** Failing to stress the market in goblin *market* is something that often undermines full engagement with the trope: the characters go to the goblin market, and while there is the potential for purchase or exchange, they leave with nothing. Consider why you would direct a character to a place that has things they can take with them—even a mundane supermarket—but then having them leave without anything special.
- **Unique or unusual forms of goods and/or payments accepted:** We want our goblin market to offer wares that we can't get in the corner shop and to require payment that doesn't come from a wallet. In *The Peculiar* (2012) by Stefan Bachmann, one price is that old-fashioned chestnut "an arm and a leg", but what isn't specified is whose appendages will do![6] Seanan McGuire's novella *In an Absent Dream* (2019) features a magical market but, except for a magic potion exchanged for good health, most of the deals and trades are for regular mundane things such as pencils or ribbons. By not taking full advantage of the setting, some of the possibilities for reader expectation and engagement can be lost.
- **Occupies some form of liminal space:** A goblin market typically exists between two worlds or only appears at certain special times, making it a rare and special place. For example, in Holly Black's 'The Night Market' (2004), the market appears in a graveyard during the full moon. Earlier examples have noted that the shop or market cannot be located when the character returns to find it. Like pumpkin spice latte, we love it when things are only available for a limited time; taking advantage of this element can give your story an extra layer of magic.

---

5. Thompson, 2021. p. 341.
6. Bachmann, 2012, ch. 15.

- **There is always small print:** If undertaken with thought, this element can only benefit your story. Many of us have a difficult time with rules and regulations that are in the fine print; we click ACCEPT on terms & conditions for technology and software all the time. This isn't because we're stupid but because it's difficult to understand, and so many little rules that are confusingly written can cause a lot of anxiety; however, we love a technicality that works in our favour. Readers also love it when a technicality of a deal—something that was earlier passed over as unimportant—ends up benefitting or even saving our protagonist. Note, this isn't a *deus ex machina* that rolls in to save the character at the last second but something that was there all along. Fairies and goblins are infamous for tricking mortals, and so a goblin market with inhuman traders should be thick with rules and regulations, terms and conditions, and various laws about how each deal works. *A Market of Dreams and Destiny* does this, with the author juggling a plethora of contracts and loopholes with which his characters must contend, making for a read that doesn't just engage a reader's love of magic but also of details.

Things That are Cool About Goblin Markets

Money comes and goes, and so do goblin markets; they're things of dreams, insubstantial and temporary, uncanny and strange. We know these markets aren't real, but they feel about as real as money, a thing that's most often nothing more than numbers on a screen. Without even describing what's on offer, just the spectre of a market appearing under a full moon can be used to create frisson in a reader. We all know how markets work, but we're so focused on money that the possibility of trading something we have but might not care much about or ascribe any value to (the sound of a favourite childhood toy, or our next view of the ocean at sunset) for something we really *really* want in this world is enticing.

Don't Get Tripped by Tropes

We bandy around the word "tropes" in SFF/H all the time, but it isn't always clear what a trope actually *is*. You'd also think that with all the academic analysis of our genres that there would be a single, clear, strong definition for what a trope is that can be applied to how we use them in SFF/H, but there isn't. The (deep breath) Aarne-Thompson-Uther Tale Type Index (ATU) as it exists now was borne out of a very early twentieth-century study of folktale types that has been translated, expanded, and revised over the past hundred years, but it only looks at folktales and fairy tales. And, despite the influence that these have on SFF/H, our genres have evolved over the years, too.

So, for the sake of simplicity, consider a trope to be a *thing*. Yes, we know, not very helpful! A trope can be an event, a character, a setting, or even an element that is repeated across stories—a vital detail to keep in mind, this repetition—such as the "chosen one" or the singularity, mad scientists or an asteroid strike. When using a trope in your writing, we suggest you do a little research to see how other writers have used it recently and consider the finer details. It can only improve your story creation! One of the best—and only—collected sources of SFF/H tropes is TVtropes.org. Beware the bunny hole it'll send you down, though!

ACTIVITIES

No price is too high: Your character has lost a loved one and will do anything to get them back (you decide whether lost means they're literally lost and never to be found again or if it's a euphemism for death). But there's a chance—the teeniest, tiniest chance—that magic can solve the problem. So, your character goes to a goblin or fairy market with the goal of making a deal to get their loved one back. Write this scene but remember: the exchange must be worth it for both sides, so what will your character offer up, and what is a step too far? (This engages the second and third items in the Spotter's Guide.)

It was here a minute ago: You've gone on a hike but get lost when a sudden gust of wind blows your map out of your hands and over a cliff (no cell reception here, sorry!). You're sure the road back to town is just over this hill, but, when you crest the hill, you find a row of tents and caravans in the middle of nowhere with no car access. Your water bottle is empty and you haven't eaten in hours. The smells coming from some of the stalls are making you salivate! What do the market and its inhabitants look like? What food and drink are on offer? But what are the rules—the risks or rewards—about ingesting anything? Is your character perfectly safe, or are they unafraid on such a sunny day? (This activity will engage with the first, fourth, and fifth items in the Spotter's Guide.)

ENCHANTED CLOTHING

We all have a favourite shirt or pair of jeans or "lucky" socks. Even for the terminally unfashionable, clothing is vital because it's illegal to take the bus to work naked! But what if your jacket had bottomless pockets or your dress made you invisible or your gloves gave you the power to put your hands through any solid material such as the walls of a bank vault? Sounds like your suitcase is full of the pieces required for the perfect enchanted outfit!

A Short History of Enchanted Clothing

Clothing is magical, even when it's not enchanted. We put on clothing to fit into a social class, to go to work or school, to fit in with a peer group, and to partake in big life ceremonies such as weddings. And fashion is where we get to fantasise about clothing. Couture houses send magical, over-the-top, and borderline unwearable clothing down runways each year in Paris, London, Milan, and New York. Sometimes the fashions are so outlandish they seem like they've been created by something beyond the human imagination. There are no lack of runway shows inspired by SFF, such as 2016's Fairy Tale Fashion exhibit in New York featuring runway looks inspired by familiar Folktales and Fairy Tales, some of them using modern fabrics and technology.[1] And, of course, since the invention of nylon, spandex, and other space-age materials, there's a plethora of clothing brands using the term "magic" in their name to indicate a promise of control over various bulges and rolls on mere mortal bodies.

More than that, however, clothing is political, in one sense because actual laws were created telling people what they could and couldn't wear, and in another because the clothing you wear can lend you power that you don't necessarily have, or even take away any power or influence you thought you carried (and in these ways it's magical again!). Put a £3,000 Saville Row suit on a bartender and people will mistake him for a VIP; put a high-powered lawyer in a boiler suit and suddenly she's a garbage collector. The same happens when school kids wear uniforms, workers wear lanyards, and gang members don red, black, or blue bandanas. We're making a statement about our identity and allegiance. We're walking billboards for who we are when we leave the house: we show love for sports teams and various nerdy IP, we show what sort of "clique" we might belong to or music we listen to (Goth kids, unite!), and some of us even wear our political affiliations on our clothing, either via logos (red baseball caps will never

---

1. Fashion Institute of Technology, 2016, n.p.

be an innocent choice again) or via the actual fabrics being used in the case of more environmentally conscious materials such as bamboo. The proverb "Clothes make the person" has been said in one way or another by a line of big thinkers for hundreds of years: Mark Twain in the early 1900s, Erasmus before him in 1500, and Homer before him in 7 or 8 B.C.E.; Shakespeare even used a variation in *Hamlet*.[2] It's been said in so many ways because it's true.

The laws mentioned above to police people's clothing—as well as regulate people's food and drink, households, and even parties—were called sumptuary laws; these were drawn up and enforced at various times around the world. The idea was "to restrict excessive personal expenditures in the interest of preventing extravagance and luxury" based on "religious or moral grounds", though such laws proved difficult to enforce.[3] In late-fourteenth-century China, the Hongwu emperor (founder of the Ming dynasty) established rules about clothing ordered by societal rank in pursuit of restoring order after nearly a century of Mongol rule.[4] At the same time, similar rules were being established in Italy: "From 1300 to 1500, Italian city-states enacted more than three hundred different sumptuary laws, 'a greater number than in all the other areas of Europe combined'".[5] And in Japan from the seventeenth to late nineteenth centuries the Tokugawa shogunate also tried to restrict clothing, but their pronouncements "were so continually flouted and revised that people mocked them as 'three days laws'".[6] Tellingly, the restrictions on clothing enacted in Elizabethan England were to keep certain classes from wearing specific fabrics and colours that could upset the status quo.[7] The Sumptuary Statute of 1574 goes into great detail on who could wear what:

> Any silk of the color of purple, cloth of gold tissued, nor fur of sables, but only the King, Queen, King's mother, children, brethren, and sisters, uncles and aunts; and except dukes, marquises, and earls, who may wear the same in doublets, jerkins, linings of cloaks, gowns, and hose; and those of the Garter, purple in mantles only.[8]

The statutes continue down the strata of society outlining everything from fabric to trim to sword length, etc. In the end, however, what these laws really "defined what was desirable—and the most desirable goods were symbols

---

2. Atkins, 2017, n.p.
3. Editors of *Encyclopaedia Britannica*, 2009, n.p.
4. Postrel, 2020, p. 186.
5. Postrel, 2020, p. 189.
6. Postrel, 2020, p. 188.
7. McGeown, 2019, n.p.
8. Elizabethan Sumptuary Statutes, 1574, n.p.

of imperial status"[9]; in effect, what's most expensive, difficult to get, or newly fashionable is magical to us. It's thus easy to see how enchanted clothing developed as a common trope in our stories. The first place we find enchanted clothing is in various mythologies:

- **Greek:** Perseus, son of Zeus, wears winged sandals that allow him to fly and the Cap of Hades, which renders him invisible, all of which helps him slay Medusa.[10] The cap appears in Rick Riordan's Percy Jackson & the Olympians series (2005–'23) disguised as a Yankees baseball cap, and a piece of clothing conferring the magic of invisibility is a trope found throughout Fantasy literature.
- **Norse:** The dwarf Andvari owns Andvaranaut, a magic ring that originally could be used to find gold but, after Loki stole it, was cursed to bring whoever owned it misfortune.[11] Such stories of magic jewellery would be highly influential on Norse mythology expert and author J.R.R. Tolkien. Meanwhile, Brísingamen (or Brísinga men), the goddess Freya's necklace,[12] inspired other stories such as Alan Garner's *The Weirdstone of Brisingamen* (1960) in which a stone in a bracelet contains within it magic that is needed to protect a realm against evil. See, too, Joel Rosenberg's Keepers of the Hidden Ways series (1995–'98) in which the dwarfs' gift to Freya is a set of jewels that, together, give the wearer power to control the universe. The jewels have been scattered, partially to keep them from Loki, and the myth echoes down to us today in the universe-controlling infinity gauntlet of Marvel comics and films that is created by combining five lost jewels.
- **Persian:** The legendary hero Rostam wears Babr-e Bayān, a coat impervious to fire, water, and weapons; some tales say it was made in heaven and others that Rostam made the coat from the skin of a sea-dwelling **Dragon** he slew.[13] We can see this source of inspiration in any number of modern SFF stories, from the Mithril shirt in *The Lord of the Rings* to Iron Man's exoskeleton and other superheroes' nearly indestructible costumes.

The next place we see a focus on special clothing is in familiar folktales and fairytales, though it isn't *always* enchanted (most of the tales mentioned here will be the European versions; in many cases, there are earlier versions

---

9. Postrel, 2020, p. 188.
10. Editors of *Encyclopaedia Britannica*, 'Perseus', 2023, n.p.
11. Editors of *Britannica Kids*, 'Andvari', n.d., n.p.
12. Editors of *Encyclopaedia Britannica*, 2022, n.p.
13. Editors of *Encyclopaedia Iranica*, 1988, n.p.

of these tales as well as versions from various non-European countries). In 'The Emperor's New Clothes' by Hans Cristian Andersen (1837), there are no clothes at all, which is the point! It's all about perception and power. In 'Cinderella' by Charles Perrault (1697), the fairy godmothers magic up a dress for Cinderella to wear to the ball, and she accidentally leaves behind a glass slipper that the prince uses to find her; neither of these items is enchanted with magic, but they do transform Cinderella into someone whom the prince notices. And then there are the references to making cloth or sewing: 'Rumpelstiltskin' (the Brothers Grimm, 1812) features spinning straw into gold, the princess in 'Sleeping Beauty' (Perrault, 1697) must avoid spinning wheels/spindles or risk death, and in 'The Brave Little Tailor' (Grimm, 1812), the tailor in question faces several tasks (though none require that he sew!).

Enchanted or magical clothing has also influenced modern Fantasy writers. In 'The Twelve Dancing Princesses' (Grimm, 1857), an enchanted cloak makes the wearer invisible; shades of Perseus's cap, for sure, but modern invisibility cloaks appear in *The Lord of the Rings* and the Harry Potter series. Andersen's tale 'The Red Shoes' (1845) is about a girl whose red shoes become enchanted and make her dance so much she has her feet chopped off (!!!); an interesting version of this is when Lily in *Legend* (dir. Ridley Scott, 1985) is woo'd into a black dress that makes her dance for Darkness, and she becomes Dark Lily. In 'Jack the Giant Killer', from Cornish folklore, Jack ends up with shoes that make him very fast, a trope similar to the "seven-league boots" in other European folklore, which give the wearer the ability to take a step equal to the length someone can walk in a day. Again, we can trace that footwear back to Perseus, but we can also see how this has influenced the use of other magic shoes such as Dorothy's ruby slippers in *The Wizard of Oz* (dir. Victor Fleming, 1939) based on the silver shoes from Frank L. Baum's original novel *The Wonderful Wizard of Oz* (1900), which magically transport Dorothy from Oz to home in faraway Kansas. Additionally, the mediaeval European tale about Old Fortunatus tells the story of a man who's gifted a purse that always contains money[14]; there's a straight line from that to Mary Poppins's bottomless carpet bag (in *Mary Poppins* by P.L. Travers, 1934) or, indeed, Hermione's magical beaded bag from which she pulls clothing, supplies, and even a tent in *Harry Potter and the Deathly Hallows* (2007). Finally, we can't miss mentioning games: Forgotten Realms, the vast world created by Ed Greenwood and countless others as the main setting for *Dungeons & Dragons* and *Baldur's Gate*, is filled with supernatural items, from belts to gauntlets to capes to mantles, some of which give the wearer strength or other magical characteristics and some of which will curse the wearer.[15]

---

14. Editors of *Britannica Kids*, 'Fortunatus', n.d., n.p.
15. Forgotten Realms Wiki, n.d., n.p.

The popularity of costume drama set in past centuries has further inspired a slew of shows and websites dedicated to better understanding historical dress, especially actual dresses. This plus the Disney-Princess-ification of Millennials and Gen Z has inspired some current YA Fantasy with a focus on fashion. In *The Dress Shop of Dreams* by Menna Van Praag (2014), Cora's grandmother can free a woman's deepest desires by adding a stitch to a piece of clothing she carries in her shop, and she secretly does this to help her granddaughter find love (it's not marketed as YA but will appeal to those readers). *Murder, Magic, and What We Wore* by Kelly Jones (2017) is set in Regency England with heroine Annis who can sew garments that disguise the wearer and uses her skills to try to catch her father's killer. *Torn* by Rowena Miller (2018) features a young seamstress who embroiders charms into the clothes she makes. In *Enchantée* by Gita Trelease (2019), newly orphaned Camille uses dark blood magic on her appearance, including her clothing, so that she can pass as aristocracy and enchant her new friends at the court of Versailles. Finally, In *Spin the Dawn* by Elizabeth Lim (2021)—which sports the brilliant logline "*Project Runway* meets *Mulan*"—Maia competes to become the emperor's tailor, using her magic scissors when tasked to make three dresses out of moonlight, sunlight, and the blood of stars.

Element Spotlight: Easy on the Eyes

All this talk about clothing leads us to consider how we describe characters' physical selves. This is something that novice writers find difficult, and one reason is that although writers love to read, they often also love television and film. But describing characters in prose is totally different from describing them for visual mediums, and that's where the confusion arises. A lot of stories and books out there describe characters from head to toe, including hair and eye colour, nose and lip shape, every piece of clothing, etc. This also comes through in descriptions of characters' eyebrows, lips, eyes, and other body parts moving in tandem with their dialogue or emotions. Count the number of times you use "eyes" or "smile" in a draft, and you might start to see that you're overusing these descriptions to the point they become meaningless. So, what do you do?

One of the best tips we gave to our students is "It's only important if it's important." This is especially significant in SFF. Say you have a character with special magical abilities, and their purple eyes are the only outward indication of this power. That detail is crucial for a reader to know; however, if they just have plain old human brown or blue eyes, it isn't necessarily that important or that interesting (unless you're writing Romance, which depends on painting a picture that links to desire, so consider your genre!). If your character is a vampire, for example, most readers will fill in the blanks: sharp canine teeth, pale skin, etc. So, what about your vampire is different or important? *That's* what should make it to the page. The same for their clothing: if what they wear helps a reader understand the character's personality (for example, they're a *D&D* nerd in a private school full of buttoned-up future cabinet ministers) mention it. And in SFF, keep in mind that clothing can indicate jobs, social class, magical or other powers, military rank, etc. So, if the detail is important for understanding the character, *then* it's important enough for a reader to know. Otherwise, consider leaving it out!

Things That are Cool About Enchanted Clothing

Creating enchanted clothing gives you the ability to add or remove magical powers more easily than explaining that a character can do X because they were born with that ability, learned it, or so on. Plus, this helps enhance story conflict. Say a character has magic, wall-scaling shoes that they use to break a relative out of prison but the shoes have a short energy reserve; when the character's teenage child finds the shoes, and they get caught halfway up a skyscraper they've climbed on a dare, not only does the kid have to be rescued but the parent is in danger of being discovered as a prison-break accomplice! Also, because clothing is so tied to various geographical places and historical eras, it's fun to scratch that costume-drama itch in Fantasy by adding magic to the clothing you would love to try on yourself.

Sometimes the Shoe Doesn't Fit

Clothing in SFF does lend itself to a few troublesome tropes:

- **"Magic pants":** No, magic pants aren't special underwear that never need to be washed! These are "magical" because when a character changes size or shape, like the Hulk or a **Werewolf**, somehow their pants change size, too, and everyone keeps their modesty! In many cases, the clothing also comes back when a character returns to human shape.
- **Fanservice:** There are many ways that stories—and the clothing within them—can be used as fanservice (here's a comics-accurate outfit in a television show; there's a character sporting colours in support of a social cause). But one thing to watch out for are situations in which female-presenting characters are depicted in a sexualised way via a lack of clothing following a supernatural transformation. This almost always serves the male gaze rather than character or plot. There's almost never a great reason for it.

- **Don't over accessorise:** Additionally, consider your characters' personalities outside of their clothing. Just like someone wearing an over-the-top outfit is described as "the clothes wearing her" instead of her wearing the clothes, you want your characters to have personalities, quirks, desires, flaws, etc., that aren't related to what they wear. The enchanted clothing is just the cherry on top.

ACTIVITIES

Inside-out: Choose a piece of clothing that's often used as a magical or enchanted item in stories and upend things. Instead of a dress making the wearer beautiful and desirable, it highlights all their personality flaws. Instead of a pair of shoes making the wearer swift, it makes them unable to understand their native language or to react to a physical threat. And instead of a coat being impenetrable, it exposes all the wearer's weaknesses. You can put a time limit on the enchantment so that the wearer is stuck in the garment for a specified length of time or until they get to a specific place. Write a scene or story in which you turn the trope inside-out.

The ties that bind: Write a story in which a seamstress or tailor can instil magic in a garment, but only at great personal consequence (you decide what the consequences of this magic are!). Unfortunately, a powerful leader in this storyworld wants the maker to create a piece of clothing that will give them even more power. If you write this from the point of view of the powerful leader, how will that person justify their desire? Who do they want the power to help or harm? If you write it from the point of view of the seamstress/tailor, what happens if they say no, or what happens if they say yes? In the end, who pays the price for this magic?

DRAGONS

The great wyrms rise! Dragons, in their many forms, are as essential a component of Fantasy as Witches, **Portals**, or elves. They're instantly recognisable, but, for all of that, they've often been misunderstood and mischaracterised. Because dragons don't all exhale fire. They don't all stockpile gold or sound like Benedict Cumberbatch. They're more varied than people realise. So come with us now on an epic quest to slay misconceptions. *Hark!* We already hear the mighty beast stirring in its lair... .

A Short History of Dragons

Born out of a long history of supernatural giant-lizard tales, the deep significance of dragons in folklore and, later, in literature cannot be overstated. The creature as we know it today comes to us through the primordial snake Vritra, said in Indian legend to have held the waters of the world hostage; through the dragon-goddess Tiamat, the personification of saltwater cloven in half by the god Marduk in the Babylonian creation epic; through the huge python overcome by Apollo and the snake-like Ladon felled by the hero Hercules (see Mythic Fantasy); through the huge worm Fáfnir in Norse mythology—killed by Sigurðr, the original dragon-slayer—and through its descendants in Anglo-Saxon literature such as Beowulf (c. 975–1025; check out the majestic translation by Seamus Heaney, 1999). Indeed, the latter two creatures prove the most influential, with no less than J.R.R. Tolkien declaring that:

> "dragons, real dragons, essential to both the machinery and the ideas of a poem or tale, are actually rare. In northern literature, there are only two that are significant. If we omit from consideration the vast and vague Encircler of the World, Miðgarðsormr, the doom of the great gods and no matter for heroes, we have but the dragon of the Völsungs, Fáfnir, and Beowulf's bane".[1]

It's from these two monsters that the figure of the dragon in the West (though that's by far not the only place you'll find it) eventually stabilised around the turn of the first millennium, finally becoming something a modern reader would recognise as dragonish.

Throughout the mediaeval period, dragons retained a sense of danger and mystery. They were something for champions, usually chivalrous knights, to prove their worth by defeating (often by outright killing them). The Middle English narrative poem *Sir Eglamour of Artois* (c. 1350) features the defeat

---
1. Tolkien, 1936, p. 253.

of a mighty dragon as one of its protagonist's many challenges. Such work perpetuated the notion of dragons as evil things that, ultimately, were destined for destruction by humanity. These were bloody years for the great beasts (and many modern works metafictionally attribute the contemporary scarcity of dragons to such historic persecution). Yet the centrality of dragons to storytelling waned with the end of the age of chivalry and the coming of modernity. Sporadic appearances would continue, but it wasn't until the mid-twentieth century that dragon fever truly returned with a wallop.

It took one titanic figure to resurrect another, with elf-language enthusiast Tolkien bringing the vicious, cunning, treasure-hording, and seemingly unstoppable dragon archetype roaring back with Smaug in *The Hobbit* (1937). Far from turn-of-the-century efforts to transform dragons into friendly figures (see the intelligent, poetry-loving creature in Kenneth Grahame's classic children's tale 'The Reluctant Dragon', 1898), Tolkien leaned heavily on his love for Fáfnir and the Beowulf dragon. His Smaug is a beast in the literal sense, the last of the great dragons of Middle-earth, a literal survivor of a mythological age. He's malicious and haughty, given to grand speeches about his terrible power and destructive deeds. He terrorises the human inhabitants around his underground lair in the Lonely Mountain and, as in the great Germanic narratives out of which Tolkien wove his Legendarium, is eventually slain by a hero out to prove his mettle and restore his reputation. Tolkien would tap the dragon vein again later, with the Nazgûl's flying beasts in *The Lord of the Rings* (1954–'55), sometimes called the Black Wings or Hell-hawks, possessing certain dragon-like characteristics—snake-like necks and heads, wings, etc.—without necessarily being fully dragonish. However, with the posthumous publication of *The Silmarillion* (1977), Tolkien readers could finally appreciate the true size, terror, and destructive ability of the author's dragons, the most destructive weapons in the arsenal of Morgoth, the first Dark Lord of the world. These were war beasts bred, essentially, to fight angels and the armies of heaven (or, in Tolkien parlance, the Valar). So enormous were these creatures that they defined historical epochs, with the death of the colossal Ancalagon the Black, the greatest dragon of all time, marking the end of the First Age of Middle-earth.

As influential as Tolkien was, of course, his dragon vision would not be the sole defining depiction of the era. Anne McCaffrey's Dragonriders of Pern series (1967–present) takes a Science Fictional approach with a story cycle set on a distant planet where human colonists, who've long since lost their technology and connection to Earth, co-exist with intelligent, fire-breathing dragons. Beginning with the Hugo and Nebula-winning *Dragonflight* (1968), McCaffrey crafts a world that's part feudal (lords, ladies, and so on) and part modern (telegraphs, chemical fertilisers, etc.), but it's her dragons, and the culture surrounding them, that truly make the series fly. These telepathic creatures are bonded with a human rider at hatching. The connection is deep and transformative for both, so much so that a dragon will commit suicide in the event its rider dies, and a rider who loses their dragon will suffer traumatic grief for the rest of their life. Meanwhile, Ursula K. Le Guin's Earthsea books (1968–2001) portray dragons with a dangerous ambiguity: they're neither good nor evil; they've accrued vast knowledge over their long lives but aren't necessarily given to sharing it with idiotic humans. Le Guin's dragons, as novelist Max Gladstone observes, are "wise, capricious, beautiful, mighty, and sometimes sad", and "she salts Tolkien's profoundly Western dragons ... with elements of the Chinese demigod. ... I don't think we would have the modern fantasy dragon—subtle, cunning, alien, wrathful and compassionate all at once—without her work".[2]

In the latter half of the twentieth century, the many avenues these authors opened continued to bear rich dragon fruits. Gordon R. Dickson's imaginative *The Dragon and the George* (1976) sees a mediaeval history professor's mind projected into a fantasy realm where it comes to inhabit a dragon's body. *Tea with the Black Dragon* (1983) by R.A. MacAvoy features a 2,000-year-old Chinese dragon who conceals himself as a linguist in 1980s San Francisco. Terry Pratchett's Discworld series features several varieties of dragons used to reliable effect by the master of **Comedic Fantasy**. Barbara Hambly's *Dragonsbane* (1985) brings real three-dimensionality to the figure of the dragon, while The Halfblood Chronicles series (1991–present) by Mercedes Lackey and SFF legend Andre Norton, though mostly focused on elves, features dragon shamans in prominent roles. The Song of Ice and Fire series by George R.R. Martin, which began in 1996, made much of dragons as weapons of mass destruction. Twenty-first-century authors have continued this trend of reimagining and, in many cases, redeeming the dragon, with prominent examples including *Eragon* (2001) and its sequels by Christopher Paolini; *Reign of Fire* (dir. Rob Bowman, 2002), which gives us a dragon Apocalypse; and Jo Walton's World Fantasy Award-winning *Tooth and Claw* (2003), a sort of Jane Austen with scales. The television series *A Game of Thrones* (2011–'19) and *House of the Dragon* (2022–present) brought Martin's particular take on the creatures as king- and queen-makers to an enormous audience in often spectacular fashion (that Loot Train attack sequence, anyone?). Marie Brennan's rather brilliant *A Natural History of Dragons* (2013) inaugurates a book series about the world's most renowned dragon naturalist. Julie Kagawa's YA Urban Fantasy *Talon* (2014) follows a dragon who disguises herself as human to operate as a sleeper agent ahead of a dragon conquest of the world. The likes of Patricia Wrede (*Dealing with Dragons* 2015), Kelly Barnhill (*When Women Were Dragons*, 2022), Kit Rocha (*Consort of Fire*, 2023), Rebecca Yarros (*Fourth Wing*, 2023), and L.R. Lam (*Dragonfall*, 2023) are also worthy of your attention.

---

2. Gladstone, 2013, n.p.

A Spotter's Guide: Here There Be Dragons

- **Western dragons:** The Western depiction of dragons descends from a combination of near-Eastern mythological entities that typically embodied some kind of primordial energy or aspect of nature (often something to do with water), and great big Nordic/Germanic mythological beasties (usually linked to the end of the world). They evolved over hundreds of years into a stereotype of evil (though it's always worth asking yourself just *who* in your story has a vested interest in perpetuating this reputation?). Some stories depict them as symbols of avarice, sitting on piles of gold. They're even incorporated into nationalist origin myths (such as England's dragonslayer St. George). Sometimes two-legged, sometimes four, and sometimes with wings, sometimes without, they usually fly and exhale fire. Oftentimes they demonstrate significant intelligence and the power of speech. Smaug in *The Hobbit* is both the classic example and, in many ways, the culmination of everything that came before.
- **Eastern dragons:** These are ubiquitous symbols of wisdom, strength, and knowledge in many Eastern cultures, particularly in China where they were long an emblem of the historical Emperors.[3] Chinese dragons are a complicated and dense subject, with many variations throughout history, literature, and art (the vast majority of which have their own lore and attributes). Yet their appearance is usually more fortuitous than that of their Western counterparts, typically evoking prosperity, spiritual enlightenment, or mastery over the elements. Marvel's *Shang-Chi and the Legend of the Ten Rings* (dir. Destin Daniel Cretton, 2021) is a recent popular representation of Chinese dragons. Do note, of course, that depictions of dragons aren't uniform across Asia, with different takes found in Japan, in Korea (said to reside in deep lakes), and in the Philippines (such as the moon-eating serpent Bakunawa), to name a few. So be sure to conduct the appropriate research to avoid problematic appropriation and to be respectful of others' cultures.
- **African dragons:** Many mythological entities across the African continent present as dragon-like serpents. The infamous Ouroboros, for example—the snake eating its own tail—originally derives from Egyptian iconography,[4] while Apophis—a primordial chaos deity—was often depicted as a serpent (used to great effect on television's *Stargate SG-1*, 1997–2007). In the rich folklores of west Africa, one

---

3. Sautman, 1977, pp. 76–77.
4. Bekhrad, 2017, n.p.

finds the reptilian Ninki Nanka in Ghana (see Natasha Bowen's 2021 YA novel *Skin of the Sea*). Stories of the rainbow serpent Ayida-Weddo, a cosmic snake that helped to create the world, travelled with enslaved peoples from what is now Benin all the way to the Caribbean, where it contributed to the Vodou religion.[5] Meanwhile, in South Africa, the legendary Grootslang—or Big Snake—is said to protect the many treasures of a deep cave known as The Bottomless Pit from which very few people have returned.[6]

- **Mesoamerican dragons:** Indigenous peoples in the Americas, especially the Aztec, the Toltec, and the Mayans, told many stories of winged beasts. Chief among these is surely the feathered serpent Quetzalcoatl, which was worshiped as a god and was said to have contributed to the creation of the world.[7] Like other dragons, Quetzalcoatl's imagery had political, religious, military, and fertility connotations depending on the context. Many Mesoamerican belief systems granted him power over the rain and the wind. The creature's name lives on as Quetzalcoatlus, an absolutely *terrifying* flying dinosaur identified in the 1970s, possibly the largest ever flying animal!
- **Sea serpents:** Sea dragons—combining the serpentine origin of dragon mythology with their repeated connection to water imagery—recur throughout the world. Stories of them are told by Aristotle in his *Historia Animalium*, in the Hebrew Bible (famously the great serpent Leviathan), and throughout Germanic/Norse mythology. The latter offers us some of the most striking depictions, including the world serpent Jörmungandr (known as Miðgarðsormr in Old Norse), a vast creature that dwells in the ocean and is so large that it encircles the planet with its tail in its mouth, ouroboros fashion. It's said to be a child of the trickster Loki, to be an enemy of Thor, and a creature with a role to play in Ragnarök, the Norse End-of-Days. Stories of sea serpents persist today, such as the Gaasyendietha said to dwell in Lake Ontario. Such contemporary folklore generally falls under the heading of **Cryptozoology**.

Things That are Cool About Dragons

Scales! Tails! Great blasts of fire! Even fur, as in Falkor the luck dragon from *Neverending Story* (dir. Wolfgang Petersen, 1984)! Dragons are one

---

5. Saint-Lot, 2003, p. 150.
6. Rose, 2001, p. 156.
7. Editors of *Encyclopaedia Britannica*, 'Quetzalcóatl', 2023, n.p.

of the most iconic images of Fantasy fiction. Writing about such enormous and multifaceted creatures can be both technically challenging and hugely satisfying. An atmosphere of barely contained power seeps into their every appearance, something that makes their moments of vulnerability even more affecting. Their size also necessitates that we think carefully about how we stage our scenes (especially when puny humans are involved). Adding a dragon to a story is like making a promise to do these remarkable creatures justice.

Quit Dragon My Heart Around

- **Dragon symbolism:** The image of a mighty dragon can evoke pride or fear depending on how it's deployed in your story. In the real world, for example, it's been used as a rallying point for national identity, such as the Welsh flag on which the dragon, the national symbol of Wales, has turned its back on England! In Martin's series, dragons are symbols of overwhelming military power (the same way, for instance, an aircraft carrier might be perceived in the real world). Yet, when paired up with protagonists on journeys of self-discovery, dragons can represent more abstract ideas. Stories can feature them as symbols of female empowerment (Daenerys Targaryen, for instance) or of literally smouldering attraction between characters. Consider the potential of dragons to enrich your fiction on a *symbolic* level.
- **How to train your dragon:** Here we don't just mean the 2010 film of this title (dirs. Chris Sanders and Dean DeBlois), itself loosely based on Cressida Cowell's 2003 book, but, instead, stories that depict the "professionalism" of dragon training, dragon riding, and so on. Because while dragon wrangling is often portrayed as an innate talent, there are just as many interesting tales to be told where it's a learned or taught skill. Consider what stories can be told about a dragon academy's rivalries and pressure (*Fourth Wing* by Yarros is a good example). Are there dragon competitions similar to showjumping or horse-riding in your storyworld? Is there a market for professional dragon-riding gear? Are there dragon vets? Are there country songs about dragons and can you please include the lyrics in your story?
- **Dragons as protagonists:** Don't forget to consider how the dragons feel about encountering people. Don't neglect their agency and do consider opportunities to allow them to be the heroes of their own stories. McCaffrey's work has things to say about this, of course. Walton's *Tooth and Claw* is also a great example of how to depict dragon society. A very recent addition that might not at first seem

evident is the Netflix film *Damsel* (dir. Juan Carlos Fresnadillo, 2024), which turns the damsel-in-distress Fantasy trope on its head in more ways than one. Questions that you may want to consider include how do dragons experience the world on a sensory level and how do their interactions with humans—both positive and negative—affect how they see us? To get the hang of this, you might start by retelling a classic Fantasy story from the dragon's perspective.

- **Dragons with jobs:** We're used to thinking of dragons as loner beasts or military assets, but there are fascinating stories to be told beyond standard expectations. What about dragons who have been bred for, or have chosen, different kinds of service? Perhaps small dragons that inspect wagons for contraband at the kingdom's border. Or seeing-eye dragons that help humans navigate the city. Maybe they deliver air cargo in your world or are "employed" by a mining company or other extractive industry (they certainly have the skills for it). So, think beyond the obvious and you might discover something unexpected.
- **Save the dragons!** Many societies in fiction fear dragons, which leads to persecution. Often, dragons are rare because humans have hunted them to near extinction. But it's also true that some characters will be more enlightened. Consider the potential for stories about dragon-preservation societies, pro-dragon environmentalism, dragon-rights activists, dragon reserves (such as the Sunshine Sanctuary for Sick dragons in Discworld), and so on (use real-world animal conservation groups as inspiration). Perhaps your protagonist is an Extinction Rebellion activist blocking runways that interfere with dragon-migration routes. Or maybe your dragons are part of your storyworld's ecosystem causing, for instance, forest fires that ultimately rejuvenate woodlands.

ACTIVITIES

Dragon diplomacy: After centuries of distrust, two rival kingdoms have reached a peace treaty. This will be symbolised by one kingdom gifting a pair of dragons to the other. Your protagonist will be one of those responsible for providing the specialised care these creatures require (perhaps they're a stablehand, perhaps a veterinarian of sorts). But the peace will be jeopardised should anything befall the dragons! Use a Fantasy setting of your choosing and write the story of how your character meets this challenge. And be warned, not everyone in the kingdom is in favour of the treaty.

Field trip: Your protagonist is a present-day dragon researcher (maybe a PhD student?) who has tagged a specimen with a GPS locator. One day the signal vanishes. Fearing the worst, they must travel deep into the mountains to find out what's happened to the animal they've spent years studying. Has it succumbed to poachers? Or has it found a mate? Write the story of this journey. Maybe include sections of your protagonist's academic research on dragons!

CRYPTOZOOLOGY

Sightings of strange creatures have been part of human culture for thousands of years, but it's only in the last century or so that these have been codified as an area of pseudoscientific inquiry or, more important for us, a whole field of amazing beastie stories. Such tales are balanced in a fascinating tension between doubt and possibility. Because of course there's nothing to prove that Bigfoot or the Loch Ness Monster actually exist... but any good spec-fic writer knows that the absence of evidence is not *necessarily* evidence of absence.

A Short History of Cryptozoology

The word "cryptozoology" was first used in the early 1940s by Scottish biologist Ivan T. Sanderson in an effort to be taken seriously by the scientific establishment when describing "the science of hidden animals".[1] The Belgian-French zoologist Bernard Heuvelmans would later coin the term independently in the late 1950s, and while he is perhaps now more associated with it, Sanderson and he would become frequent correspondents and supporters of each other's work. Later, in the early 1980s, J.E. Wall contributed the term "cryptid" for the discipline's subject of inquiry, a conscious effort to replace "monster" with something less sensational (the result has been, shall we say, a mixed success). Wall's term means "a living thing having the quality of being hidden or unknown".[2] We use it as an umbrella for stories about creatures whose existence is denied by the academic establishment, but while this terminology is recent, the kind of beings it describes have a long history intertwined with **Folk Horror** and **Mythic Fantasy**. For example, Tibetan tales of the Yeti, the so-called Abominable Snowman, are several thousand years old, while stories about the Loch Ness Monster—potentially embellishments of Scottish Kelpie legends—allegedly date to a sighting by Irish monk St. Columba in 565.

Cryptids past and present tend to be sparked by a local myth before going on to serve as mutable embodiments of wider social-political, racial, or even economic discourses. A good example is the Jersey Devil, sometimes described as "America's original Cryptid", which is said to have prowled that state since at least the 1780s.[3] Supposedly a deformed "devil child" that, upon its birth, immediately flew up a chimney and away into the forest, the Jersey Devil is a good example of a cryptid whose physical description varies

---

1. Heuvelmans, 1968, p. 508.
2. Wall, 1983, n.p.
3. Mart and Cabre, 2021. p. 9.

throughout its reported history (indeed, in many cases, the "manifestations and motivations" of individual cryptids are "so diverse that only the name could possibly connect them"[4]). Sometimes the Jersey Devil is child-sized, sometimes adult-sized; it variably displays wings, claws, horns, and a tail; sometimes it can fly, sometimes it's invisible; it attacks cattle and children depending on the time period. It typifies how cryptids are whatever people— and specifically *you* as a writer—want them to be. More than that, the Jersey Devil tells us about how cryptozoology stories come to be, derived as it is from the weirdness of a 1700s folk tale rooted in white-colonist fears of the sheer vastness of the American continent. We might connect this tale to Mark Fisher's observation that "the sense of wrongness associated with the weird" serves as "a signal that the concepts and frameworks which we have previously employed are now obsolete".[5] No surprise so that cryptid tales can so often be traced to historical settler anxieties.

A more modern example is El Chupacabra—the "goat sucker"—a vampiric cryptid that first emerged in Puerto Rico in the 1980s and whose narrative presence now extends across Mexico and the southern border regions of the US (where, at the peak of its notoriety, it channelled white anxieties about rocketing Latino immigration). El Chupacabra is blamed for countless animal deaths and is well known via depictions in television and film throughout the 1990s. Some see this cryptid as a manifestation of anti-imperialist energies, finding in its Puerto Rican origins "fears of United States sponsored medical experimentation and sterilization, the decline of agriculture affecting the southwestern economy, and popular unrest regarding United States military radar projects".[6] It is, in many ways, the perfect urban legend.

Of course, the universality of stories about strange creatures means that it's impossible to cover more than just a pawful of them in any single text. American writer Charles Fort (from whom we derive the term "Fortean" for strange phenomena, later to give its name to the popular magazine *Fortean Times*) did much early work to popularise the breadth of their cultural footprint. Also important in this early period was *American Myths and Legends* (1903) by Charles Montgomery Skinner, which laid the groundwork for some of the most famous cryptids. Meanwhile, writers including Sanderson and Heuvelmans gathered global examples, and explorers and adventurers such as Roy Chapman Andrews reported anecdotes (Andrews's 1926 book *On the Trail of Ancient Man* introduced western readers to the Mongolian Death Worm, which would serve as inspiration for the much larger creatures of *Tremors*, dir. Ron Underwood, 1990). Later in the century, sightings of "new"

---

4. Genge, 1996, p. 23.
5. Ficher, 2016, p. 13.
6. Ahuja, 2009, p. 561.

cryptids spawned huge numbers of books and journalistic accounts. A case in point is the terrifying, red-eyed flying creature known as Mothman, said to appear before disasters, which caused a cryptid scare in West Virginia in 1966 and '67. The story garnered media attention and inspired the cryptid text *The Mothman Prophecies* (1975) by John Keel. Later again, the prevalence of tabloid newspapers, especially in the 1980s and '90s in the US, fuelled a market for stories about the unexplained (see, too, the likes of the television series *Arthur C. Clarke's Mysterious World*, 1980). Sporadic claims of cryptid sightings have continued ever since (consider the "Owlman" of Cornwall or the shapeshifting Popobawa—Swahili for "Bat Wing"—which caused an outbreak of mass hysteria in Zanzibar in the mid-1990s).

A representative sample of texts from the fictional side of things—or at least the side that *acknowledges* itself as fictional—might begin with the ancestor of the modern form, *The Lost World* (1912) by Arthur Conan Doyle, a pre-*Jurassic Park* dinosaur tale "in which the Cryptozoologist's wildest dreams come true".[7] Stories such as William J. Makin's 'The Monster of the Loch' (1934), Leslie Charteris's 'The Convenient Monster' (1959), and Lionel Fanthorpe's 'The Loch Ness Terror' (1960) all take Scotland's most famous cryptid as their subject. A true Yeti appears in Hergé's graphic novel *Tintin in Tibet* (1960) while a Robot version serves as the antagonist on television's *Doctor Who* in the Second Doctor serial 'The Abominable Snowmen' (1967). Ape-men and underground lizard people were among the strange creatures investigated by *Kolchak: The Night Stalker* on his eponymous television series (1974–'75). *Kolchak* would directly inspire writer Chris Carter to create *The X-Files* (1993–2002), which famously flirted with classic cryptids such as the Jersey Devil, El Chupacabra, and even lake monsters throughout its run, but also invented and popularised original creatures at the intersection of folklore and urban legend.

As with other subgenres, the twenty-first century has brough increased diversity, narrative sophistication, and tonal variety to cryptozoology. The award-winning *Wild Life* (2000) by Molly Gloss is an example that tells the masterful story of a "a cigar-smoking, feminist writer of popular adventure" lost in Washington State's Cascade Mountains who survives with the help of a gentle family of "apes or erect bears of immense size": the Sasquatch.[8] It's serious, profound writing, which treats its subject with dignity and respect. For younger readers, the YA novel *Cryptid Hunters* (2005) by Roland Smith follows a pair of teenage siblings sent to live with their uncle, an anthropologist searching for cryptids, on a **Mysterious Island**. Yan Ge's *Strange Beasts of China* (2006; trans. 2021) blends SF and magical realism for a story of an amateur cryptozoologist writing an account of unusual

---

7. Heuvelmans, 1968, p. 433.
8. Anonymous, 2000, n.p.

species in a fictional Chinese city (and, with big Spotter's Guide energy, is structured around its own idiosyncratic cryptid-classification system). Seanan McGuire's InCryptid sequence (2012–'24) offers a generational tale of a cryptozoologist family fighting to protect supernatural beings from cryptid hunters. Elsewhere, sasquatches, this time a vicious variety, occur again in Max Brooks's *Devolution: A Firsthand Account of the Rainier Sasquatch Massacre* (2020), which features a small town under siege from a savage clan of Bigfeet. The book incorporates fictional diary entries, interviews, and research by its journalist protagonist in a parody of typical cryptozoological practices. Further afield, the West African Ninki Nanka—a large and dangerous **Dragon**ish reptilian—appears in Joseph J. Grant's *Kaytch* (2016), Natasha Bowen's *Skin of the Sea* (2021), and in *Moon Witch, Spider King* (2022) by Marlon James. Finally, *Cryptid Club* (2020) by Sarah Andersen celebrates the inherent daftness of cryptozoology in a comic that takes a humous look at the life of creatures such as Nessie and Mothman.

A Spotter's Guide: What's That Coming Over the Hill?

While it's difficult to capture the sheer variety of cryptids in folklore and fiction, some general categories can be discerned:

- **Hominids:** These include such classics as the Sasquatch/Bigfoot, the Yeti, the Australian Yowie, and the Siberian Chuchuna. These are large bipedal creatures glimpsed on the mountainside or in the forests. Hairy and wary, they shun contact with humans and leave only footprints as evidence of their presence. For westerners, they personify the wilderness and the threatening nature of the unknown. For indigenous populations they often serve as guardians or protectors. John Zada's *In the Valleys of the Noble Beyond: In Search of Sasquatch* (2019) explores the history of that creature in British Columbia, but there's absolutely nothing to say you can't make up a hominid cryptid of your own.
- **Sea and lake monsters:** Like hominid cryptids, sea and lake monsters tend to reflect the danger, vastness, and, in the case of the ocean, the inherent unknowability of their environment. Scotland's Nessie is the obvious example, but lake-monster stories are a global phenomenon. These cryptids can also be found in deep water, such as the Pacific Northwest's sea serpents or the giant squids and megasharks that harry the protagonists of **Submarine** fiction. Many stories reveal such creatures to be descendants of plesiosaurs, but, for storytelling, how they force our characters to face the limits of their knowledge is more important.

- **Postcolonial prowlers:** Some cryptids, such as El Chupacabra or the Pishtaco in Peru, serve both as avatars of extractive colonial oppressors (it's not for nothing that the Pishtaco is frequently depicted as a white man in stories that first emerged during the Spanish conquest of South America), and as embodiments of the resulting economic disparities. Like <u>Vampires</u>, they draw blood from their victims, or, famously, they prey on literal capital investment in terms of livestock. While they manifest as deadly, opportunistic killers, their real threat—and something that places them firmly in the Horror camp—comes from destabilising the distinctions upon which social, economic, and even racial power depend. These cryptids collapse species identity and are frequently described in hybrid terms combining mammalian and reptilian characteristics.
- **Big cats:** Sometimes known as Alien Big Cats or ABCs, the sightings of giant felines in unexpected places (yes, we know, that could be a description of *any* cat!) was a staple of paranormal magazines throughout the 1980s and '90s. They were frequently reported in Britain, often on moorland, and earned names such as the Beast of Exmoor, the Surrey Puma, or the Staffordshire Panther. Farmers attributed hundreds of sheep deaths to them and eventually the government deployed Marine snipers to tackle the worst offenders (they found nothing). The most logical explanation is that they were (or are the offspring of) illegal exotic animals dumped in the wild after the UK's Dangerous Wild Animals Act came into effect in 1976. Yet for writers, ABCs make for ideal intrusion narratives and—given the constant tabloid emphasis on the dangers of their non-native origins—offer a potent metaphor for addressing themes of racism and belonging.
- **Aerialists:** Skyborne cryptids, such as the Mothman or the "Batsquatch" of Washington state, bring terror and dread from above. The enormous eagle-like Roc has long plagued Middle Eastern mythology, while Ivan Sanderson's interest in cryptozoology was inspired by his claim of being attacked by a giant monkey-headed bat known as an "olitiau" in west Africa. Yet aerialist cryptids have a particular resonance with the North American imagination (#BigSkyCountry). Such imagery has travelled to modern times through thousands—if not millions!—of years. Adrienne Mayor, in the fascinating *Fossil Legends of the First Americans* (2005), makes the point that vast graveyards of dinosaur bones underlie lands later populated by tribes such as the Sioux, the Crow, and the Blackfeet. Indigenous American storytellers likely encountered fossils exposed by the elements, and so it isn't impossible that the petrified skeletons

of huge flying animals (later catalogued by scientists in Kansas, Nebraska, Wyoming, and South Dakota) inspired the various tales of huge Thunderbirds in Native American mythology.

Things That are Cool About Cryptozoology

Writing about cryptids is an easy route into atmospheric or scary stories. The basic models are straightforward fits for SF, Fantasy, or Horror, and a good spooky monster story never goes out of fashion. Such tales have long been a way for people to make sense of the inexplicable and the unjust, of the shapes they glimpsed on the hillside, of footprints they found in the forest, or of the prejudicial violence of the world. In that way, cryptozoology—like more traditional folk horror—can often be hyperlocal, allowing us to say a lot (perhaps more than we realise) about the circumstances of its composition.

Maps and Legends

- **Let's get weird:** Cryptozoology stories are about *weird* things. They involve, as Fisher put it, "a weird entity or object so strange that it makes us feel that it should not exist, or at least it should not exist here" (such as, for instance, a panther on an English moor).[9] That these stories come with this built-in form of affect is useful for writers to remember. Cryptid narratives should—for the most part—be unsettling (though other registers are of course possible, such as the comedic television series *Harry and the Hendersons*, 1991–'93, in which a suburban family adopts a Bigfoot).
- **Evidence:** Many stories revolve around the presence of, or search for, objective evidence of cryptids, be that footprints, scat or hair, photos and videos, or other materials. Expeditions in search of cryptids can provide a great spine for a story, as straightforward as people tramping into the woods or as technically challenging as deploying submarines into Loch Ness (which has actually happened)! Expeditions can sometimes be connected to conservative or religious organisations keen to, for example, discredit evolution, so stories in this vein have the potential for meatier commentary on the ideological fault lines in contemporary society.
- **Cryptidcore:** If your characters are searching for cryptids then they've got to be properly kitted out. The aesthetic in question is known as cryptidcore. First codified via social media in the 2010s, the look draws on popular representations of cryptid hunters in *Kolchak*, *The X-Files*, or animated series *Gravity Falls* (2012–'16).

---

9. Ficher, 2016, p. 15.

Embrace the dorkiness with flannel shirts, woolly hats, combat boots, and backpacks festooned with patches. Think of how members of the band The Automatic are decked out in the video for their 2006 song 'Monster'!

- **How we see the world:** The way we write about cryptids tells us a lot about characters and settings. So, consider whose story you're privileging—accidentally or intentionally—in your fiction. One good example is how "for millennia, indigenous peoples have recounted the existence of giant sea creatures along the coasts of what is now Washington State and British Columbia".[10] For these cultures, the creatures were guardian spirits with an intimate connection to the environment; but for the white settlers who came later, the same tales described monsters to be feared.
- **Biohoaxing:** Cryptozoology is replete with scams and deception! Fraudulent photographs of Nessie kicked off the modern Loch Ness Monster craze, and it's not difficult to imagine that many sasquatch sightings have been pranks. Thus, there are great stories to be told about people faking the existence of cryptids (and, just perhaps, learning that the creatures are actually real…!). After all, a story about a good hoax is at least as compelling as a story about a real cryptid encounter.

---

10. Teorey, 2019, p. 128.

ACTIVITIES

Building a better beast: Design your own cryptid by exaggerating an existing animal or hybridising a pair of animals. Perhaps the cryptid displays partially human characteristics or maybe they are entirely beastlike. Consider sensory detail beyond visual description: what does your creature smell or sound like? Do they live in the forest, on a mountainside, or in a lake? How do they react when they encounter people; are they monstrous or kindly? How long have they been hiding from the world?

Podcast: Your protagonist researches, writes, and presents a podcast on cryptid themes. Their latest investigation takes them to a small town in search of the creature you designed in the first activity. Write the script for the resulting episode. Be sure to set the scene and the disquieting tone with vivid description of the town and its surroundings. Include interviews with locals (both witnesses and more sceptical perspectives) as well as some historical background on your cryptid. Will your podcaster discover that the creature is real or a hoax, or will their conclusions be more ambiguous?

BODY SWAPPING

Ever find yourself wondering "Why is my kid having more fun than I did when I was young?" or "Why is my dad such a stress head?" Ever think everyone else around you has it all figured out? Ever wish you could understand those questions but then wake up to discover that you're expected to give an important presentation at a job you don't know how to do or deliver a book report to a high school history class that you don't attend? Hate to break it to you, but you might have swapped bodies!

A Short History of Body Swapping

Body swapping is two beings exchanging their physical forms. The contemporary manifestation is mostly teen comedies, but in mythology and classic literature, it didn't always have to be parent and child. It didn't even always have to be two *humans*! In Ovid's mega-epic poem *Metamorphosis* (c. 8 C.E.), for example, we find tales of people turning into plants or animals (Daphne turned into a tree, Actaeon turned into a stag, Lycaeon into a wolf; see **Werewolves**!), and people even changed gender without too much fuss. The Japanese *Torikaebaya Monogatari* ("If only I could exchange! (them) story"), translated as *The Changelings*, is a tale of unknown authorship (c. 800–1200) about two children, a girl and boy, who exhibit various characteristics of the opposite sex, and so grow up having "swapped" their genders; the tale's four volumes follow their lives and adventures (and it influences, among others, 2016's *Your Name* from dir. Makoto Shinkai, in which two teenagers who've never met begin to inexplicably swap bodies).

One of the first examples to introduce the body swap into modern Western literature is 'Transformation' by SF's originator, Mary Shelley. Written in 1831, it's the story of a man who swaps bodies with a mysterious creature for the promise of treasure. Soon after comes the French novella *Avatar* (1856) by Théophile Gautier in which a physician who's spent some time in India performs a magic trick on a heartbroken young man, switching the latter's body with that of the husband of the Lithuanian Countess he loves; when the two men realise what's happened, they go to the physician to change back, but the young man decides not to live without the woman he loves and allows his mind to evaporate. The doctor then takes over his cadaver! *Vice Versa: A Lesson to Fathers* (1882) by F. Anstey (pseudonym of Thomas Anstey Guthrie) introduced the now classic parent-swaps-with-child trope as a father and son swap bodies and learn lessons about each other's lives in the process. This novel inspired a radio play in 1947, a 1981 television adaptation, and several films including the 1988 version directed by Brad

Gilbert. Not long after Anstey's novel, Arthur Conan Doyle published 'The Great Keinplatz Experiment' (1885), a story about mesmerism (see **Ghost Stories**) in which two people's souls are swapped when they're hypnotised simultaneously; whereas *Vice Versa* uses magic to swap the bodies, this story employs pseudo-scientific ideas being explored at the time. A decade later, in 1896, H.G. Wells wrote 'The Story of the Late Mr. Elvesham', in which an older man tricks a younger man into switching bodies with him, leaving the younger man with a terrible choice. Another early use of body swapping, and a more comical one, is in P.G. Wodehouse's *Laughing Gas* (1936), in which a child star and an unmarried earl swap bodies via nitrous oxide that's administered to each as they're having dental work performed; hijinks ensue, of course, and they end up swapping back after simultaneously being knocked unconscious.

The story potential of body swaps, especially to tell comedy tales (see **Comedic Fantasy**), has ensured its popularity down to modern times. Everyone has heard of *Freaky Friday*, for instance, which has now become an almost genericised term for body swapping. First appearing as a novel by Mary Rogers in 1972, *Freaky Friday* was filmed in 1976 (dir. Gary Nelson) and stars Barbara Harris and Jodie Foster as the mother and daughter who swap bodies; it was filmed again, this time for television, in 1995 (dir. Melanie Mayron), then in 2003 (dir. Mark Waters) with Jamie Lee Curtis and Lindsay Lohan, then *again* as a television musical in 2018 (dir. Steve Carr). But it's not just parents and children who swap bodies. In Tim Powers's *The Anubis Gates* (1983) the character Dog-Faced Joe is a body-swapping werewolf, part of a complex storyline that contains Time Travel, magicians, and Egyptian mythology. David Mitchell uses body-swapping characters to link several novels such as *The Thousand Autumns of Jacob de Zoet* (2010), *The Bone Clocks* (2014), and *Slade House* (2015). In Sylvia McNicoll's *Body Swap* (2018), a teenage girl and an elderly woman swap bodies and come back to life after a fatal car wreck. The trope has also been employed in popular media franchises, such as 2006's *Doctor Who* episode 'New Earth' (dir. James Hawes) in which Rose's body is taken over by Lady Cassandra, and the *Star Trek: Strange New Worlds* episode 'Spock Amok' (dir. Rachel Leiterman, 2022) in which Spock and his fiancée T'Pring swap bodies with hilarious results. One aspect of body swapping that isn't always explored is sex, so of course *What We Do in the Shadows*, not known for shying away from the carnal, *goes there* in 'Pride Parade' (dir. Yana Gorskaya, 2023); Nadja and her doll, which contains the spirit of human Nadja before she was turned into a Vampire, trade bodies so that Doll-Nadja can finally get some afternoon delight. Beyond English-language media, we have the Japanese *I am Him and He is Me* by Hisashi Yamanaka (serialised from 1979–'80; first filmed as *Transfer Student* in 1982 by director Nobuhiko Obayashi); in this story, a young girl and boy switch bodies and learn about the opposite sex's experiences. Satoshi Kitamura's *Me and My Cat* (1999), a children's picture book, is the story of a boy who swaps bodies with his cat due to a witch's spell. From India, we have 'Wish Fulfilment' ('Icchapuron', 1895) by Rabindranath Tagore, about a father and son who swap bodies, similar to *Vice Versa*, in that each thinks the other has the better life. A more recent example is *Ithihasa* (dir. Binu Sadanandan, 2014) in which a strait-laced professional and a pickpocket each end up with one of a pair of magical rings which cause them to swap bodies.

A Spotter's Guide: The Old Switcheroo

Writers use many methods to prompt the swap:

- **Technology:** The machine method includes various inventions or even <u>Alien</u> devices. *The Master Mind of Mars* by Edgar Rice Burroughs (1928), one of his Barsoom books, is an early example in which a mad scientist can swap brains between bodies. The *Help! I'm Trapped...* series (1993–2001) by Todd Strasser includes a machine a science teacher is building to swap intelligence/education between people (plot hole alert: wouldn't that put the science teacher out of a job?). One day the machine is triggered by a bolt of lightning and sixth-grader Jake swaps bodies with his teacher Mr Dirksen. In the sequels, Jake swaps bodies with more people and even animals. In a double episode of the *X-Files*, 'Dreamland' and 'Dreamland II' (dirs. Kim Manners and Michael Watkins respectively, 1998), Fox Mulder and a Man in Black swap bodies when the rays from an alien craft sweep over their vehicles.
- **Magic:** This method includes spells, potions, curses, various magical items, and supernatural rituals. In Shelley's 'Transformation' a mysterious shipwrecked creature performs a ritual to swap bodies with the unlucky Guido. In 2020's comedy slasher film *Freaky* (dir. Christopher Landon) a magical stolen dagger causes a high school girl and a serial killer to swap bodies. In some cases, the magic occurs when either or both parties wish for a swap. Golden-age television show *I Dream of Jeannie* includes the body-swap episode 'Haven't I Seen Me Someplace Before?' (dir. Claudio Guzmán, 1968), in which Jeannie gives Roger a wish for his birthday but he wishes to trade places with Tony, who is soon to go on a space mission.
- **Physical contact:** Some stories dance along the line between magic, genetics, and physics, with everything from bumping into someone to kissing them bringing on a body swap. An example is 'Chapter 1'

of the *X-Men* adjacent television show *Legion* (dir. Noah Hawley, 2017) in which mutant David kisses Syd, who possesses the ability to involuntarily swap bodies with anyone she makes skin contact with. The resulting swap leads to chaos and deaths when Syd can't control David's body and psychic powers.

- **Random accident:** This method includes falling, colliding, or suffering a bump to the head, but it often requires some other intervention such as one party carrying a magic item or someone performing a ritual of some sort at the exact moment of impact. In *Dream a Little Dream* (dir. Mark Rocco, 1989) teenagers Bobby and Lainie collide in an alley at the exact moment older couple Coleman and Gina are performing a meditative exercise to try to be together forever. Coleman wakes up in Bobby's body and Gina is stuck in the "dream state" only accessible to Coleman/Bobby when he's asleep; Coleman is now against the clock to swap back and save his wife. Random accidents often overlap with or involve...
- **Natural Phenomenon:** This method includes lightning, wind, eclipses, storms, etc. In the Filipino film *Here Comes the Bride* (dir. Chris Martinez, 2010), when a wedding party make their way via car up Magnetic Hill in Laguna during a solar eclipse, there's an accident and the five passengers all discover that they've swapped bodies; they have to wait for another solar eclipse to try to swap back, but it takes a many attempts (and car crashes) before it works.
- **Urinating in a magical fountain:** This method is so weird and specific that it demands an extra bonus section! It occurs in *The Change-Up* (dir. David Dobkin, 2011) and, inexplicably, also in the *Aqua Teen Hunger Force* episode 'Rabbit, Not Rabbot' (2015). In the movie it's enough for Ryan Reynolds and Jason Bateman to wish for each other's lives when drunkenly urinating in a fountain (yes, we watched that so you don't have to!). In the cartoon, however, the swap requires locking eyes with the other person urinating just as the fountain is struck by lightning.

Things That are Cool About Body Swapping

Body swapping, whether one- or both-sided, can challenge you to put your characters through their paces, to have a new experience with someone of a different sex or gender, age, or even race or culture. This can give you the chance to try out a new way of seeing the world through your characters' eyes and provide you with the opportunity to stretch your story-telling skills.

You're Only Trading Skin Suits

- **Go beyond the obvious:** Just as with any instance of writing a character who's outside of your immediate experience (sex/gender/age/culture/etc.), you'll need to do some research so that you don't fall back on stereotypes. Body-swap stories are usually a way for each person to build a better understanding of the other by, literally, "walking in their shoes"; therefore, having a character trade bodies with someone else but then experience the world only through pre-existing stereotypes wouldn't be taking full advantage of the possibilities (say, for example, a story in which a teenage boy swaps bodies with a teenage girl, it would be a waste if all the girl is interested in is make-up and clothes instead of grabbing this opportunity to smash the patriarchy!). Because we should always be thinking about what it is we're trying to say with our SFF stories.
- **Know your history:** Early examples of body swapping can in part be accounted for with philosophical ideas born out of the Enlightenment and the development of psychology. In the eighteenth century, Scottish philosopher David Hume argued that "the minds of men are mirrors to one another".[1] This idea of mind mirroring is vital to empathy, a term that wasn't introduced to the English language—from German—by psychologist Edward Titchener until 1909[2]; though the concept of empathy in a psychological setting was new over a hundred years ago, we now know it as the ability to understand other people's feelings because we've experienced the same. Psychology is all about understanding how our minds work, so it isn't a stretch to consider that expanding the knowledge of our minds, including how we identify ourselves in relation to others, would influence literature.
- **Remember to forget:** A bit before Titchener, Hermann Ebbinghaus, a German psychologist, was one of the first people to scientifically study memory; his findings include "the well-known 'forgetting curve' that relates forgetting to the passage of time" reported in 1885.[3] Combining empathy and forgetting leads us to see in body-swap stories an adult longing for the "good old days" of their youth, which when re-experienced really aren't all that great!
- **Physicality:** A lot of work has been done in the past century to better understand human sexuality and gender identity, so isn't surprising to see that explored in books and films using the body-swap trope. While

---

1. Quoted in Stueber, 2019, n.p.
2. Quoted in Stueber, 2019, n.p.
3. Editors of *Encyclopaedia Britannica*, 'Hermann Ebbinghaus', 2023, n.p.

most often the gender-swapping aspect of the trope is employed for laughs (or for too many pornographic possibilities), such as in *The Hot Chick* (dir. Tom Brady, 2002), there are others, such as Shinkai's film *Your Name*, that centre empathy. Consider, too, how body swap stories—especially characters waking up as other genders—have a powerful built-in allegory for trans identity.

ACTIVITIES

Close to home: If you're privileged to have elder relatives or even family friends you can interview, take the chance to sit and ask them questions about what their life was like when they were your age. Ask questions about mundane daily life (schedules, school, meals, jobs, etc.) and about any big events they might have experienced (military service, winning an award, inventing something, meeting someone famous, etc.). Be sure to ask them—as long as it's okay with them—how they felt at those moments or if they had the experience that we all do of knowing that something big and important is happening but being distracted by "daily" stuff. Then, see if you can write a draft of a story (that nobody has to see! This is just for practice) in which you swap bodies with that person. The swap can happen now with you both at your current ages, or you can body swap your interviewee with someone else during one of the events they described.

Opposites attract: This activity will require you to observe how other people act, not in the way we think they act (due to stereotypes or cultural expectations) but how they *actually* act. Choose someone, either a friend or stranger, who's the opposite of you—either another sex or gender, another age, from another culture, etc.—and take notes on how they behave in a random situation (ordering a coffee, riding a bus, shopping for food, at a cinema) over just a few minutes. Though remember that you don't want to seem like a stalker! Then, try to observe yourself objectively and note how you behave in the same situation. You'll likely find differences. Use these notes to start a story in which, via one of the methods listed above, you swap bodies with this other person. Try to write it from the point of view of the other person experiencing your world.

PORTAL FANTASY

You open a door, step over a threshold, fall down a hole, exit an elevator, or jump in a pool and—*blammo!*—you're in a different world. Everything might be strange, or magical, or even dangerous, but, basically, it's not the place you left behind. Surprise! You're in a portal fantasy.

A Short History of Portal Fantasy

One way of better understanding types of Fantasy stories is by looking at how the fantastical elements—the magic, the creatures, etc.—are encountered by the (usually human) protagonists; that is, by looking at how the characters engage with or even understand the fantastic happening around them. Critic and academic Farah Mendlesohn, in her study *Rhetorics of Fantasy* (2008), developed a taxonomy of Fantasy types: intrusion, immersive, liminal, and portal-quest. In intrusion, the magical comes to the mundane (fairies in your kitchen); in immersive, the whole story is set in the fantasy (secondary) world and the characters are from that place; liminal describes a fantasy story in which the fantastical elements are at the edges, or the characters take the magic for granted, which unsettles a reader who sees that they're magical; and in portal fantasy, a character crosses a line from mundane to fantastical and then often undertakes a quest to gain something, rescue someone, or to get home, etc.[1] The latter in particular is an *immensely* popular form of storytelling. That's because portal fantasies are a special creature: they speak to the child in us who wished for a means of escape, or for the magic we saw on television or read about in books to be a simple doorway away. And they do the same thing for the adult in us who's tired of a mundane life and wants to explore a different—or even better—world.

Portals or thresholds between one world and the next can be found throughout ancient myths and legends. In Norse mythology, Asgard, the realm of the gods, can only be reached via the rainbow bridge, the Bifrost, a transitional portal separating here and there.[2] In **Fairy** folklore portals in hillsides often provide access to the otherworld where time doesn't flow like it does in the real world, and visitors will often find decades or even centuries have passed while they've been gone. The collection of early Welsh stories called the *Mabinogion* (see **Mythic Fantasy**) calls this place Annwn,[3] however "access is seldom physical in the normal sense" with the "most common methods of access … going Into the Woods, by River,

---

1. Mendlesohn, 2008, pp. 1–58.
2. Editors of *Encyclopaedia Britannica*, 'Asgard', 2023, n.p.
3. *Encyclopedia of Religion*, 2024, n.p.

by being transported by the winds (usually the North Wind) or by Dreams (though Faerie is seldom portrayed as a dreamland; rather, memory of being there is as of a dream)".[4] As a result, the portal itself isn't a clear physical border, matching the difficulty in pinning down stories from folklore and mythology to a single version.

As Science Fiction and Fantasy developed into more clearly demarcated genres, portals, too, gained definition. One of the first SFF stories to contain a portal is *The Blazing World* (1666) by Margaret Cavendish in which a Utopia is reached by boat by sailing "not onely ... to the very end or point of the [North] Pole of that World, but even to another Pole of another World, which joined close to it".[5] Cavendish's imaginary world beyond our own North Pole is populated by people who look like bears and foxes but walk upright, as well as satyrs and green-skinned people. In 1864, Jules Verne published *Journey to the Centre of the Earth*, an early hollow-Earth tale, in which a professor and his nephew, following details found in an Icelandic saga, journey into a dormant volcano—serving as a portal in the narrative sense—and down into the earth to find a whole new world full of prehistoric plants and animals as well as a giant-sized humanoid. The following year saw *Alice's Adventures in Wonderland* (1865) by Lewis Carroll, in which the titular heroine tumbles down a magical rabbit hole. Carroll's tale illustrates a defining characteristic of portal-fantasy stories in that the new world must be navigated and that situations often become weirder and more mysterious.[6] Wonderland does this by throwing up absurd and dangerous roadblocks, making Alice shrink or grow huge, and pitting her against the Queen of Hearts in a possibly deadly croquet game. Another good example is *The Wonderful Wizard of Oz* (1900) by L. Frank Baum, which follows Dorothy as she's transported from Kansas to Oz via a cyclone that serves the function of the portal. It is, however, the 1939 film version *The Wizard of Oz* (dir. Victor Fleming) that most aligns with our imagining of how someone transported via portal will experience the transition: in the film, the tornado transports Dorothy from a black-and-white Great Depression to a Technicolor, and therefore hopeful, fantasy realm. In Oz, her quest, as in many portal stories, is about trying to get home; however, Dorothy's trip is complicated by the Wicked Witch's desires and her companions' own needs.

The use of portals in Fantasy, and the development of the portal-quests, expanded with the evolution of Fantasy in the twentieth century. In C.S. Lewis's *The Lion, the Witch, and the Wardrobe* (1950), the Pevensie children climb through a wardrobe from World War II-era England into Narnia, a magical land with mythical, talking creatures, where it's "always

---

4. Ashley, 1997, n.p.
5. Cavendish, 1668, n.p.
6. Mendlesohn, 2008, pp. 1–58.

winter but never Christmas". The siblings become the kings and queens of Narnia, undertaking many quests and battles in its defence. In 1963, Andre Norton expanded on Lewis's idea in her *Witch World* series (1963–2005), containing over twenty SF/Sword and Sorcery/High Fantasy books, some published after the author's death. These are set in a world of many portals and many universes (see **The Multiverse**), showing the possibilities that fantastical portals can give a writer when it comes to building new worlds. The film *Stargate* (dir. Roland Emmerich, 1994) and its many television spin-offs, particularly *Stargate SG-1* (1997–2007) take a Science Fictional approach to portals, with an ancient technology that allows human explorers "instantaneous travel across interstellar distances, reducing the galaxy itself to an analogy of the global village".[7] *Stargate SG-1* is notable for its consistent approach to the rules of its portal travel, often generating clever plots from efforts to bypass the limitations the series itself has imposed on the fictional technology. A more recent example, Lev Grossman's *The Magicians* series (2009–'14; also a television series 2015–'20), contains two portals; one is between the mundane world and Brakebills (a university for magicians); the other is between the regular world or Brakebills and Fillory, accessed with a button via a middle space called the Neitherlands. Fillory is a secondary world created by fictional author Christopher Plover (read a clever bio of him that weaves in Grossman here[8]) that Quentin, our main protagonist, has grown up loving but didn't know was real. Quentin and his classmates end up as queens and kings of Fillory—a reference to the Narnia series—but Fillory is much more dangerous than anyone suspects.

A Spotter's Guide: Some Doors Revolve

- **It doesn't have to be this way:** The portal fantasy can be a vehicle to build a world that we wish our own reality looked like. It can also be a world that takes our own negatives to an extreme as a warning. In the MG/YA *Un Lun Dun* (2007), China Miéville considers the environmental price of unchecked progress. Zanna and Deeba cross from our London to UnLundon, a broken Wonderland-inspired mirror city where litter from the real world is sentient (and forgotten by the real world, because that's what we do); furthermore, an evil Smog, originally created in London, is growing more menacing, supported by those who exploit UnLondon despite the price to the environment. Sarah Rees Brennan's *In Other Lands* (2017) features young Elliot, who's invited to a magical military school in the Borderlands (on the other side of a wall only few can see) where he's trained, along with

---

7. Nolan, 2020, p. 42.
8. Liptak, 2014, n.p.

mermaids, fairies, and other imaginary beings. Because he doesn't want to be a soldier, he subverts primary-world expectations for boys and gravitates towards diplomacy; additionally, fairy women are the warriors, there to protect their men (because women deal with blood all the time!).

- **New world, new you:** Crossing a portal into a different world will often force a character to face their own shortcomings and flaws. *Coraline* (2002) by Neil Gaiman features a door through which his young protagonist finds a mirror universe of her own, a twisted and sinister place, where her "Other Mother" and "Other Father" have buttons for eyes (not a story for anyone with koumpounophobia!). When she discovers her own parents are missing from the real world, she must find the courage to go back into the mirror world to save them. In *Labyrinth Lost* (2016) by Zoraida Cordova, new bruja Alex, who hates magic, wishes her powers away on her Death Day, inadvertently banishing her family to Los Lagos (a purgatorial realm with trolls, harpies, giants, etc.). As a result, she must learn to work with Nova, a brujo, to get them back. While the story is full of elements linking it to the mythologies of Central and South American cultures, of particular note is the lack of any White characters.

- **Magic of stories themselves:** One of our favourite twists on stories is when they're *about* storytelling, and portal fantasy has often used this power for good. In the classic *Seven-Day Magic* (1962) by Edward Eager, five children check out what seems to be a blank book from the library, only to discover it's writing the story *of* them. They learn that making a wish on the book turns it into a sort of portal, making the wish come true, but the wishes are often connected to other stories that they've read. Melissa Albert's *The Hazel Wood* (2018) is an unsettling look at the thin line between the imagination that builds stories and real life when Alice's mother is taken by a supernatural creature from the Hinterland—the setting of her grandmother's twisted fairy tales—and she must venture into the Hazel Wood to find her. Finally, multi-award finalist *The Ten Thousand Doors of January* (2019) by Alix E. Harrow is the story of a book that can create doors between worlds and the girl, January, who navigates the worlds to unravel the mysteries of her missing family members.

- **It's literally just a game:** Sometimes portals take characters to another plane or universe as a sort of test, much like many episodes of *Doctor Who* in which the Doctor and their companions get stuck figuring out the solution just so they can escape (because failing means being stuck there forever!). In *The Gauntlet* (2017) by Karuna

Riazi, twelve-year-old Farah and her two friends get sucked into a mechanical board game and must dismantle it to save everyone trapped inside. Based on Chris Van Allsburg's 1981 picture book, the film *Jumanji* (dir. Joe Johnston, 1995) is about schoolboy Alan who, in 1969, is transported into a board game that had been buried for a century; twenty-six years later, when two new kids play the game, Alan and animals from the jungle are released into the real world. The story was resurrected for the sequels *Jumanji: Welcome to the Jungle* (2017) and *Jumanji: The Next Level* (2019), both directed by Jake Kasdan. In each, kids from our world are magically transported into the Jumanji jungle world, though this time they show up there as avatars from the video-game version (trading genders and body shapes!), and dangerous monkey business follows with Dwayne "The Rock" Johnson on hand to beat up the bad guys.

- **A door as therapy?** Being faced with unexpected situations can bring out the best—or the worst—in our characters, and those we find in portal fantasies are no different. Creatures from the other side, for example, aren't always nice. This is the case in Mishell Baker's Urban Fantasy Arcadia Project series (2106–'18), in which protagonist Millie is hired to help police the portal between Hollywood and Fairy through which the "fey" access our world as film stars. Millie, a double amputee with borderline personality disorder, isn't always easy to work or live with. She faces many setbacks throughout the series but also learns a lot about herself from beings on either side of the portal.

Things That are Cool About Portal Fantasy

Portal fantasies give us the opportunity to create infinite new worlds for our characters to discover. They give us a break from reality; when a character crosses the threshold into another realm, this allows readers room to imagine that a magical world is just on the other side of their bedroom wall. The fantasy world also gives us a way to explore issues in our own time and place, everything from inequality to political strife to environmental factors. We can build a world that's closer to what we want this world to be or create a world that's so terrible that either our world looks better by contrast or we're warned of the road to avoid continuing down.

You Know, It's Like, Weird and Everything…

- **Tune your language:** In *Rhetorics of Fantasy*, Mendlesohn investigates how the language of different types of fantasy should match. For example, in immersive fantasy the characters are of the world, so nothing they encounter is surprising. The rhetoric, then, won't have the same effect as that of a character in an invasive or portal-quest fantasy, where the fantastic is unexpected. In the latter, the characters' experiences will be conveyed with descriptions that express this surprise. A fairy appears in your flour jar? You'll be shocked. You fall through a grate in the street and end up in another world? Your time will be spent getting to grips with where you are, how the world works, what's safe, what's dangerous, etc. And the way you describe the surroundings and creatures or people there will be full of *feeling*: Fantasy is about the magical and impossible.

- **Order of description:** When a character encounters a new, unexpected place, think of the order in which they experience it. If they fall through a portal and are immediately in danger (monster!), the prose shouldn't stop to describe the landscape. Instead, the character's experience of the world will be quick flashes of imagery as they try to find a means of escape. Only when they're safe will they get a chance to look around. And that's when the order of description will be important: what will they notice first? It'll likely be what's closest or most immediate, or easiest to understand (or put into a familiar context). For example, a character who's in a new world that looks much like their origin world will maybe take the trees and sky for granted; but the strange birds with four wings, if one is on the ground right there, will be noticeable.
- **Depth of description:** A character with time to absorb their surroundings gives you, the author, a chance to describe the world in more depth. But readers tend to like characters that are taking action—and it's called a portal-*quest* because often the character is on their way to somewhere or something—so your challenge will be to build the world around the character as they proceed. Some elements will require more description than others. Some readers love a worldbuilding "info dump", but lots don't. Also, it's not just how things look that you can describe. Use sensory detail to describe how things smell, taste, feel and sound.
- **Pacing:** Keep in mind that stopping to describe something in the new world will slow the pace of your story down for that passage. You might not want to do this when you're in the middle of an exciting chase scene. But after a scene with a lot of action and snappy dialogue, spending a few sentences describing the setting or a strange new creature will slow things down to give the reader a chance to breathe. This is, essentially, going back and forth between showing (slow writing) and telling (fast writing) as appropriate.

ACTIVITIES

No sampling the wares: Your character is a gatekeeper at the portal between this world and another, but a requirement is that they never set foot over the threshold. One day, a trespasser jumps through the gate before running into the other world. Forgetting the rule, your character—shocked at the event—chases after the trespasser. Alarms go off immediately when the gatekeeper crosses, but not when the trespasser does. What does the gatekeeper see as soon as they cross the threshold? What has the "boss" (or whoever oversees the portal) been keeping secret about the other world? Why has the gatekeeper never been allowed to cross the border? And why did the trespasser jump the gate?

For better or for worse: Consider how you can use a portal fantasy to say something about the real world. Either build a fantasy world where the expectation or current situation of our world/culture is subverted (maybe all the world leaders are women, for example, as in Barbie, dir. Greta Gerwig, 2023), or where whatever you find troubling here is even worse there (as in Miéville's UnLondon). Will you go for "better" or "worse" in your portal world? Will your protagonist want to stay or return home? What obstacles lie in their way?

CARNIVALESQUE

Are you ready to let loose? Or, at least, are you ready to suspend the habitual rules of your day-to-day existence for a while? Are you ready to put on a costume and get a bit chaotic? To celebrate our bodies and our senses and the fact that we're alive? To rag on The Powers That Be while normal service is postponed? *You are?* Then hold onto your various bits, because here comes the most debauched thing of all… literary criticism!

A Short History of Carnivalesque

Carnivalesque is about turning our characters' worlds upside down. It allows us insight into our fictional societies and permits our protagonists to be someone else—or perhaps who they truly wish to be—for a little while. Carnivalesque is less a true subgenre than a mood or technique that subverts a storyworld's established rules and pieties. A well-placed instance of carnivalesque can serve as a grenade thrown into your narrative! Such episodes often serve as points around which character arcs and plots will pivot and can be deployed with equal impact in Fantasy, SF, or Horror, and even—*shock*—in realist texts. To best understand carnivalesque, however, we need to go back to the source: Mikhail Bakhtin (1895–1975), a Russian philosopher, critic, and literary theorist who wrote a book called *Rabelais and His World* (1968), a study of François Rabelais (1532–'64), a French polymath best known for a satirical, vulgar, larger-than-life tale of a giant and his son (*Gargantua and Pantagruel* or, to give its full title, *The Horrible and Terrifying Deeds and Words of the Very Renowned Pantagruel King of the Dipsodes, Son of the Great Giant Gargantua!*). In studying Rabelais, Bakhtin found himself interested in the history of festivals and carnivals in mediaeval and Renaissance Europe. These events, he said, were occasions during which rulers permitted (even openly sanctioned) boisterous merriment and celebration. The logic here was that of the pressure value: if peasants were to be made to work all year, then it was necessary to permit them an opportunity to cut loose occasionally (office Christmas party, much?). Part of this involves an inversion of established hierarchies, with satirical speech and action permitted. This dissolution of norms allows for characters who might never find themselves together to freely interact without a power imbalance. The queen and the pauper might, for example, find themselves dancing together, and this temporary suspension of the rules often results in characters laughing with each other at the absurdities of social convention.

Bakhtin places the roots of carnivalesque in old-school Socratic dialogues and Greek Menippean Satire (which, sadly, has nothing to do with Muppets;

you're thinking of *Meep*ippean Satire). He nonetheless considered one of the earliest examples of "a purely Carnivalesque vision" to be a comic play called *The Play in the Bower* (1262) by troubadour (great word) Adam de la Halle.¹ Closely based on its author's real life, family, and friends, the play "presents a feast of carnival type ... the right to emerge from the routine of life, the right to be free from all that is official and consecrated".² More accessible to modern readers is William Shakespeare's comedy *A Midsummer Night's Dream* (1595) in which carnivalesque techniques create the perfect atmosphere for the play's interconnected plots and confused lovers, as well as its collision of aristocracy and "rude mechanicals" (and its subplot about **Fairies** further illustrates how carnivalesque represents an intrusion of the fantastic into mundane reality).³ In bringing together characters from across the socio-economic spectrum, the play sends the message that people are not all that different from each other despite the artifice of social standing, wealth, or responsibility. At their best, carnivalesque episodes like this promise the possibility that disparate characters can understand each other better through the simple process of interaction. Because the most effective carnivalesque allows for what is supposedly sacred to be cut down to size. And perhaps from this, later Bakhtin proposes, the resulting creative energies might see "a clearing away of dogma so that new creation can take place".⁴

Modern examples of this pattern can be found in many cult classics, including Mexican director Luis Buñuel's sharply satirical film *The Exterminating Angel* (1962), in which the aristocratic guests at a lavish party find they cannot leave, and, especially, Jim Sharman's rollocking *Rocky Horror Picture Show* (1975) in which a restrained young couple find themselves part of a chaotic, sexually liberated celebration of excess overseen by an alien transvestite ("Don't dream it, be it!"). Back on the page, one might point to the elements of "carnivalesque misrule" throughout J.G. Ballard's *High-Rise* (1975; brilliantly adapted for film by Ben Wheatley in 2015), though that book's tale of social collapse in a London tower block veers off into a very violent direction.⁵ We see further echoes in Angela Carter's multifaceted feminist *Nights at the Circus* (1984), not just in its reality-suspending circus setting but also in its "challenge to subversive patriarchal norms and deconstruction of arbitrary patriarchal hierarchies".⁶ Another good example is Turkish author Elif Şafak's *The Gaze* (1999) in which an overweight woman and her dwarf lover tire of being stared at so take control of their experience by attempting to reverse aspects of their

---

1. Bakhtin, 1984, p. 15.
2. Bakhtin, 1984, p. 257.
3. Shakespeare, n.d., n.p.
4. Morson and Emerson, 1990, p. 95.
5. Crawford, 2016, n.p.
6. Abdullah, 2017, p. 114.

appearances (the man adopts make-up and crossdressing, the woman draws a moustache on her face). One might also include the adolescent humour of infamous MTV stunt series *Jackass* (2000–'02) and any number of gross-out comedies from the same era. Many interpretations of the Joker from the Batman franchise exhibit carnivalesque characteristics, especially the phenomenal portrayal by Heath Ledger in *The Dark Night* (dir. Christopher Nolan, 2008). Meanwhile, the idea of carnivalesque as pressure valve in society recurs in *The Purge* (dir. James DeMonaco, 2013), which takes an aggressive approach to the suspension of social norms with a US where, for one night, all crime—including murder—is legal. Though the many sequels dilute the concept, eventually abandoning the Bakhtinian time-limit with *The Forever Purge* (dir. Everardo Valerio, 2021), the first film remains a shocking and vicious take on the initial concept. That franchise aside, one of the hallmarks of the carnivalesque is that it comes to an end. Some semblance of—often transformed—reality will almost always be restored at its conclusion. And, thus, it is for us. So, quickly now, everybody make haste; let's get back to writing....

A Spotter's Guide: Dancing in the Streets

- **Upside-down world:** Pieties are suspended in episodes of carnivalesque. Rules are reversed—sometimes metaphorically, sometimes literally—and disparate strata of society are brought together in boisterous fashion as though *Drunk History* has collided with *Undercover Boss*. This topsy-turvy period has several important consequences. In terms of worldbuilding, it's a chance for oddball behaviour that might normally arouse suspicion or concern to be accepted without question. Because remember, social norms are hardly absolutes: they're artificial constructs that vary from time to time and culture to culture, and your storyworld can and arguably should reflect this (even if only in trace elements such as different generational perspectives among your characters). In terms of character, the rejection of norms will likely make your protagonists feel things that make them uncomfortable—sympathy for those worse off, or maybe sexual desires of an unexpected nature—but this period of inversion is temporary. Your characters will return to their ordinary lives, but the resulting changes can be (and often are) quiet and profound adjustments in how they see their world.
- **Exaggeration:** A key part of carnivalesque as a literary style is the "exaggeration of the inappropriate to incredible and monstrous dimensions".[7] It tends to apply this principle—in fact, *delights* in

---

7. Bakhtin, 1984, p. 306.

applying it—to bodily imagery and function, what official narratives tend to repress as rude or unclean. "Polite" society doesn't want you talking about genitalia, for example, despite so many people's lives literally revolving around them (though of course not everyone's lives; shout-out to the asexuals, we see you!). Equally, our societies have, for a long time, hidden women away during menstruation or childbirth. Yet for Bakhtin, folk celebrations involve bringing such things into the open through vulgar, profane, and sexual images of exaggerated bodies in acts of "fertility, growth, and a brimming-over abundance" (though let's keep consent in mind here as not everyone wants wobblies up in their space; it's often enough to add some dancing and moving bodies to a scene in order to convey this effect!).[8] Indeed, carnivalesque maintains that our physicality is nothing to be ashamed of. Its humour can consequently be puerile and scatological with emphasis on the physical rather than the intellectual.

- **The people's laughter:** During carnivalesque episodes, your characters not only get to openly laugh with the people in charge but *at* them. Because laughter—in fiction, at least—can conquer emperors and, in some cases, even overcome the supernatural. Permitting our characters to lampoon figures or institutions of authority whom they're otherwise expected to respect is a useful string on any writer's bow. It allows us to satirise real-life issues of inequality, enables us to manoeuvre protagonists into moments of revelation, or do both. Here, too, we might connect the mechanisms of carnivalesque with **Comedic Fantasy** and even meta SF.
- **Dialogism:** Woah, woah, woah, that's a big word for a party! But dialogism simply means that people who normally don't get a chance to speak have an opportunity to do so. Because authorities are monologic, the state, the church, any Powers That Be tend to speak with a single voice (and it's usually telling you to behave yourself according to their rules). By contrast, a multitude of voices—and so perspectives—are on offer during instances of the carnivalesque, important given how often our characters' interactions with their world are shaped through dialogue. In this way, dialogism is closely related to…
- **Real talk:** Bakhtin was a champion of what he called "Marketplace Speech".[9] This isn't the heightened formality of the state or the church, which are actively deprivileged during carnivalesque, but instead the linguistic reality of the individual on the street "permitting no distance between those who came in contact with each other and

---
8. Bakhtin, 1984, p. 19.
9. Bakhtin, 1984, p. 10.

liberating from norms of etiquette and decency imposed at other times".[10] In practice this means cussing and obscenity, the more outlandish and colourful the better (such as the satirical political comedy *The Thick of It*, 2005–'12, which raised vulgarity to a baroque art form). A consequence of marketplace speech, loosely, is a ground-up revelling in how things are rather than the top-down condemnation about how they "should" be. In the process, this permits a sexual frankness and openness, one that is largely body-positive and kink friendly. Characters will say **** and **** not for shock value, but because *people* **** and ****. It's acknowledged and delighted in. Carnivalesque isn't about shaming, but about full-bodied celebration in every sense of the word.

Things That are Cool About Carnivalesque

Carnivalesque is *fun*! Though it's not just that. It also serves as a versatile narrative tool for writers. Characters get dressed up! Characters hook up! They exchange their real lives for transformative encounters with (usually) out-of-bounds individuals. In the process they speak truth to power and share laughter across normally immutable social boundaries. Episodes of carnivalesque can tell the reader or viewer about how your characters secretly see themselves; it can even motivate them to become who they would like to be. It is, in some respects, like going to a SFF convention!

Na-na-na-na-na-na-na-na Bakhtin!

- **Masks:** Identity is fluid in the carnivalesque. Royalty can be paupers and paupers can be royalty. Masks—in both the literal and the metaphorical sense—permit this kind of role reversal or roleplay. It's an aspect of Bakhtin's upside-down world. And we still practice it today in, for example, cosplay when we assume the roles of superheroes, pop stars, or video-game characters and temporarily take on associated traits (we can be more confident, sexier, etc.). The more adult version, the fancy masked gala seen in so many stories and films, taps a similar energy to generate a frisson of sexual excitement for characters and titillate audiences with flirtatious possibilities.
- **Nights at the circus:** It's almost too obvious to say that carnivalesque often involves a carnival but, well, it certainly helps! A party atmosphere enables the reader to suspend their disbelief that such unlikely character interactions can occur. A celebratory event, in particular one that takes over a whole town or country, explains how

---

10. Bakhtin, 1984, p. 10.

your detective ends up drinking shots with her quarry or how soldiers from opposing factions wind up in bed together. Such interactions—especially because of their temporary nature—can precipitate any number of story developments firmly rooted in character. Thus, you might play with carnivalesque in your writing by including a fair, fete, or carnival where the repressed is released, the straight is queered, and mischievousness (and even debasement) is the order of the day. These are often occasions of heightened physicality and sexual energies (but, again, please acknowledge consent). Good real-world examples include Brazilian Carnival, Mardi Gras in New Orleans, burlesque shows, or the notorious Spring Break of US colleges. Though you can of course make up your own event in your Fantasy or SF setting!

- **Liminal spaces:** Liminality is a sense of in-betweenness. Liminal spaces are neither one place nor another (think of transient structures such as circus tents or places people just pass through such as railway-station waiting rooms). This effect also occurs during carnivalesque episodes, with the normally certain "here" becoming indistinct as specific locations—bars, clubs, palaces, etc.—spill out across streets and thoroughfares. Familiar spaces—the city park, the town square—are transformed into sites of wonder and possibility in the process. This erasure of physical boundaries obviously symbolises the dissolution of social ones. For as much as alcohol or hormones are involved, it's liminality that enables Bakhtin's "free and familiar contact" between people.[11]
- **Inhibition McGuffins:** A great thing about SFF/H stories is that sometimes the carnivalesque happens because… a wizard did it. Or because something… reversed the polarity. Any number of preposterous explanations for carnivalesque behaviour suddenly becomes plausible. Many episodes of *Star Trek* do just this, such as 'Fascination' (dir. Avery Brooks, 1994), an instalment of *Deep Space Nine* loosely based on *A Midsummer's Night Dream*. The episode sees an alien festival turned upside down by a visiting telepath's amorous thoughts stripping the characters of their inhibitions, which leads to a breakdown of social and professional norms. See, too, the *Buffy the Vampire Slayer* episode 'Halloween' (dir. Bruce Seth Green, 1997) in which a magic spell transforms people into the characters they're dressed as, thoroughly upending the power dynamics between the Scooby Gang (powerful Buffy becomes a timid noblewoman, goofball Xander becomes a soldier, etc.) and, in the process, revealing their fears and desires.

---

11. Bakhtin, 1984, p. 11.

- **Renewal:** A consequence of turning the world upside down—degrading it, to use Bakhtin's terminology—is that sometimes interesting things are shaken loose. Instances of carnivalesque in our stories offer our characters the chance to conceive of new approaches to their lives, their relationships, and, in extreme examples, their societies. Because "to degrade something," Bakhtin says, "is to bury, to sow, and to kill simultaneously, in order to bring forth something more and better".[12] Because bringing someone or something down to earth isn't the metaphor we think it is in the carnivalesque; it's instead an act of bringing them into contact with "the reproductive and generating power of the earth and of the body".[13] It's a measure of how mockery and parody can be expressions of just where a system needs to be reimagined or renewed by our protagonists.

---

12. Bakhtin, 1984, p. 21.
13. Bakhtin, 1984, p. 22.

ACTIVITIES

Big-banquet energy: Alongside bodily functions, one of Bakhtin's go-tos for excessive imagery in carnivalesque is food. So, imagine a character attending a feast in honour of a local festival (this can be either a Fantasy or historical setting). Place emphasis on the preposterous overindulgence in food and drink, on the processes of ingestion and digestion, flatulence, and even defecation! Exaggerate it as much as you can! Make the food as over-the-top as you can describe! Make the event *messy*, with wine dribbling down people's chins and close focus on chewing mouths and bulging bellies and sensational belching. Have fun with making it borderline disgusting!

Party's over: Some critics, such as Terry Eagleton, have asked whether the seeming anti-establishment nature of carnivalesque is, in the end, serving a conservative purpose. Remember the pressure-valve metaphor: perhaps permitting the occasional release of social energies allows not for real change but instead for the perpetuation of the establishment? Maybe it is just another way of keeping people in line? Considering this, return to the banquet above and insert a character sceptical of carnivalesque's ability to renew society. Place them in dialogue with another reveller and see where the discussion leads.

COMEDIC FANTASY

And now for something completely different.... People sometimes think Fantasy is all *grr argh* swords and monsters, but, if we want our writing to truly resonate with readers, we need to reflect all aspects of the human/elvish/orcish condition. And humour is a crucial part of that. Hence comedic fantasy, which ranges from jokey asides and snarky characters to full-on parody and satire. So, permit yourself a bit of silliness. Allow your protagonists to have a laugh once in a while. Let yourself believe that comedic fantasy is actually a very serious business.

A Short History of Comedic Fantasy

The *short* short history of comedic fantasy is to just say "Terry Pratchett", drop the mic, and walk away from the resulting explosion in slow motion, but in fact there's a lot more to discover beyond the great man's insanely popular Discworld novels. That said, the subgenre has often had a hard time of it. If Fantasy isn't "serious" enough for a lot of writing courses (boo!), then the notion of writing *comedic* Fantasy is something too many of them consider downright scandalous (though that could also be because it's quite hard to teach comedy!). The broader ecosystem of literary criticism can, with a couple of exceptions, be similarly suspicious of this "low" art. Because heaven forbid that anyone follow in the footsteps of disreputable comedy writers such as <checks notes> William Shakespeare (the Witches of *Macbeth*, for instance, were for centuries played for comedy rather than for unease).[1] Such broad scepticism means that comedic fantasy's fan base has long been forced "to defend their reading choices—especially in the 80s, before the 90s geek revolution made our obsessions cool—against charges of meaninglessness or childishness".[2] That would make anyone protective and sarcastic!

As a subgenre, comedic fantasy comes into focus during the nineteenth century. The seeds of it are sprinkled throughout the (Folktales and) Fairy Tales and Christmas stories of Very Serious Authors Hans Christian Andersen and Charles Dickens respectively. The first true example, however, comes from the brilliantly pseudonymous 'F. Anstey' (in actuality the English humourist Thomas Anstey Guthrie) who published an early **Body Swapping** comedy called *Vice Versa* in 1882. In this novel, magic causes a father and son to switch places. The father is forced to attend his son's boarding school

---
1. Taylor, 2020, n.p.
2. Harkaway, 2015, n.p.

beneath the cane of an evil headmaster, while the son finds himself running his father's business in the City of London. In typical fashion, both gain a new understanding of the challenges facing the other (and the reader gains an insight into Victorian values). The novel was quite popular at the time, though comedic fantasy nonetheless remained thin on the ground for many decades. Indeed, it would not trouble the public imagination much for almost forty years, this time in the US, when author James Branch Cabell published a satirical Fantasy that served as the model for much of what followed (including Monty Python, Pratchett, and, unexpectedly, even Robert A. Heinlein's 1961 SF novel *Stranger in a Strange Land*). Titled *Jurgen, A Comedy of Justice* (1919), Cabell's novel romps its way through **Mythic Fantasy** and, in the process, parodies everything from Arthurian legend to Dante's *The Divine Comedy* (c. 1321). *Jurgen*, which was highly praised by infamous English occultist Aleister Crowley, was a notorious novel (as all good satire should be). It notably found itself the subject of an obscenity case taken by the New York Society for the Suppression of Vice (wow, they sound *fun*). Cabell would swipe back satirically four years later with a revised edition including a section where the protagonist is placed on trial by the Philistines. The prosecutor in the fictional case? An enormous dung-beetle!

The first half of the twentieth century wasn't exactly a parade of happy fun times, yet one important exception was *Unknown Worlds* magazine (1939–'43), which favoured Fantasy stories with a comedic inflection. Many authors known for their use of humour—if not necessarily as humourists—graced its pages. These include work by Fletcher Pratt and L. Sprague de Camp; H.L. Gold's 'Trouble with Water' (1939), a whimsical fairytale about a water gnome in New York; and, perhaps the most enduring, Fritz Leiber's playful take on Sword and Sorcery with the Fafhrd and the Gray Mouser tales. Such writers engaged in a kind of comedic conversation with the tropes and conventions of the Fantasy genre. However, after another two decades, this drifted into parody, as it would with *Bored of the Rings* (1969) by National Lampoon magazine founders Henry Beard and Douglas Kenney, a comedic take on J.R.R. Tolkien's *The Lord of the Rings* (1954–'55). The book follows the general outline of the original but approaches it with irreverence (Merry and Pippin, for instance, become Moxie and Pepsi) as well as slapstick humour. It's been continually in print for half a century, which, for a parody, is remarkable longevity! Five years later, another commercial (and, indeed, critical) success arrived with the Mel Brooks film *Young Frankenstein* (1974), which parodies the various adaptations of Mary Shelley's seminal *Frankenstein* (1818) as well as the horror-film genre more generally. The film tells the story of the original scientist's grandson, utilised many props from 1930s films, and was shot in black and white to further spoof the appropriate atmosphere. It's regularly listed among the best comedy films ever made.

Around the same time, a young English journalist named Terry Pratchett was poised to change the face of comedic fantasy forever. After dabbling in SF novels (check out *The Dark Side of the Sun*, 1976), Pratchett began writing comedic fantasy in the early 1980s set on his fictional Discworld, a flat planet carried through space by four gigantic elephants standing on the back of an enormous turtle. Pratchett's stated aim was to "have fun with some of the clichés" of Fantasy fiction but, across three decades, the series became much more than that.[3] The first novel, *The Colour of Magic*, appeared in 1983, and the series quickly brought enough success for the author to quit his job (as a press officer for the Central Electricity Generating Board) and focus full time on writing. As he progressed, the immensely popular Discworld series, though ostensibly comprising stand-alone books, developed several distinct story arcs and novel sequences following beloved characters and groups such as the wizard Rincewind, the young witch Tiffany Aching, the City Watch, and more. Along the way, the brilliantly read Pratchett poked fun at the entire Fantasy genre, as well as SF and mainstream literature, in works rich in allusion and reference. Crucially, he also found time for social commentary on issues such as religion, racial prejudice, inner-city discord, and more, believing (quite rightly) in comedic fantasy's power to sneak past the gatekeepers both inside and outside our heads. "Laughter," he said, "can get through the keyhole while seriousness is still hammering on the door. New ideas can ride in on the back of a joke, old ideas can be given an added edge".[4] The series eventually grew to an amazing forty-one books and has earned a pride of place in not just comedic fantasy but in literature full stop!

By the 1990s, comedic fantasy seemed to have achieved critical mass. Mary Gentle's *Grunts!* (1992) offered a satirical approach to typical Fantasy worlds by positioning orcs—usually the villains—as her protagonists (and also by showing up the noble characters as anything but). The always humorous Diana Wynne Jones would expand comedic fantasy further with *The Tough Guide to Fantasyland* (1996), a *non*-fiction take on the material. The book presents as a tongue-in-cheek travel guide (a parody of the popular Rough Guides format) detailing the archetypical characters and situations found in fantasy realms/literature. The comedic Time Travel novel *To Say Nothing of the Dog: or, How We Found the Bishop's Bird Stump at Last* (1997) by Connie Willis makes much of the absurd possibilities of visiting the past. More recently, the animated film *Shrek* (dirs. Andrew Adamson and Vicky Jenson, 2001) found a huge audience with its self-aware parody

---

3. Young, 2005, n.p.
4. Quoted in Villiers, 2014, p. 77.

of fairy tales—and fairy tale adaptations—as well as its brilliant characters who deconstruct a variety of Fantasy stereotypes (among them an antisocial ogre, a princess under a magical curse, a wise-cracking donkey, and a **Dragon**). The film's success led to many sequels. *Disenchantment* (2018–'23), from *Simpsons* creator Matt Groening, brought animated comedic fantasy to the streaming age. Anchored by its parody of recognisable Fantasy tropes and conventions, the series follows a rebellious, alcoholic princess on her adventures with a naïve elf and her literal personal demon. Meanwhile, the film *Dungeons and Dragons: Honour Among Thieves* (dirs. Jonathan Goldstein and John Francis Daley, 2023) applies a similar wry eye to the storyworld of the famous tabletop role-playing game (players will find much amusement in, for instance, how the film characters' quest repeatedly gets sidetracked). Other contemporary Fantasy authors with a penchant for laughs include the inimitable Seanan McGuire, T. Kingfisher (pseudonym for Ursula Vernon), Sarah Kuhn (see 2018's superhero novel *Heroine's Journey*), Kim M. Watt (see the Beaufort Scales Mysteries), and Chandra Clarke (check out *Pundragon*, 2020).

A Spotter's Guide: Is This Some Kind of Joke?

- **Parody and pastiche:** This is probably the first thing that comes to mind when people think of comedic fantasy: deliberately exaggerated imitation of other works in the genre for the purposes of comedy or ridicule. Parody tends to be focused on a specific work or series, offering a new spin on something familiar. It's not plagiarism—*wash out your mouth right now!*—but instead a kind of homage. Parody can be quite critical of the perceived shortcomings of the original work (though it doesn't have to be) and will twist it in whatever way it needs to in order to generate the most laughs even if it has to demolish cornerstones of the original in the process. A good parody of High Fantasy is *The Dark Lord of Derkholm* (1998) by Diana Wynne Jones. Adam Roberts also has form in this, with his work including a pair of Tolkien parodies titled *The Soddit* (2003) and *The Sellamillion* (2004), which he published as A.R.R.R. Roberts. Parody also tends to be incredibly popular on the big screen. For instance, Edgar Wright's 2004 *Shaun of the Dead* parodies the Night of the Living Dead films (dir. George A. Romero, 1979–2009). Though, in his affectionate approach to the material, Wright illustrates how readily parody overlaps with—and is often discussed alongside—the broad celebratory mode of pastiche. Think of the latter as a love letter that utilises recognisable signifiers to make something new from a genre's familiar tropes, styles, or incidents.

- **Satire:** Fantasy is fertile ground for satirical riffs on life, society, and politics. By satire, we mean the humorous use of exaggeration, irony, and *cutting* ridicule to criticise power, authority, and injustice. It can be as straightforward as cartoons in the newspaper (remember newspapers?) and impressions of public figures on the radio (the weird little talking box your parents had), or it can be as complicated as elaborate, seasons-long television deconstructions of governance (Scottish writer Armando Iannucci is an acknowledged *master* of the latter, with mainstream television shows such as *The Thick of It*, 2005–'12, and *VEEP*, 2012–'19). Satire tends to be more prickly and more political than parody in its intent. It is cheeky humour that does well in situations in which you want to bring attention to outrageous real-life issues. It often presents itself as something serious before taking its assertions to outlandish extremes. Satire has long been intertwined with Fantasy fiction, with one of the most famous and imitated—possibly too imitated—satires being *A Modest Proposal* (1729) by Jonathan Swift, author of *Gulliver's Travels* (1726). The essay mocks heartless accounts of Irish starvation in the British press at the time by suggesting, with a straight face, that poor people might sell their children to the rich as food.
- **Absurdism:** Sometimes humour is weird. Like, *really* weird (which, in Fantasy, always seems like a great fit!). Absurdist comedy juxtaposes rational belief and motivation with nonsensical situations by taking the latter to their extreme. It tells mundane stories in grandiloquent or epic fashion, often highlighting how preposterous the things we take for granted really are. The classic example is *Monty Python's Flying Circus* (1969–'74), whose comedy troupe took on mediaeval and Arthurian Fantasy in the film *Monty Python and the Holy Grail* (1975). Contemporary examples include the spec-fic friendly sitcom *Community* (2009–'15; check out its amazing *Dungeons and Dragons* episodes!). Though be warned, while some people are super into absurdist comedy, others never seem to get it.
- **Mime:**

- **Situation comedy:** We're used to thinking about sitcoms as a modern, urban form of storytelling, but there's no reason Fantasy can't mine humour from the same basic model: a group of people thrown together by geography, employment, or familial relationships. After all, what makes a sitcom pop is its *characters*. Set it in a tavern (*Cheers* with monsters!), or in a castle among the royal servants (*The Office* with scribes and jesters!). Or take a Fantasy staple, such as Witches, and place them in our world, as classic comedies *Bewitched* (1964–'72) and the original *Sabrina the Teenage Witch* (1996–2000) successfully did. More recently, *The Good Place* (2016–'20) offered an exceptional example of a sitcom set in a Fantasy version of the afterlife. Meanwhile, on the page, Travis Baldree's super wholesome *Legends and Lattes* (2022) installs its orcish protagonist in a coffeeshop. Subtle humour and low-stake Fantasy delights are on the menu here.

Things That are Cool About Comedic Fantasy

Writing comedy is one of the most difficult challenges you can set yourself (well, writing *funny* comedy is anyway!). That's because humour is subjective: what one person finds hilarious leaves another staring at you like you're some sort of Gollum. Consequently, comedy can be a hard sell, though not an impossible one. Successfully placing such a story—especially one in a genre that has historically had difficulty being taken seriously—always feels like a win. For writers at least, that's no laughing matter!

An Elf, a Princess, and a Demon Walk into a Bar…

- **Workshop your jokes:** The best draft of your comedy is almost never the first draft. This is true of most writing, of course, but the process of fine-tuning humour is a particularly good example, even if it's counterintuitive. Comedy often reads as or sounds natural and off-the-cuff but, in reality, an awful lot of it is carefully honed, rehearsed, and refined. Consider how professional stand-up comedians often sharpen new material in small clubs before taking it to a bigger stage. Follow their example (just this once) and test out your jokes on your friends or writing group.
- **Mock the king, not the peasant:** It should go without saying that making fun of people who can't respond, for whatever reason, isn't cool. That's called bullying. Too often comedy dresses up this kind of behaviour in the guise of humour (or, worse, as "edgy" stand-up). There's no call for mocking people disadvantaged by history or race

or gender or physical condition. By contrast, comedy *does* have a role to play in punching up, in speaking truth to power (as court jesters often did), and in highlighting the absurdities of socio-economic and political inequality (see **Carnivalesque**). Fantasy worlds, modelled in many cases on reality, are prime territory for this kind of satirical discourse and for the kind of jokes that make people think.

- **Pundemonium:** Some people will tell you that clever wordplay is the lowest form of humour, but those people are no pun at all. Because, sure, some puns are terrible, but they're also a marker of real skill. They require considerable knowledge of and control of language (see, for instance, the rabbit hole of multi-lingual puns in the writing of James Joyce!). So don't be afraid of the pun! Don't let grinches steal your joy!
- **Use moments of levity in serious stories:** Humour is like seasoning in your Fantasy in that it brings other elements of your writing—be that character or structure or even worldbuilding—into definition. It offers a means of supplying useful tonal variance to your work. There is, after all, a reason why even Grimdark frequently includes wisecracking characters (Tyrion Lannister, anybody?) to comment, often sarcastically, on the proceedings. An otherwise overly serious, pessimistic, or nihilistic work of fiction would be little more than drudgery without an occasional laugh to punctuate it!
- **Commit to the bit:** A key route to successful comedic fantasy is displaying a firm belief in the material. A writer needs to ensure that any hint of embarrassment or self-consciousness on their part is expunged: *Fakelatinis disappearis!* Because maybe you're writing a dorky moment set in a dragon lair, or a farcical misunderstanding atop a wizard's tower, but either way you want your reader invested in that scenario and not distracted by wondering if the writer is thinking, "This is a bit goofy really, isn't it?". Readers need to trust that the writer thinks the material is funny. Sure, the jokes aren't always going to land, but you've got to commit to them nonetheless. Writing comedy is like a marriage: it's for better or worse! Plus, it helps if you can laugh at yourself. Trust us, that's healthy in both cases.

ACTIVITIES

Stand-up: You're a resident of a Fantasy world hoping to make it as a professional jester. Write a ten-minute stand-up routine that you could perform in the local tavern. Set the tone at the outset: Are you going to concentrate on observational humour (knightly behaviour, for example) or are you going to be bawdy (maybe discussing courtly relationships)? Watch some stand-up online for inspiration but be sure to remain in the Fantasy storyworld throughout your routine. For bonus marks (we're not actually grading you, don't worry), perform the results for your friends!

Parody: Pick your favourite guilty-pleasure Fantasy movie or television show and spend twenty minutes jotting down everything that's objectively silly about it (the clothes, the food, the dialogue, the monsters, the plot...). Then imagine what would happen if a character from our reality finds themselves in this world. Write a short scene in which this person tries to find someone to explain how to navigate the Fantasy city. Contrast their disbelief with how the Fantasy character regards everything in this bamboozling reality as completely normal.

CHAPTER THREE

HORROR

Allegory

People think Speculative Fiction is all about other worlds or the far future or depravities beyond human comprehension, but the truth is—and always has been—that Science Fiction, Fantasy, and Horror actually address what we—the author or our society or our world—are going through, even if the story itself isn't set in the author's hometown during their lives. Which is to say that storytelling does not exist in a vacuum. Original blend *Star Trek?* That's about race relations in 1960s America, the Cold War, and the fallout from the conflict in Vietnam. Contemporary *Doctor Who?* That features trans actors and includes plotlines about self-identification, hybridity, and how violent individualism is endangering the fabric of society. Horror is no different. In the 1880s it tackled anxieties about the human mind and body. In the 1980s it allegorically addressed the AIDS epidemic and video censorship. In the present day it has a lot to work with in terms of our, shall we say, *interesting times.*

Such world turmoil affects people in different ways: some drink and take risks; others turn into hermits, finding solace in hot chocolate, thick socks, blanket forts on the couch, and *The Lord of the Rings* trilogy extended editions marathons. We often seek comfort in what we read and watch and, surprisingly perhaps, this has recently happened in Horror, too. The 2020s in particular have seen the rise of so-called "cozy horror". What is cozy horror, you ask? Well, it's Horror that's still scary (for some), but that might end happily; or Horror that doesn't have such huge stakes, or maybe has a romantic subplot. We like to think of it as Tim Burton vibes: it's ooky and spooky but can also be funny and, well, *cozy*. It addresses our contemporary anxieties in classic Horror fashion, but what makes it different is its willingness to also sooth them.

Be a Keymaster, Not a Gatekeeper

The likes of cosy horror shed light on one of our pet peeves here at *Spec Fic for Newbies*: the notion of gatekeeping. Because there are those out there who say that cosy horror isn't really Horror because it isn't scary/traumatic/nihilistic enough. This is perhaps, and as Julia Glassman in the *Mary Sue* has said, because Horror is sometimes framed as an "endurance contest" and the more you can handle, the "better" a fan you are.[1] Which is categorically not true. Certainly, we believe that all subgenres have merit and worth. If someone wants to have the wigglies frightened out of them by a story, then that's cool. If someone wants a couple of jump scares and a happy ending, that's also fine! Horror, like everything else in the world, is a spectrum.

In this section we explore subgenres and tropes all along that spectrum, from traditional (such as **Ghost Stories** and **Werewolves**) to more modern examples (such as **Ecohorror**). Within each, however, is another tonal spectrum that depends on the effect you wish to have on your reader. Each one can be written in a way that evokes chilling or terrifying responses or, dare we say it, can leave the reader feeling *cozy*. So don't be a gatekeeper, be a keymaster, and, whether it chills you to your very soul or reaffirms your belief in the wonderfulness of life, write the Horror that *you* want to read.

---

1. Glassman, 2023, n.p.

FOLK HORROR

Something feels wrong.... You've left the highway and now the roads have more goat skulls than signposts. The locals are looking at you funny, dancing around maypoles, and gathering for their special seasonal festival. There's a creeping vibe that neither you nor your doomed companions can explain, or reason with, or escape. You took the wrong turn at that last fork in the road and now you're smack dab in the middle of—*gasp*—folk horror!

A Short History of Folk Horror

Folk horror is appropriately difficult to pin down. It's a mood as much as anything else. It's the eyes of a close-knit community watching as you pass through their town. It's the odd ceremonies you see performed on a hillside or a village square. It's a subgenre in which your protagonist will always be the outsider. It's a type of storytelling deeply beholden to half-forgotten histories and (often very local) folklore, one filled with ideocratic supernatural beliefs, warped versions of Christianity, sexual acts in the service of pagan fertility cults, ritualistic killings (so many killings), and yet, for all of that, it's a relatively recent development. It first appeared as a specific term in 1970 "when reviewer Rod Cooper used it to describe Piers Haggard's amazingly titled *The Blood on Satan's Claw* (1971)".[1] This film, about a demonic force that's unleashed on a seventeenth-century English village, is one of the holy trinity of early folk-horror films along with *Witchfinder General* (dir. Michael Reeves, 1968) and Robin Hardy's 1973 masterpiece *The Wicker Man* (but don't worry, we'll get to those!). Folk horror is, in the words of academic and filmmaker Adam Scovell, "a prism of a term", a subgenre "best seen, not simply as a set of criteria to be read with hindsight into all sorts of media, but as a way of opening up discussions on subtly interconnected work and how we now interact with such work".[2] With academic rigour—which is its own kind of perverse ritual impenetrable to outsiders—Scovell has broken the term into its constituent parts—folk and horror—and discussed how even defining those as concrete things is nigh on impossible. Nonetheless, like someone who has stumbled into a small village and is about to have their fancy city certainties torn asunder, let's give it a try....

Folk horror is deeply anchored in the roots of Horror literature, the roots of our history, and the roots of the most ancient of forests. The word

---

1. Pilkington, 2023, n.p.
2. Scovell, 2017, pp. 5–6.

folk comes from the Old English *folc*, meaning "common people" or "tribe"[3]; folklore, then, is a culture's collection of stories, songs, rhymes, superstitions, and other "common" wisdoms (see Folktales and Fairy Tales). These are the stories that aren't quite as codified as literature. They're more slippery: they're the sayings your grandparents muttered underneath their breaths and the whispered tales about the local murder house. Folklore is hyperlocal and in that way was neglected by scholars and historians for generations (though various projects in various countries have by now gathered up much of this material in accessible databases). Some of this material has evolved over the years to become the fairy tales, legends, and tall tales that are familiar to us now, everything from Cinderella to King Arthur to American folk heroes such as John Henry and Paul Bunyan. Yet folklore—true, scary, *weird* folklore—is, to an extent, still seen by the literary establishment as something backwards, a kind of degenerative storytelling that remains the preserve of rural communities and the unrefined. It's ironic that the victims in folk horror are so often the self-described sophisticates, intellectuals, or authority figures who wander into isolated communities they don't understand either by accident (the fateful missed turn on the road), for indulgent holidays (come for Instagrammable views, stay for the ritual sacrifice), or to investigate a disappearance ("We don't know what you're talking about, Inspector"). In almost all cases they discover that the folk belief they've disparaged has a powerful connection to nature and the past, more often than not to ancient beliefs in various spirits or deities (beneficial and otherwise) and to other creatures, such as animals, connected to nature. Folk horror is the subgenre that executes these elements to gruesome effect. Deer-headed gods stalk the unwary through the night. Cloaked figures draw virgin blood on a devil-consecrated rock by moonlight. People—the scariest creatures of all—perpetrate horrific crimes in the service of depraved beliefs passed down from generation to generation because *that's how we have always done things*. Such practices may not be part of official history in either reality or in your storyworld, but they exist beneath our technologically savvy present and their very presence undermines it. Folk horror can, in that way, be thought of as a narrative rupture in the nice and tidy story we tell ourselves about how the world works. Which is to say we might have smart phones and air fryers and cars with heated seats, but when up against a nature deity that wants to pull us into the darkness beneath the trees, we're pretty powerless. There is, after all, no GPS in Hell.

    We can say that the initial threads of folk horror as a distinct subgenre emerged in the late nineteenth century and it initially shares strands of its DNA with Gothic Horror. This was a potent moment in which vernacular beliefs and superstitions (often in the guise of "Celtic" symbolism) pressed

---

3. Online Etymology Dictionary, 'folk', n.d., n.p.

up against the modern world and created a productive tension for writers, and it was into this strange world that the earliest folk horror slouched towards its grotesque birth. Among the first creators were Welsh author Arthur Machen, an occultist whose *The Great God Pan* (1894) explores the destructive influence of the titular deity who finds, in the daughter of a woman who underwent medical experiments, a conduit into this world. The book was denounced as a work of degeneracy (Oscar Wilde is said to have loved it!) and, in that way, sets the tone for folk horror's particular mix of "occultism, paganism, non-mainstream eroticism, sexual diversity, the femme fatale, violent and strange deaths, and the simultaneous investment in and disavowal of bourgeois identities".[4] Other early practitioners include English author Algernon Blackwood (another occultist, this time a disciple of theosophy, and author of *The Willows*, 1907, in which two men encounter mystical and unknown strangeness in the wilderness), and English author and medievalist M.R. James (see **Ghost Stories**) whose work explores themes of ancient spirits being encountered in the modern world. Indeed, it's that idea of a (usually remote) place clinging onto ancient spirits and practices that will help us follow folk horror's unsettling thread from these early examples to modern and contemporary classics such as Shirley Jackson's phenomenal 'The Lottery' (1948), Thomas Tryon's influential *Harvest Home* (1973), or Ari Aster's disturbing film *Midsommar* (2019).

A Spotter's Guide: Here We Go Around the Maypole High

At this point, writers may find it useful to consider what Scovell calls the "Folk Horror Chain," a sequence in which each of the following elements naturally proceeds from the one before it:

- **Landscape:** The setting for folk horror usually has clear "adverse effects on the social and moral identity of the inhabitants'.[5] Media specialist Cathy Pilkington describes the landscape of folk horror as "almost becom[ing] a character in itself—isolated villages, barren fields and claustrophobic woods all play host to folkloric creatures, sacrifices, rituals and superstition".[6] Little details will help to sell this unsettling feeling: lack of phone reception, animal skeletons, strange carvings, and sticks and twigs fashioned into geometric shapes.
- **Isolation:** Folk horror often works best when set in a rural or "inhospitable place", not just because of bleakness (though this helps!) but because such remoteness allows for a setting "in some

---

4. Denisoff, 2018, p. 4.
5. Scovell, 2017, p. 17.
6. Pilkington, 2023, n.p.

way different from general society as a whole".[7] When folk horror set in the past is placed in villages, small towns, and even islands, the isolation is clear because of the lack of large urban centres. In more current folk horror, characters visiting or banished to a remote location experience isolation in the juxtaposition of where they were from versus where they find themselves.[8] Folk horror classic *The Wicker Man* (inspired by David Pinner's 1967 novel *Ritual*; unnecessarily remade in 2006 by dir. Neil LaBute to negative reviews) is a good example of this as it's set on an island that's isolated but still reachable by seaplane. What's just as important here, of course, is the idea of being *culturally* isolated and of visitors being literal strangers in a strange land.

- **Skewed belief systems and morality:** It's unsurprising that a horror story set in an isolated place that has adverse effects would also contain people with a skewed belief system. In *The Wicker Man*, the islanders' beliefs are skewed when compared to the status quo of life back on the mainland. However, the islanders' paganism is viewed through the eyes of a devout Catholic policeman whose death as a human sacrifice is ironic when one considers the representation of consuming the body and blood of Christ in church rituals. In Jackson's 'The Lottery', a small New England community practises the annual tradition of randomly selecting a person to be stoned to death as a sacrifice to ensure a bountiful harvest. Meanwhile, in the book-length poem *Gaudete* by Ted Hughes (1977), the Christian mission of an English vicar—to prepare for the return of his messiah—is literalised by a changeling who establishes a sex cult in order to father the second coming.
- **Happening/summoning:** Scovell describes this as the weakest of the four links because its manifestation can take so many forms. He explains that "Folk Horror is often about death, in the slowest, most ritualistic of ways, occasionally encompassing supernatural elements, where the group belief systems summon up something demonic or generally supernatural".[9] In *Midsommar*, for example, the every-ninety-years "happening" point is death via a series of nine ritual sacrifices, though without any supernatural elements. But in so much folk horror, the common ending is ritualistic death for the chosen sacrifices (usually visitors or outsiders).

---

7. Scovell, 2017, p. 18.
8. Scovell, 2017, pp. 17–18.
9. Scovell, 2017, p. 18.

Things That are Cool About Folk Horror

Because every culture has its own folklore, superstitions, beliefs, etc., folk horror offers a doorway into writing Horror that allows you to incorporate elements of your own culture or background into fiction (note, too, the existence of a more "modern" folk horror—weird stories about abandoned factories, ghostly taxi drivers, that sort of thing—that might relate more clearly to your urban existence). Folk horror gives writers a means to deal with *cultural* isolation, that feeling of being different or alone in a community where the accepted practices and behaviours perplex us. In this way you can write folk horror set in non-rural locations that still carries recognisable themes.

Asking for Directions

As with other subgenres that exist in slightly different ways in diverse places, the topics or focus of a story might need to be handled carefully to avoid insensitive and even racist elements. Delving into a culture's folklore beliefs gives us a way to explore themes that resonate with us as humans— isolation, family, love, etc.—and so folk horror can be a way to explore these common themes as long as we don't use another culture's folklore in a way that "others" that culture. Note that there are *many* cultures (such as those in Nigeria, Guatemala, Poland, Australia, Italy, Mexico, and Japan, for example) that engage with folk horror, giving writers numerous examples to explore.

A recurring folk horror-trope is the lost visitor who must stop and ask for directions. They generally ignore the warning to turn around and proceed to their slow, ritualistic, and horrifying deaths. So, in that spirit, let's take a closer look at some of places we can go to find folk horror:

- **Britain:** The English-language origins of folk horror lie in Britain, in part because of its cultural melting pot of folklore (English, Welsh, Scottish, Cornish, and even Scandinavian influences), its history of religious upheaval, and its importance in the witchcraft trials in the early modern era (see <u>Witches</u>). One of the original folk-horror films, *Witchfinder General*, focuses on the mid-seventeenth-century witch hunts in East Anglia (home of one of your authors!) that led to the torture and death of over 200 people.[10] Other recent examples include the brilliantly constructed *Wylding Hall* by Elizabeth Hand (2015), in which a folk band encounters the supernatural; *Starve Acre* (2020) by Andrew Michael Hurley, which evokes the best of 1970's

---

10. Morrill, 2022, n.p.

English folk horror; *Pine* (2020) by Francine Toon, which tackles the eeriness of the Scottish Highlands; *The Green Knight* (dir. David Lowery, 2021), which adapts the staple of university Intro to English Literature courses as a revisionist mediaeval fantasy with undeniable folk horror sensibilities; and *Enys Men* (dir. Mark Jenkin, 2022), an experimental film set on an uninhabited island off the Cornish coast.

- **Scandinavia:** This is a location known for extremes of cold, dark, isolation, and a distinct folklore, mythology, and history thrown in for good measure (all recently popularised by not just the plethora of Viking-inspired shows and films but also the crime subgenre Scandi-Noir). An early Finnish entry is *The White Reindeer* (originally *Valkoinen peura*; dir Erik Blomberg, 1952), in which a lonely new bride living in isolated Lapland is transformed into a vampiric, shapeshifting white reindeer. Good recent examples include *The Ritual* (2011), set in Sweden though written by British author Adam Neville (in which isolation and skewed beliefs are delivered with a giant dollop of supernatural hijinks), along with *Midsommar* and *Lamb* (dir. Valdimar Jóhannsson, 2021).

- **North America:** The sheer size of North America means that folk-horror settings here run the gamut from the recognisable to the surreal. New England, for example, has never quite shaken its reputation as an isolated and strange place for the first White colonists. Stories set here include *The VVitch* (dir. Robert Eggers, 2015), about a seventeenth-century family barely surviving in the wilderness whose eldest daughter ends up joining a coven after the rest of the family is killed. Elsewhere, America's agricultural heartlands have inspired work such as Stephen King's 'Children of the Corn' (1978, with nearly uncountable filmed versions!) about a couple travelling through rural Nebraska caught by a cult populated by children who worship a monster that lives in the cornfields. See, too, a couple of terrifying episodes of *The X-Files*, such as the infamous 'Home' (dir. Kim Manners, 1996) about an incestuous, murderous family in rural Pennsylvania. One example that hoodwinked viewers into believing it was real "found footage"—similar to popular ghost-hunter television shows—is *The Blair Witch Project* (dirs. Daniel Myrick and Eduardo Sánchez, 1999), about a trio of students researching a local legend who go into the woods and never return. Of course, North America was home to vibrant and varied cultures before the European settlers, and those peoples had their own beliefs and practices; *The Only Good Indians* (2020) by Stephen Graham Jones is an example of folk horror focused on indigenous cultures and themes about an elk's spirit seeking revenge on a group of Native American men who, as teenagers, massacred her herd.

- **Southeast Asia:** Director Kong Rithdee explains that "Southeast Asian horror has always been Folk Horror. It's our default mode, our modus operandi, it's what audiences in this part of the world grew up with".[11] Examples include 1980s *Satan's Slave* (Indonesian: *Pengabdi Setan*) directed by Sisworo Gautama Putra, and the 1981 cult classic *Mystics in Bali* (Indonesian: *Punahnya Rahasia Ilmu Iblis Leak*) directed by Tjut Djalil; though while those films feature local folklore, neither exactly matches with Scovell's "Folk Horror Chain". This suggests limits to "universal" story structures and, indeed, to the application of Western-centric criticism to global storytelling. That said, the impact of globalisation is as real on narrative as on anything else, with some newer work adhering more closely to the "Folk Horror Chain". A good example is the 2019 Malaysian film *Roh* (*Soul*) directed by Emir Ezwan, with its location (an "atmospheric rain forest setting"), isolation, skewed belief system and a "happening" at the end.[12]

---

11. Rithdee, 2021, n.p.
12. Ferrarese, 2021, n.p.

ACTIVITIES

Family ties: If you're lucky enough to have a family history of superstition or family lore, or if you're from a place with strong ties to cultural folklore, take advantage of it! Interview family members or to do research at libraries or online to find stories that you didn't know about. Did Aunt Dot have an encounter with a mysterious older relative who gave her an ominous warning? What about the time Cousin Rick went camping in the forest and found a campfire surrounded by human bones? Use even small bits of stories to expand them into something that you can use to slot into the "Folk Horror Chain" to develop a more filled-in tale.

Get lost: Pull out a map of the world, whether it's a paper atlas (love those!) or an online map. Place it upside-down (or in some way mess with your ability to easily recognise where certain countries or continents are), close your eyes, and play pin-the-tail-on-the-map. The world is huge, and there's lots of empty space, so hopefully your finger lands on an isolated spot. Now, place yourself there in your imagination. You can conduct online visual research to learn what it looks like, as well as about sounds and smells. Then do a bit of digging into local cultures and their belief systems, either now or in the past. This is the start of your Folk Horror Chain: you have a landscape and the start of "skewed" beliefs; now you just need to place yourself there (in isolation or isolated because you're new to the place and so isolated from your own life). Ramp up the horror with a ritual/summoning/happening.

GHOST STORIES

Phantasm. Spirit. Wraith. Shadow. Ghoul. Ghost. No matter what you call it, it's the dead coming back from beyond the grave to interfere with the living, enact revenge, or just hang around. We've been distracted—obsessed?—by them for millennia, and they've made their way into our oral and written stories to the point where "Do you believe in ghosts?" is a run-of-the-mill second-date question. So, join hands with us and let's call forth to the spirits from the beyond….

A Short History of Ghost Stories

All cultures have beliefs about what happens after we die. All have works of fiction that explore these ideas. They're tales of hauntings and tales of what's haunting us. As a narrative form, they've evolved considerably across the millennia. Academic Roger Clark explains it:

> The earliest ghosts in the Epic of Gilgamesh, for example, bear little relation to what came afterwards. Babylon's dead seemed to hover between the human and the inhuman. The ghosts of Ancient Greece were strange wraith-like creatures, pathetic and winged, who had no power over the living. Medieval ghosts were reanimated corpses or holy apparitions; Jacobean ghosts, demons pretending to be human. Post-Restoration ghosts returned to correct injustices, right wrongs, or supply information about lost documents and valuables. Regency ghosts were gothic. In Victorian times, ghosts were to be questioned in séances, and ghost-seeing became far more associated with women. Late Victorians embraced paranormality, seeing the ghostly as a manifestation of as yet understood laws of nature. The 1930s found the poltergeist.[1]

The ghost story as we know it in popular Western literature today can be strongly linked to what happened in the past two hundred years. And, as with other subgenres and tropes in SFF/H, the development and popularity of contemporary ghost stories have a formidable link with scientific "progress".

In the nineteenth century, as the world convulsed with the ramifications of industrialisation—including advances in transportation via trains, the invention and installation of gas lights and then electricity in cities and homes, and the evolution of medicine and the new science of psychology—it was also looking "beyond" at the mysteries that had bewildered populations for generations. The hope was that applying science would lead to solutions

---
1. Clarke, 2012, pp. 23–24.

that would allow people to talk to the dead, read minds, and perform other formerly "misunderstood" feats. As a result, the Western world was questioning religious beliefs during the "so-called nineteenth-century crisis-of-faith" when "scientific and medical explanations of the natural world began to displace older religious ones", leading to "a rise in secular thinking".[2] This "bashing together" of science and religion contributed—as it often does—to people feeling off-kilter about their place in the world and their understanding of how the world worked. Enter Spiritualism, the belief that the living and the dead could communicate, a practice that became all the rage in the Western world right in the middle of the nineteenth century.[3] The movement itself started in 1848: in New York, the young Fox sisters—Margaretta and Catherine—"claimed to have come into contact with the unquiet spirit of a murdered man in their house, who communicated with them by loud knocks on wood".[4] Though they weren't exposed as frauds for decades, cracking their toe knuckles to trick paying customers took them (and their older sister, Leah, who figured out how to monetise the talent) across the ocean to perform in Britain.[5] The spectacle resulted in a belief that mediums—mostly women, who "were deemed to have more delicate, sensitive nervous systems than men"—could communicate with the dead.[6] The more ghost-related part of the Spiritualist movement included mediums contacting the dead via seances and Ouija boards, images we find in Horror stories even today.

That the popularity of Spiritualism influenced literature is no surprise, especially considering the Gothic sensibilities found in stories written before the Fox sisters ever cracked a toe knuckle, such as those by Horace Walpole, Mary Shelley, and Edgar Allen Poe. Spiritualism along with "mesmerism, clairvoyance, electro-biology, crystal-gazing [and] thought-reading" attracted believers, among them popular writers such as Elizabeth Barrett Browning[7], Arthur Conan Doyle, Charles Dickens (who "believed himself an expert Mesmerist" or someone who could cause "miraculous medical cures ... by manipulating the invisible flows of 'animal magnetism'"[8]), Margaret Oliphant, Vernon Lee, Edith Wharton, Henry James, and William Butler Yeats.

At the time, it was the emergence of technology that helped influence the explosion of ghost stories in the public sphere. Nineteenth-century America and Europe saw technological advancements in paper making and publishing

---

2. Sera-Shriar, 2022, n.p.
3. Diniejko, 2016, n.p.
4. Luckhurst, 2014, n.p.
5. White, 2016, n.p.
6. Luckhurst, 2014, n.p.
7. Diniejko, 2016, n.p.
8. Luckhurst, 2014, n.p.

as well as transportation; paired with an increase in literacy rates, this all led to the burgeoning magazine and journal markets. These materials made getting sensational stories into the hands of readers easier, cheaper, and quicker, and led to the surge in the ghost story (the Penny Dreadfuls are one example, but a lot of magazines and journals published fiction or chapters of novels). The ghost-story author Montague Rhodes (M.R.) James (1862–1936) himself studied the birth of the modern Horror story and credited the popularity of magazines in the first half of the nineteenth century: "the real happy hunting ground, the proper habitat of our game is the magazine, the annual, the periodical publication destined to amuse the family circle. They came up thick and fast, the magazines, in the thirties and forties, and many died young".[9]

A contemporary to some of the authors mentioned, James changed the ghost story by taking the spirits out of their gothic surroundings—the falling-down houses and castle ruins—and bringing them into contemporary life, although a link to the past is usually still there. When investigating why the stories published in the 1860s were popular, he concludes that it's the juxtaposition of the supernatural with his contemporary world that matters: "The setting and the personages are those of the writer's own day; they have nothing antique about them. Now this mode is not absolutely essential to success, but it is characteristic of the majority of successful stories".[10] James created the "antiquarian ghost story" that featured academic protagonists who studied old books, artefacts, etc., that often end up being the source of the hauntings, with one of his most famous stories 'Oh, Whistle, and I'll Come to You, My Lad' (1904) about a professor who finds an ancient whistle that calls a spirit to him. He further cemented the British connection of ghost stories with Christmas[11], a tradition that continues today.

But what about stories of "real" hauntings? Enter the media and its interest in investigating the spirit world. In the late nineteenth century, journalist W.T. Stead, an editor of the *Pall Mall Gazette* (a newspaper that itself is referenced in several SFF/H tales including *Dracula* and *War of the Worlds*), founded the journal *Borderlands*, "perhaps the most eccentric journal of the century, in which news about ghosts, spirit séances, astrological predictions, psychical research findings, book reviews on anything occult, and news of breakthroughs in physics and chemistry were mixed together in a potent cocktail of weirdness".[12] We see echoes of this type of journal in the likes of the *Fortean Times* (founded 1973) on one end of the spectrum to the American tabloid *Weekly World News* (home of the infamous Bat Boy stories) on the

---

9. James, 2015 (originally published 1929), n.p.
10. James, 2015 (originally published 1929), n.p.
11. Luckhurst, 2014, n.p.
12. Luckhurst, 2014, n.p.

other.[13] These days, reality television has fortunately (or unfortunately?) given us free rein to follow our fears and curiosity. Simply google "paranormal reality television series" and dozens of international shows materialise, including *Ghost Hunter* (USA), *Derek Acora's Ghost Towns* (UK), *Bhoot Aaya* (*Ghost Has Come*, India), *Extranormal* (Mexico), *Knock Knock Ghost* (Canada), *Haunting: Australia*, and *Spøgelsesjægerne* (*The Ghosthunters*, Denmark). And that's before you get to the well-known on-screen fictional examples such as *Ghostbusters* (dir. Ivan Reitman, 1984), *Ghost* (dir. Jerry Zucker, 1990), or the Paranormal Activity series (2007–'21).

A Spotter's Guide: More Than Just a Sheet with Holes Cut in It

Author and parapsychologist Peter Underwood has identified several types of ghosts:

- **Elementals:** These "are often 'ghosts connected to burial grounds' and are 'primitive or race-memory manifestations'. An American ghost-hunter would probably call them demonic. Many of the ghosts of Wales and Scotland are elementals, fragments broken off from a pagan past, such as the 'kelpies' in lochs" (see **Cryptozoology**).[14] Underwood identifies the spirits in James's stories as elementals "connected to black magic practices, or reanimated corpses in the medieval and Scandinavian style".[15] We might consider the ghosts (or, rather, reanimated corpses "possessed" by spirits) in Stephen King's *Pet Sematary* (1983), which was made into a film twice (dir., Mary Lambert, 1989; dir. Kevin Kölsch, 2019), as this type; the protagonist buries the family's cat, his young son, and later his wife in a burial ground so that they can come back from the dead, but they don't come back happy or "right".
- **Poltergeists:** We're familiar with this type of ghost because of the proliferation of stories about them. They "present themselves as violent energies connected to a focus person…. The focus is generally a teenager, usually a girl" in an extension of the belief that girls/women were better receptors to spirits in the Victorian era.[16] The film *Poltergeist* (dir. Tobe Hooper, 1982) in which the ghost attaches itself to young Carol Anne, is the best known. Underwood additionally claims that "The world of ghost stories is riddled with class, and the poltergeist is occasionally tagged as the 'council

---

13. See Heller, 2014, if you're curious for more!
14. Underwood quoted in Clarke, 2012, p. 17.
15. Underwood quoted in Clarke, 2012, p. 18.
16. Underwood quoted in Clarke, 2012, p. 18.

house ghost'".[17] While we think of ghost stories as connected to big, drafty mansions or castles, poltergeists pop up in regular homes, such as with The Battersea Poltergeist, which haunted a house in South London and connected itself to the family's teenage daughter, Shirley (see Suburban Horror).[18]

- **Traditional or historical ghosts:** These are a very familiar type: "they are the souls of the dead, aware of the living and able to interact with them".[19] We find this type in more stories than we can list, though we might single out Susan Hill's *The Woman in Black* (1983) in which the ghost of a wronged woman takes her revenge, and Liz Williams's *Fallow Sisters* novel series (2020–'23), in which sister Bee has a relationship with the spirit of a sixteenth-century privateer.
- **Mental imprint manifestations:** These ghosts are "an effusion of mental energy soak[ed] into a particular place, usually a room, and represents a psychic model of an extreme state of mind"; they repeat the same actions, often at the same time of day or on anniversaries.[20] One example is Lady Jane Grey, who "is said to appear on the date of her execution—though, since the calendar was adjusted in the eighteenth century, this can be thought nonsensical."[21] A recent example is on BBC's *Ghosts* (dirs. Tom Kingsley, et al., 2019–'23): Fanny the Edwardian ghost does this when she screams and falls out the window at the same time each night (despite her existence as a spirit who interacts with everyone else daily), so they change the clock to keep from being woken up by her!
- **Time slips:** The ghosts in this type of Time Travel are all about nostalgia: they "are usually rather picturesque and decorative, almost like stepping onto a movie set, and they especially appeal to the imaginative with a sense of history" and "became all the rage from 1911 till the end of World War One" likely "as nostalgia for a lost world, or perhaps one that was about to be shattered".[22] One of the most popular in literature is *An Adventure* (1911) by Elizabeth Morison and Frances Lamont (pseudonyms of Charlotte Anne Elizabeth Moberly and Eleanor Frances Jourdain), who claimed to have time slipped back to the eighteenth century while walking through the gardens of Versailles.

---

17. Underwood quoted in Clarke, 2012, p. 19.
18. You can learn more via BBC 4's *The Battersea Poltergeist*, link listed under Robins, 2021.
19. Underwood quoted in Clarke, 2012, p. 19.
20. Underwood quoted in Clarke, 2012, pp. 19–20.
21. Underwood quoted in Clarke, 2012, pp. 19–20.
22. Underwood quoted in Clarke, 2012, p. 20.

Things That are Cool About Ghost Stories

Ghost stories aren't just about the dead coming back. We can use stories about the dead returning as a way of investigating some of the darker aspects of contemporary life. For example, Edith Wharton's 'The Lady Maid's Bell' (1902), about a lady's maid who gets a job caring for a sickly woman after the previous lady's maid dies, is about "how domestic servants were used up and seen as replaceable by the upper class"[23]; Toni Morrison's *Beloved* (1987), about a woman who kills her infant so that the child won't grow up to be enslaved, shines a light on the psychological aftereffects of slavery on the people who experienced it; and in Hari Kunzru's *White Tears* (2017) a pair of white hipsters remix a song they hear by a Black musician in a park and attribute it to an imaginary musician from decades before only for the musician to become real and haunt them in a tale about cultural appropriation.

Who You Gonna Call?

- **The Native American burial-ground trope:** One issue to avoid is what we call the Native American burial-ground trope, particularly apparent in North American popular culture (though it can apply to any number of indigenous cultures around the world). This appears in stories and films where the explanation for supernatural goings on is that a building has been constructed on an indigenous burial site. One of the classic instances of this is in *The Amityville Horror* (dir. Stuart Rosenberg, 1979). The trope plays on outdated stereotypes that indigenous peoples are somehow inherently magical and likely to curse those who've wronged them (and that's before we get to how the trope whitewashes the issues of how indigenous lands and artifacts were violently seized by settlers).
- **Haunted inanimate objects:** Some ghosts are linked to an item that the deceased previously owned or used, and "the ghost moves with the item".[24] Haunted objects like this abound in literature (see **Possessed, Haunted,** and **Cursed Items**), and there's even "a brisk eBay trade in 'haunted furniture' and, in the United States, a strong belief in haunted toys".[25] An older example is James's 'A Warning to the Curious' (1925) in which a man finds one of the crowns of the kings of East Anglia and the king's ghost isn't happy about it. More current is *Heart-Shaped Box* by Joe Hill (2007) in which the

---

23. Dickey, 2022, n.p.
24. Underwood quoted in Clarke, 2012, p. 22.
25. Underwood quoted in Clarke, 2012, p. 22.

protagonist buys a box containing a dead man's suit on an online auction site and ends up "buying" the ghost that comes with it.
- **Ghosts of the living:** Does a ghost have to be dead? Because some ghost stories are more about our brains than about the occult. Instead of the dead coming to haunt us, they "seem to suggest something of the brain function behind certain paranormal phenomena and seem to indicate that such phenomena are nothing to do with the dead at all. Somehow, using ESP and the ability of the brain to generate images, some invisible signal is accessed and processed".[26] This type of ghost also exists in other cultures, among them the Japanese belief in Ikiryō, as seen in *The Tale of Genji* (c. 1000) by Murasaki Shikibu, in which the spirit of Genji's living mistress leaves her body to haunt and harm his wife; she even haunts his other lovers after her own death.
- **Crisis or death-survival apparitions:** Many wartime stories feature ghosts that are seen by "someone with whom they have a close bond at the moment of their death, or at the moment they experience a life-threatening ordeal".[27] This can be a useful inciting incident in a story or a way of illustrating a particularly intimate connection between characters.

---

26. Underwood quoted in Clarke, 2012, p. 22.
27. Underwood quoted in Clarke, 2012, p. 20.

ACTIVITIES

Blast from the past: Consider the type of ghost story that M.R. James made popular, with academic protagonists who come to harm via the study—and disturbance of—antiquities. Your protagonist doesn't have to have a PhD, just an interest in an academic discipline and enough curiosity to kill a cat (or get them in great peril!). Do a bit of research into folklore or history in your area to pin down something for your protagonist to either search for or stumble across and see what happens next.

Back to the future: Choose a type of ghost from the examples above and bring it to the present, even to your own geographic place. Will you write about a haunted object in your own kitchen? A traditional ghost in your own garage? Or perhaps a death-survival apparition happening on a street or in a factory nearby.

WEREWOLVES

Like Vampires and Witches, werewolves are a staple of fiction, shedding their fur all over Horror and Fantasy stories with a history that reaches back to ancient Greece and beyond. So, the next time the moon is full and you think you hear a coyote or an owl, maybe you should get inside and bolt the door, load up on silver bullets, and cross your fingers. Because a werewolf is on the prowl….

A Short History of Werewolves

One of the earliest known mentions of human-to-animal transformation is in *The Epic of Gilgamesh* (c. 1700 B.C.E.) when Ishtar, the goddess of love, turns a shepherd into a wolf because he spurns her.[1] Next comes Virgil's *Eclogues* (37 B.C.E.), a pastoral poem in which a magician turns himself into a wolf and hides in the woods.[2] However, in neither case does the person become a werewolf. For that we must wait until the story of King Lycaon in Ovid's *Metamorphosis* (c. 8 C.E.), the first instance of a werewolf showing man's true animal nature. Lycaon "was turned into a wolf because he tested the divinity of Zeus by serving up to him 'a hash of human flesh'" that was possibly one of his own sons.[3] If Zeus had eaten the meal, he'd have accidentally been a cannibal.[4] When changed into a wolf, Lycaon is much like himself—violent and bloodthirsty—and the metamorphosis is a "deepening of what already was, since Lycaon's appearance now matches his true character."[5] In another version of the tale, Zeus is offended when Lycaon sacrifices a child to him, so Zeus orders that "each time a sacrifice was made" on the altar Lycaon built for Zeus, "a man was turned into a wolf but if, after eight years, he had not eaten human flesh he became a human again."[6] In these early tales, men are changed—or change into—wolves, but the rules of werewolf-ness aren't yet solid. Nonetheless, this Greek myth gives us the terms *lycanthrope* (someone who can change into a wolf) and *lycanthropy* (the ability to change or the curse itself) from *lukos*, for "wolf" and *anthropos*, for "man"; this term, used "for this supposed transformation and for the form of insanity in which the subject exhibits depraved animal

---

1. Sconduto, 2008, p. 7.
2. Sconduto, 2008, p. 7.
3. Room, 2001, p. 1257.
4. Sconduto, 2008, p. 9.
5. Sconduto, 2008, p.10.
6. Room, 2001, p. 1257.

traits", pops up more as the werewolf legend grows.[7] A while later, Patronius's *Satyricon* (first century C.E.), an early version of a novel written as fiction rather than "history", contains a tale of a werewolf; one night, a man loses track of his travelling companion (the friend undresses and his clothes turn to stone) and, later, realises the friend is a werewolf when the friend turns up with a neck wound after reports of a wolf being stabbed in the neck while bothering some sheep.[8]

Soon, the changed human became known as a werewolf ("A 'man-wolf'; Old English *wer*, 'man'")[9], or a *loup-garou* in French. The first known use of the actual term "werewolf" appeared in the Ecclesiastical ordinances of King Cnut (c. 1000) as a synonym for the Devil."[10] Ireland has a strong history of werewolf tales, the most popular being the mediaeval werewolves of Ossory.[11] These stories might come from the descriptions of Irish warriors' wild hairstyles and the wolf skins they wore (an accusation of "savagery" linking humans to animals), as well as the pre-Norman "kings of Ossory [that] claimed descent from one Laignech Faelad who was said to be the first to adopt the wolf-shape."[12] Gerald of Wales's twelfth-century *Topographia Hibernica* (*Geography of Ireland*) recounts the tale of a priest meeting two werewolves and giving last rites to the female of the pair, further cementing a belief in the battle between the animal (wolf) and human nature, at least in religious terms.[13] Even St Patrick has werewolf ties in the story of a stubborn pagan tribe mocking him and howling at him like wolves; when he asks God to intervene, God curses the tribesmen and their descendants to be trapped as wolves for "seven years in a row, while some of them have to go through the transformation every seven years" (a clear link back to one version of Zeus's curse of Lycaon).[14] A few centuries later, female werewolves terrorised Levonia (current-day Estonia and Latvia). Sebastian Münster, in a 1550 reprint of his *Cosmographia*, describes a "belief in werewolves shared by the inhabitants of Livonia: 'In this land there are many sorcerers and witch-women, who adhere to the erroneous belief—which they have often confessed before court—that they become wolves, roam about, and cause harm to all they encounter. Afterwards they transform back into human shape. Such people are called werewolves' (warwölff)".[15] However, the process of becoming a werewolf still hadn't reached our current understanding: in the

---

7. Room, 2001, p. 1257.
8. Ogden, 2021, n.p.
9. Room, 2001, p. 1257.
10. Sconduto, 2008, p. 7.
11. Kenny, 2021, n.p.
12. Kenny, 2021, n.p.
13. Kenny, 2021, n.p.
14. Su, 2020, n.p.
15. Metsvahi, 2015, p. 206.

1550 record, "To become a werewolf, the werewolf-to-be has to share a mug of beer with an experienced werewolf who has to recite a certain spell while doing this."[16] Honestly, it sounds like becoming a writer!

The modern werewolf's rules and make-up can be traced to folklore reports and fiction from the nineteenth century and to films from the early twentieth century. J.D.H. Temme, who mostly wrote about crime and criminals in the early 1800s, was one of many folktale collectors from what's now Germany. His recounting of 'The Werewolves in Greifswald' (recorded in 1840) contains the earliest reference to silver as a werewolf repellent: in the story the people under attack fight back by pooling together all of their silver buttons.[17] Later stories describe inscribing a cross onto regular lead bullets, but it's not sufficient to stop the creatures. A hundred year later, in 1935, the film *Werewolf of London* (dir. Stuart Walker) gave us the rule about lycanthropy being passed on via a bite by a pre-existing werewolf "and often in foreign locations (similar to infection by vampire bites)"[18]; the fear of the foreigner in werewolf tales mirrors that of vampire stories. But it's 1943's Lon Chaney, Jr., vehicle *Frankenstein Meets the Wolf Man* (dir. Roy William Neill), the first sequel to 1941's *The Wolf Man* (dir. George Waggner), that rounds out our list of werewolf "rules" when Larry Talbot—the lycanthropy-afflicted protagonist of the first film—rises from the dead when grave robbers expose his corpse to the full moon and remove the wolfsbane buried with him (an herb that has folklore connections). The werewolf with which we're all familiar has finally arrived.

This figure came into its heyday as a Horror staple in mid-twentieth-century films. In *The Werewolf* (dir. Fred F. Sears, 1956), doctors inject an amnesiac with an "irradiated wolf serum" in hopes of creating a means by which a select few people can survive a nuclear attack—because science!—but he turns into a werewolf before going on a killing spree; this obviously reflects the fear of nuclear holocaust, something the era's children and teenagers grew up with. A year later, *I Was a Teenage Werewolf* (dir. Gene Fowler, Jr.) combined a heady mix of rebellious teenagers with an experimental serum that turns a boy into a werewolf. Any semblance of science was dropped in favour of camp by 1962's *House on Bare Mountain* (dirs. Lee Frost and Wes Bishop), in which the Wolfman along with Dracula and Frankenstein's monster invade a nudist girls' school.

While there's no end to cult-horror films featuring werewolves in the 1970s, the creature really became a fixture of pop culture in the 1980s and beyond. The touchstone has to be *An American Werewolf in London* (dir. John Landis, 1981), with its cutting-edge special effects and make-up that shows

---

16. Metsvahi, 2015, p. 206.
17. Temme, 1840, no. 259, p. 308.
18. Rosens, 2020, n.p.

bitten David suffering the metamorphosis from man to wolf. Noteworthy, too, is the fact that David wears a bright red jacket in the first act of the film: an obvious hark back to 'Little Red Riding Hood'. That movie can't be mentioned without also noting Warren Zevon's 1978 song 'Werewolves of London' (*Ah-hooooo!* You're welcome for the earworm!). Of further note is Neil Jordan's eerie and atmospheric film *The Company of Wolves* (1984; co-written by Jordan and modern Fairytale grande dame Angela Carter, adapted from one of her stories). The werewolf transformation scene is one of the most unsettling in cinema! In the mid-eighties, werewolves howled for teenage audiences, starting with Michael J. Fox in *Teen Wolf* (dir. Rod Daniel, 1985), in which high schooler Scott, who's inherited the werewolf "curse", is forced to deal with its physical demands in addition to the challenges of being an adolescent. The film's popularity (its numerous sequels and television series have lasted up until 2023) predicted the popular fur-a-thon to come.

In the past two decades, many works have brought werewolf and vampires together. The *Underworld* series (2003–'16; the first starring Kate Beckinsale as Selene, a vampire who hunts werewolves who are led by Michael Sheen's Lucian), the *Twilight* series of books (by Stephenie Meyer, 2005–'20) and films (2008–'12), the *Vampire Diaries* book series (1991–2014; the 2012 instalment included werewolf characters) and television series (2009–'17), and the *Southern Vampire Mystery Series* books by Charlaine Harris (2001–'13) and its television version known as *True Blood* (2008–'14) all feature vampires and werewolves. In some cases, the werewolves are antagonists to the vampires (*Underworld*) and in others they're just another type of creature for teenage viewers to crush on. We'd be remiss not to mention the *What We Do in the Shadows* film (dirs. Jemaine Clement and Taika Waititi, 2014) and television series (2019–present), which, while focused on vampires, contain occasional werewolves who're working on their better nature (their motto: "We're werewolves, not swearwolves"!).

While there's been a huge explosion of werewolf-heavy Paranormal Romance in recent years, many authors have approached the trope as a means of further exploring human nature and how changeable—and damaging—we can be (shades here of *The Company of Wolves*). In *The Wolfman* (2008) by Nicholas Pekearo, Vietnam Vet/werewolf Marlowe takes it upon himself to be a sort of Dexter for the fur-clad set, only killing the worst of humanity each month. Japanese novel *Loups-Garous* (2010) by Natsuhiko Kyougoku, set in a near future in which people basically live online and have no personal contact, is about a string of murders, which should be impossible in a world as controlled as this. The murders bring terror and superstition to the surface, with the spectre of a werewolf hanging over it all as a sort of metaphor questioning humanity in a sterilised world. And in *The Devourers*

(2017) by Indra Das, a professor encounters a stranger who shares his story, partially set in seventeenth-century India. The novel doesn't shy away from visceral shapeshifting moments, containing scenes of Body Horror as well as touching on themes of gender fluidity and sexual politics.

Element Spotlight: More Than Skin Deep

Anthropomorphism is giving animals or inanimate objects human characteristics, and in Fantasy and Horror, humans changing into animals and back is par for the course. These genres have a long list of tales told from the point of view of animals, but often they're animals that act like humans wearing fur or feathers. In Richard Adams's *Watership Down* (1972), for example, the rabbits have social rules—much like real animals do—but, like humans, also have history and mythology. They feel "rabbity" but they're not. A suspension of disbelief is important for many if not all SFF/H stories; writing animal characters is one way to achieve this (see also **Uplifted Animals**). Consider how to approach writing a scene in which your human character turns into and then exists as an animal that isn't just a human in an animal suit. Lev Grossman explores this in his novel series *The Magicians* (2009–'14), and it was depicted in the television series (2015–'20), with his student characters turned into geese, whales, and foxes. They live as animals with very little acknowledgement or memory of having been humans. Luanne G. Smith opens her novel *The Vine Witch* (2019) with the protagonist having been turned into a frog several years previous: "*The skin. It was time to shed again.*"[19]. The character reads as a frog, surprising the reader when it's revealed that she's a human under a curse. One way to accomplish what might seem impossible (because you can only know things from a human's point of view and experience) is to start by researching animal behaviour. Wolves have been extensively studied, but, unfortunately, misreported (for example, the alpha doesn't behave the way online men's rights activists would have you believe!). Consider how you'd respond physically to life from a four-legged perspective. Animals act on instinct, and whether they have fur, feathers, or scales, their experience of the world will be very different from a human's; capturing that difference can help make for a more immersive reading experience.

Things That are Cool About Werewolves

Where vampires are attractive because they bring us closer to the heady combination of sex and death, and witches turn our heads because they promise power, werewolves let us tap into our baser natures. They're about

---
19. Smith, 2019, p. 1.

the animal inside of us bursting out, about giving in to our instincts and escaping the boxes we live inside, even if it's only on the full moon. Writing about werewolves allows you to create a character who can do those things that they only think about in the dark of night. Also, the legend has such a long history that it's ripe for reinvention; for example, the 2020 film *Wolfwalker*, by *The Secret of Kells* director Tomm Moore, takes inspiration from the mediaeval Ossory tales, while Joyce Chng's Starfang series (2017–'18) feature werewolves in space.

Werewolf by Night

Writing werewolves allows you to explore various aspects of human experience, including their foibles and mistakes. Some will free you, but older elements of the trope and how it's been used should be closely considered. Early popular literature that features werewolves grappled with societal expectations for women and even displayed racist beliefs in the "savagery" of certain peoples.

- **Going through the change:** The transformation from human to werewolf mirrors in some ways the changes we all go through as we age from child to adult (and even beyond): we get hair in weird places, we smell different, and sometimes there's blood. In *Ginger Snaps* (dir. John Fawcett, 2000) a girl reaching puberty turns into a werewolf after being attacked and bitten; her supernatural metamorphosis is reminiscent of puberty. In the *Being Human* series (2008–'13), which has a ghost, a vampire, and a werewolf living in a houseshare, werewolf George is focused on controlling his monthly change and not passing on the "curse" as he calls it, akin to controlling sexual urges and not passing on a disease. As you write, think of how you could use the shift from human to wolf to explore embarrassing or even distressing bodily changes.
- **Alphas are female, too:** One of the earliest pieces of popular literature to star a werewolf is Frederick Marryat's Gothic novel *The Phantom Ship* (1839), which contains a section titled 'The White Wolf of the Hartz Mountains' that features a female werewolf who, in the day, is an abusive stepmother; at night, she changes into a wolf and begins to eat the children one by one, an inversion of the Victorian expectations for matrimony and motherhood. Several decades later, Clemence Houseman, a leading figure of the suffrage movement in Britain, published *The Were-Wolf* (1896), the story of a mysterious woman who arrives at the lodge in a distant Scandinavian village; it depicts White Fell (the female character) as a "New Woman":

she's bold, a hunter, and doesn't follow the scripted roles of wife and mother. It was originally published in a magazine for young women, *Atalanta*, and Houseman made the choice to "[take] the frequently stereotyped figure of the New Woman and [alter] her portrayal in *The Were-Wolf* to comment upon the restrictive nature of prescriptive gender roles".[20] Consider how a trope about humans experiencing such extreme physical alteration can be a means to explore switching gender or sex.

- **Brother wolf:** Early modern werewolf stories suffered from Western culture's more racist beliefs. Henry Beaugrand's 'The Werewolves' (1898) contains unfortunate racist language, describing Native Americans (in this case Iroquois) as "savage" loups-garous who are "constantly intent on capturing some misguided Christian, to drink his blood and to eat his flesh in their horrible fricots"[21] (a type of stew). In *Werewolf of London* the protagonist meets his foil, Dr Yogami, in Tibet, and "the choice to make the antagonist Asian rather than European is perhaps indicative of U.S. relations and attitudes towards China, Tibet and other Asian countries at the time (not to mention contemporary attitudes towards Asian-Americans)".[22] 'Bright is the Water, Dark is the Land' (2013), by one of your present authors, Tiffani Angus, explores the invasion of "Old World" creatures in colonial America. So, when considering where to set your werewolf story, think about how the trope can be a means of examining our beliefs about "the other" and how we frame those experiences or expectations.

---

20. Purdue, n.d., n.p.
21. Beaugrand, 1898, n.p.
22. Rosens, 2020, n.p.

ACTIVITIES

Tween wolf: Your character is an introverted twelve-year-old student whose classmates relentlessly bully her. One evening, on her walk home from school, she's attacked and bitten by what she thinks is a dog. Soon, she begins to experience changes that clue her in that she's now a werewolf. However, she's offered a cure (you decide who offers it to her!). Does she take the cure, or does she use her newfound powers to take revenge on those who've abused her? Consider how being a werewolf will benefit her or make things even worse.

A sheep in wolf's clothing: Your protagonist is a zoologist or a wolf biologist studying the wolves in a zoo or other research centre. They notice one of the wolves, a newer import from a far-off land, acting unexpectedly. The wolf seems to understand commands in whatever language your character speaks, and it doesn't fit in with the other captive wolves. Where did the wolf come from, and what's on the report that accompanied it to the centre? What's going on with this animal, and what does your zoologist hypothesise is happening? What will your zoologist do to test their hypothesis? And how will the wolf react? Is it a werewolf, or something else?

POSSESSED, HAUNTED, AND CURSED ITEMS

Human beings have always found meaning in inanimate objects: a pen we "can't write without", a grandparent's ring of sentimental value, a "lucky" item of clothing we wear on a date. Our stories ascribe powerful associations to such things—a rabbit's foot is good luck; a monkey's paw is cursed—and in that we give them authority over how we see the world. Thus, objects become talismans, talismans become personal truths, and, before you know it, your bad luck isn't random chance, it's because *that thing* is haunted, cursed, or possessed!

A Short History of Possessed, Haunted, and Cursed Items

We are a ridiculously superstitious species. We believe that wearing the same underwear or socks will lead our sports team to victory. We throw salt over our shoulder if we spill any, despite not understanding why we do it anymore. It's super common that we attach such superstition to things: everything from jewellery to dolls to paintings to books have been considered either bad luck, haunted, or actually possessed by evil spirits. Television shows, tabloids, and listicles (itself a cursed word!) fuel our obsession with cursed items. Some venues even offer advice on how to sell them in the brisk trade that occurs through online auction sites. There's even a museum of cursed and haunted items: Zak Bagan's The Haunted Museum, in Las Vegas. Tickets aren't cheap, and visitors must sign a waiver because "management wants to ensure every visitor is aware of potential risks that could be caused by unseen forces" (as gimmicks go, it's a great one!).[1] Obviously we can't get enough of these stories, which have often been quite significant from a socio-historically perspective, so where to start?

First of all, terminology: items that are possessed are believed to have a demonic spirit inside them, so they are in some way sentient; a cursed item isn't sentient but only under a magic spell or hex, which can cause bad luck to befall anyone who owns or, in some cases, touches it; meanwhile haunted items are similar to possessed items but, instead of a supernatural evil, they are inhabited by the spirt of a dead person (see **Ghost Stories**). There's obviously a lot of overlap here, but J.W. Ocker, who wrote a whole book on this subject, explains that "both haunted and possessed objects can function practically as cursed objects if they bring misfortune to enough people, but if they merely act spooky, then they're not cursed".[2]

---

1. Zak Bagan's The Haunted Museum, 2020, FAQ page.
2. Ocker, 2020, n.p.

In terms of fiction, Oscar Wilde's *The Picture of Dorian Gray* (1890) deploys an aspect of the trope (though it's more of a Gothic tale about someone making a demonic deal or selling his soul). The story famously features a young aristocrat who keeps a portrait of himself hidden, with the image in the painting aging while he stays young. One of the clearest and earliest modern examples—and the most well-known due to it being assigned so often in school—is 1902's 'The Monkey's Paw' by W.W. Jacobs. The animal artifact in question, cursed in India, is said to grant three wishes... though always with a terrible consequence. Many of M.R. James's tales also focus on items as the locus of the haunting or odd goings-on, such as a doll's house in, you guessed it, 'The Haunted Doll's House' (1923) and a legendary crown in 'A Warning to the Curious' (1925).

Around the same time, the cursed-item trope became particularly popular among women authors. Much of that writing, which spoke to women's changing roles in society, the difficulty of forcing those changes, and the repression many women faced at the hands of the patriarchy, has been made accessible to modern readers by editor Melissa Edmundson in *Women's Weird: Strange Stories by Women, 1890–1940* (2019) and *Women's Weird 2: More Strange Stories by Women, 1891–1937* (2020). In reviewing the former, author Sarah Jackson explains that "part of the reason many of these stories are so effective 100 years later is that the strange events unfold on a much more familiar stage (for most of us!) than in classic gothic tales of windswept moors and crumbling manor houses".[3] The stories—and items—run the gamut from a haunted saucepan to a mysterious plate to scissors with a life of their own. One writer whose work is featured is Margery H. Lawrence, who was one of the most prolific authors of the supernatural and weird in the early twentieth century. Her story 'The Mask' (1923, first published in *The Tatler*) tells of a mysterious mask that seems to demand blood sacrifice, first from the shop owner who sells it to a young married man (the shop owner has killed his wife before selling it, then kills himself afterwards), and then from the new owner, his wife, and her cousin (echoes of this story survive in the cursed masks of the *Buffy the Vampire Slayer* episode 'Dead Man's Party', dir. James Whitmore, Jr, 1998). Another Lawrence tale 'The Mystery of the Crystal Snuff-box' (1929, first published in *Cosmopolitan*) depicts an ornamental container haunted by the spirit of a woman who was burnt as a witch in 1668. The spirit is out for revenge on men in particular—here represented by the young man who purchases the box as a gift—by leaching their strength so she can "come back" to life. In all such stories, the employment of daily items "render[s] the familiar in objects and garments as uncanny and malign".[4] It allows writers, especially

---

3. Jackson, S. 2021, n.p.
4. Masters, n.d., n.p.

women, to use objects as metaphors for wider situations that aren't under their control. So instead of a generic rabbit's foot bringing you good luck, an item a woman owns and uses daily (a saucepan, say, or scissors) comes to represent her, her quiet desperation, and her inner rage, imbuing the item with powers beyond its original function.

A Spotter's Guide: Possession is 9/10 of the Law (of the Occult)

Stories about dangerous items benefitted from the Horror renaissance of the 1980s. For the past forty years or so, Horror writers have employed a huge variety of items as their loci of terror. They've also reflected on what these objects *are* when they're at home. This is because different types of items and how we interact with them will convey different reactions in readers. We can categorise the types of objects:

- **Things with faces:** We don't know about the rest of you, but we find dolls, especially large collections of antique dolls, super creepy. Anything made to look like a human—dolls, Robots, etc.—will ping the uncanny valley response in us. According to the DSM-5 (the Diagnostic and Statistical Manual of Mental Disorders, Fifth Edition, 2013), automatonophobia is "a fear of human-like figures, such as mannequins, wax figures, statues, dummies, animatronics, or robots" and its related phobia is pediophobia, "a fear of dolls".[5] In Ruby Jean Jensen's *Annabell* (1987, and not her only "evil doll" novel!), haunted/possessed dolls adopt little Jessica, who has come to play with them after her own family has fallen apart. One of the most popular evil dolls arrives in 1988 with Chucky, star of *Child's Play* (dir. Tom Holland) and its six sequels (plus a television show, a reboot, comics, etc.), about a Good Guy doll possessed by the soul of a serial killer. The film *Annabell* (dir. John R. Leonetti, 2014), not related to the Jensen novel but part of the Conjuring series, concerns a doll possessed by a demon summoned by a cult. Andrew Shaffer's *Secret Santa* (2020), set in a publishing house during the 1980s (how meta!) sees a cursed secret Santa gift, a German devil doll called a Percht, wreak havoc. Most recently, Grady Hendrix explored the creepy dolls/puppets trope in *How to Sell a Haunted House* (2023); trust us, you'll never look at a hand puppet the same way again!
- **Things we name:** Humans like to name things that aren't alive, such as ships and boats, houses and cars. Some people even name home appliances. We build relationships with items, some of which we use every day and come to depend on. So, it's not a jump from

---
5. PIERS, n.d., n.p.

thinking of a thing as a friend (or enemy, in the case of cars that like to conk out on you at inopportune times!) to thinking of it as alive. Theodore Sturgeon's novella *Killdozer* (1944) tells the story of a bulldozer named Daisy Etta that's possessed by Aliens of pure energy that take over metal machines and start killing people. Stephen King's *Christine* (1983), about a cherry-red 1958 Plymouth Fury, is one of the most famous possessed-items stories; the car is possessed by the spirit of its original driver, who then takes over its new teenaged owner and goes on a killing spree. Tales of haunted ships—often called "ghost" ships because the fate of their crews remains a mystery—abound through history; the idea was brought to the big screen in *Ghost Ship* (dir. Steve Beck, 2002), about a ship lost in 1962 and found 40 years later haunted by Jack Ferriman, a soul collector for Hell ("ferry man", get it?). More contemporary is Gus Moreno's *This Thing Between Us* (2021), which cleverly tackles that disembodied presence whispering and behaving strangely in many of our homes today: smart speakers ("Alexa, what is possession?").

- **Things that are completely mundane:** The thing that's "so insidious about cursed objects is how mundane they are".[6] Author Graham Masterton has employed this angle in *The Heirloom* (1981) about an antique chair that's possessed by the Devil (and is a sort of **Portal**), as well in the creepy *Mirror* (1988) in which the titular object is haunted by a slain child star from the 1930s (again, the mirror serves as a portal to a Hell dimension). *Oculus* (dir. Mike Flanagan, 2014) is also about a mirror, in this case the Lasser Glass, which causes several hundred years of murder, suicide, and madness. Meanwhile, Iain Rob Wright's *The Picture Frame* (2014) concerns a mystery writer whose child finds an antique picture frame buried outside their new home in the country, but the frame is cursed and harms those whose photo it contains.

Things That are Cool About Possessed, Haunted, and Cursed Items

You can find inspiration for these tales everywhere in real life. There is no end to the lists of "possessed" items in the world. For example, there is a plethora of tales about cursed gemstones, especially diamonds, and there are Horror stories about cursed jewellery, such as Michael McDowell's *Amulet* (1979).[7] But, as Ocker explains in an interview when asked about the Hope diamond, "Rich people will always fall into weird troubles, and it's usually generational" so it's easier to blame an object than on "the fact

---

6. Castrodale, 2020, n.p.
7. Newman, 2022, n.p.

that you never got the tools to exist as a human being".⁸ The great thing about using everyday items is that they gain gravitas by how they're used and by who, historically or usually, uses them. Because while a story about a possessed or cursed item seems to be about the item, it's really about the people interacting with the item, or the pain or revenge or unfinished business related to the person—or entity—who has cursed or haunted it. The trope also overlaps with other subgenres, such as Techno Horror, most popularly with Koji Suzuki's *Ring* (1991, translated by Glynne Walley) about a cursed VHS tape.

Do You Have a Receipt for That?

Be careful here of the Native American burial-ground trope discussed elsewhere. This involves stories in which items from another culture are imbued with evil spirits that, in terms of how the author/story presents and frames them, are depicted as a "natural" or "expected" part of that culture. Lawrence's story 'The Mask' did this, which isn't a complete surprise for a story from a hundred years ago. Lawrence's racially tinted description of the mask is at pains to present it as from an exoticised non-white culture: it has "narrow eye-holes squinting sideways at the firelight … One wisp of coarse black hair hung straight each side of the long thin face, dull yellow-brown in colour, creased with a thousand lines and wrinkles; a huge gilt tassel swung from the cap's crown, and the thin-lipped mouth was bitterly sardonic".⁹ In contrast, the hero is "Jack Trelawney—clean, healthy Englishman" who is hypnotised by the mask to see "strange and dreadful lands"¹⁰ and "unspeakable obscenities, vileness beyond power of human imagination, sin at the mere sight of which his very soul sickened and shrank within him—cowered, shrivelled and whimpering, in the storm of blood and fire and evil unspeakable that swept it".¹¹ The result is an object lesson in how bias—conscious or unconscious—tints a text with meaning, presenting the fit, wholesome, White hero as being corrupted by another culture. While it's common for an object in these stories to be from a place other than the story's setting, be careful to avoid framing an equation in which anything "other" is bad or suspect entirely because of its otherness.

---

8. Castrodale, 2020, n.p.
9. Lawrence, M.H., 1923, p. 44 (pdf p. 1).
10. Lawrence, M.H., 1923, p. xxii (pdf p. 6).
11. Lawrence, M.H., 1923, p. xxii (pdf p. 7).

ACTIVITIES

Mary Poppins's handbag: What do you carry with you on a daily basis, either in a purse, a backpack, or even just your pockets? Empty it all out and take a look at each item. Try to see it as if you're excavating a long-lost tomb. These items are important for various reasons: practical, necessary, nostalgic, etc. What would result from one of them being possessed, haunted, or cursed? How would your identity as a person (and this is a long line from one end to the other, so give it a bit of thought: your cultural, career, sexual, gender, educational, familial identities, etc.) change if something you carried every day was out to get you? Choose the object, decide whether it is possessed (by whom or what), haunted (by whom or what), or cursed (by whom and why), and write a scene or story in which your character discovers the problem with the object. Can your protagonist solve the problem or even survive?

Crossed wires: Write a story in which a piece of technology becomes possessed, haunted, or cursed. This can be a cell phone, a smart television, a smart speaker, a pair of wireless headphones, or something else. These items don't have long histories—they're usually not inherited or handed down—so how has it come about becoming more than it seems? And what does the possession/haunting/curse mean to the protagonist who depends on the item to do the job it was purchased to do and not the "hidden extras" it's shown itself to be capable of? Technology is already difficult enough to understand (we use it but usually can't fix it!), so examine the situation of having a character learn that the "features" the item is exhibiting aren't on the product list, the possible uncanny valley moments that might erupt, and the consequences of the character's search for help from another human. Who will believe them, and why or why not? And what does this say about our dependence on technology?

ANIMALS THAT ATTACK

You're an animal lover. Your family always had a dog, a cat or two, maybe a budgie or goldfish. You loved the zoo or the aquarium. And then your mother took you to see *Jaws* for your birthday, rendering you terrified of the toilet for months afterward and giving you a healthy and not-at-all neurotic wariness of wild—and not wild—animals *just in case*, which came in handy when you started to hear random growls and snarls in the dark. So, grab your bear spray and bee-keeper costume because these animals are in attack mode!

A Short History of Animals That Attack

Humans have long lived surrounded by animals and insects with, in some cases, a wary respect. Pre-Industrial Revolution towns in Western Europe were often surrounded by walls built to keep marauders out. However, they often didn't repel animals that were attracted by food, rubbish, animal waste, and dead livestock, such as in Carmarthen, Wales in 1166, when wolves attacked 22 people, as well as other wolf attacks in Evreux in 1400 and Rouen in 1445.[1] Nonetheless, one of our favourite early examples of attacking animals are the "killer bunnies" found in the margins of mediaeval-era illuminated manuscripts. These rabbits don't attack with fangs bared, à la the rabbit in *Monty Python and the Holy Grail* (dirs. Terry Gilliam and Terry Jones, 1975), but use swords and arrows against human hunters, showing the rabbits and hounds in a topsy-turvy world "where roles are reversed and the impossible becomes the norm".[2]

Fast-forward to contemporary times and the closest most of us get to a wild beast is when feeding pigeons in the park or visiting a zoo to view animals behind glass or in enclosures with—we hope—a lot of security built in to protect us *and* them. But this hasn't stopped us from freaking out about animals and conjuring up all sorts of stories following the "What if?" to its furriest, scaliest, and most feathered conclusions. One of the earliest modern examples is Henry Kuttner's 'The Graveyard Rats' (1936) in which a cemetery caretaker/grave robber in storied Salem, Massachusetts, fights off—you guessed it!—giant rodents. The tale was reprinted in 1983 and later made into an episode of *Guillermo del Toro's Cabinet of Curiosities* (dir. Vincenzo Natali, 2022). A couple of decades later, Daphne du Maurier's short story 'The Birds' (1952) shocked readers with gigantic flocks of avian

---

1. Medievalists.net, n.d., n.p.
2. Jackson, E., 2021, n.p.

antagonists attacking people all across Britain. It was later adapted as Alfred Hitchcock's film of the same name (1963), in which a California town is attacked by the feathered fiends (see **Ecohorror**). Of course, it wasn't just the du Maurier story that got Hitchcock thinking about horror with wings; he was also inspired by an event in 1961 in California during which sea birds "regurgitated anchovies, flew into objects and died on the streets" because of eating toxic algae, although that reason wasn't discovered until a similar event thirty years later.[3]

In the 1950s and '60s, the "atomic age" led to fears of what science was doing to the natural world. One of the first films to exploit this fear is 1954's *Them!* (dir. Gordon Douglas), featuring man-eating ants that have grown to the size of military tanks as the result of being irradiated; and this despite the fact that, scientifically, an ant that size wouldn't be possible because their legs would collapse under their weight (but, hey, who lets science get in the way of fantastical films?). Around the same time, we can chart the rise of men's magazines that featured stories revisiting the "pulp" mode of previous decades, among them *Man's Life* magazine, which ran from 1952 to 1975. Its full-colour cover illustrations would show humans (usually manly men and sometimes scantily clad women) being attacked by the expected bears, tigers, and lions, but also by unexpected hordes of flying squirrels, weasels, and snapping turtles![4] Coinciding with the later years of these adventure magazines was the rise of environmental groups working to save the planet, many as an offshoot of the hippie movement of the 1960s and '70s. Groups that had been around for decades such as the Sierra Club (founded 1892) were joined by Friends of the Earth (1969) and Greenpeace (1971). Meanwhile, the first Earth Day was celebrated in 1970. The US government also turned its attention to the environment at this time by passing the Clean Air Act (1963) and the Clean Water Act (1972), as well as establishing the independent Environmental Protection Agency (1970). People were concerned about nuclear waste, acid rain, pollution, littering, pesticides, and more; consequently, the fact that so many animal-attack novels and films were created in the 1970s isn't a surprise considering how many people were aware of and concerned about the environment.

Following *Them!*, Western audiences were treated to a plethora of animal-attack novels in the 1970s and 80s. Horror writer Grady Hendrix thoroughly investigates this era of Horror literature in his award-winning 2017 book *Paperbacks from Hell*. What's interesting is that the animal attacks in so many of these stories—books and films—are rooted in the actions of those same "manly men" described above: these men take part in military or government experiments on animals to turn them into weapons; their

---

3. Parry, 2012, n.p.
4. Deis, 2013, n.p.

scientific experiments or need for energy lead to the dumping of nuclear or other dangerous waste into the natural world; they invade the animals' environment for money or sport; or they retaliate against the animals for doing what animals do. Indeed, Hendrix finds a common thread in novels about rogue insects in particular that can be applied to so many other "animal attack" tales:

> These books take place almost exclusively during the hottest day/week/month of the year after radiation/evolution/untested insecticide causes fauna to mutate. Insect-attack books are basically morality tales in which unscrupulous developers, ethics-free businessmen, and ineffectual local leaders find their scale-balancing comeuppances between chitinous mandibles.[5]

All of which is to say that, in the end, it isn't so much natural behaviour that's usually the catalyst for animal attacks. It's human behaviour itself.

A Spotter's Guide: Fur, Scales, Feathers, and Skin

- **Rodents:** *Rats* (1974) by James Herbert does what it says on the cover or, as Hendrix summarises: "What is it about? Rats. What do they do? Eat everyone".[6] The novel, arguably the start of the popularity of this trope in late-twentieth-century Horror novels, features giant rats that—you guessed it—have become mutants due to nuclear waste; they run rampant all over London and then into the English countryside in the sequel *Lair* (1979) but return to a now post-Apocalyptic London in the trilogy finale *Domain* (1984).
- **Big sea life:** Sharing the limelight with *Rats* as the granddaddy of this trope is, without a doubt, *Jaws* (dir. Steven Spielberg, 1975), based on Peter Benchley's 1974 novel of the same name. Unfortunately, its sequels never live up to the greatness of the original but make for a fun night of *MST3K*-esque quips. A couple of years later, Horror fans were scared by another massive denizen of the deep in *Orca* (1977) by Arthur Herzog, later filmed as *Orca: The Killer Whale* (dir. Michael Anderson, 1977), about a man hunting an orca that's out for revenge because the man killed the fish's mate and offspring. The trope of military-trained animals going awry can be found in Peter Tonkin's novel *Killer* (1979) about an orca, again, attacking a group of people. Not to be left behind, a giant mutant octopus is the star of *Tentacles* (dir. Ovidio G. Assonitis,1977). But our attention returned to the shark

---

5. Hendrix, 2017, p. 94.
6. Hendrix, 2017, p. 82.

with such films as *The Meg* (dir. Jon Turteltaub, 2018), loosely based on the novel *Meg: A Novel of Deep Terror* (1997) by Steve Altenin. In *The Meg*, Jason Statham goes mano-a-fin-o with a 75-foot long megalodon, a prehistoric species, that's been hiding in a very deep section of the Marianas Trench. Other entries in this category include the ridiculous but fun *Sharknado* (dir. Anthony C. Ferrante, 2013) and its five sequels as well as *Shark Bait* (dir. James Nunn, 2022), in which a group of five college kids are marooned far from shore on two broken-down jets skis and picked off, one by one, by an angry shark.

- **Smaller sea life:** The ocean or any large body of water, where humans can't breathe (see **Places People Shouldn't Go**), is ripe as a site of terror, and plenty of twisted writers took advantage of this, especially in the Horror heyday of the 1970s and '80s. For readers, one of the most out-there series in this category are the crab books by Guy N. Smith featuring enormous crabs attacking people at various locations along the British coast, starting with *Night of the Crabs* (1976) and ending with *The Charnel Caves: A Crabs Novel* (2019). In *Piranha* (dir. Joe Dante, 1978) flesh-eating swarms of genetically altered fish (part of a defunct experiment to create killer fish during the Vietnam War) terrorise tourists in a riverside summer resort. *Barracuda* (dirs. Harry Kerwin and Wayne Crawford, 1978) continues with the trope of war veterans experimenting on fish and turning them into killers. In *Fleshbait* by David Holman and Larry Pryce (1979), nuclear waste has leaked into the sea and turned schools of fish, including tuna, into killers.

- **Insects and spiders:** Writers have banked on the fact that the tiniest of critters, *en masse* or even alone, can freak people out. (I mean, who of us hasn't screamed when we discovered we were sharing the bath with a spider?) In addition to the ants in *Them!*, we have *The Ants* (1980) by Peter Tremayne with more, well, ant-sized ants in the Brazilian jungle, and *Legion of Fire: Fire Ants* (dirs. Jim Charleston and George Manasse, 1998), in which fire ants are jostled out of hibernation by seismic activity and terrorize a small town. *The Spiders* (1978) by Richard Lewis features a horde of genetically altered spiders (created to be a weapon, of course!) out for blood, and in his sequel *The Web* (1981) the spiders return for more. Although we all do what we can now to save the bees, they weren't cute, fuzzy-bottomed lifesavers in Arthur Herzog's *The Swarm* (1978), in which "Africanised" bees (yes, the term carries racist tones) are turned into killers and bring on the downfall of the US.

- **Ssssssssnakes and reptiles:** Enter the mid-size terrestrial creepy-crawlies! *Venom* (1979) by Russell O'Neil, which we'll nickname

"Snakes in an Apartment Building", is about cobras accidentally let loose by a man who's smuggled them home from India so he can use one to murder his mother. Because matricide has to be *complicated*. *Anaconda* (dir. Luis Llosa, 1997) follows a giant snake that attacks a documentary crew on the Amazon River. The infamous film *Snakes on a Plane* (dir. David R. Ellis, 2006; and written by, it feels like, the Internet) is probably the snake-attack story that most readily comes to mind: terror ensues when a box of snakes is stowed aboard a plane and the passengers sprayed with a substance that makes the snakes want to attack them in this bonkers-level Samuel L. Jackson vehicle. Meanwhile, in 2019's *Crawl* (dir. Alexandre Aja), an alligator traps a daughter and father in a flooding house during a hurricane.

- **Lions & tigers & bears, oh my!** Because lions, bears, tigers, and wolves have always been a danger to people, Horror narratives about them "going rogue" and attacking humans aren't as easy to come by. *The Ghost and the Darkness* (dir. Stephen Hopkins,1996) is loosely based on the historical accounts of a pair of rogue lions attacking workers building a railway in Kenya in 1898. In *The Grey* (dir. Joe Carnahan, 2011), based on the short story 'Ghost Walker' by Ian MacKenzie Jeffers, packs of wolves attack plane-crash survivors in the Alaskan wilderness. Finally, one of the most outlandish and funny-gory bear-attack narratives based partially on fact (yes!) has to be *Cocaine Bear* (dir. Elizabeth Banks, 2023) in which a bear goes all Scarface in a Georgia forest after huffing its way through parcels of cocaine dumped out of a smuggler's aircraft.

- **Domesticated animals gone wrong:** Many of us can't live without our beloved pets, but are we really safe? In *The Pack* (1976) by David Fisher, dogs abandoned on a vacation island join forces to get revenge on humanity. In Nick Sharman's *The Cats* (1977), lab animals used in bacterial-weapon tests get loose and you can guess what happens next. The well-known *Cujo* (1981) by Stephen King pits a rabies-infected St Bernard against a mom and her young son trapped in their broken-down car, with the book's ending much darker than the film adaptation (dir. Lewis Teague, 1983).

Things That are Cool About Animals That Attack

With so many different species of animals out there, as well as so many potential causes for the attacks, you can use this trope to explore various situations that are troubling to some of us, such as the encroachment of humans onto once-wild land and the Anthropocene's impact on the natural world. Do note that readers/viewers will often care more about the animal character than the human ones! So you can, as a writer, use that affection for animals as a means to investigate the effects of our modern world and its excesses in a way that your audience might be more prone to engaging with than if you use human characters only.

Animal Control

Jaws, while a nearly perfectly formed film, spawned a set of sequels that do *not* live up to its reputation. One reason is that despite the first film featuring a scientist who studies sharks and their behaviour, the sequels do no such thing, and nobody ever asks *why would a shark do this?* Instead, characters anthropomorphise the sharks (a caring mama protecting her young, which doesn't match with what we know about great white sharks: they give birth to live young that then swim away). With so many reasons for bizarre animal behaviour, from toxic algae to rabies to—as farfetched as it is—poisoning from nuclear waste, a reason for the animal attacking is bound to interest a reader more than "it happened just because". So do some research into your chosen animal's behaviour. Sure, the idea is to take the information you find and twist it, but if you can find some nugget of fact you can scare your readers more.

ACTIVITIES

Wolf in the henhouse: For this activity, choose the animal that, by itself, scares you the most. It doesn't necessarily have to be a predator, but this will be an animal not under any sort of outside influence such as pollution poisoning or medical testing. Describe what about that animal freaks you out the most: is it the way it looks? Is it how it moves? or what it eats? Whatever it is, give that animal a full character profile. Then, place it in your house. It's you vs it, in a place that you know intimately. Remember, it's an animal and you're a human; it will act according to instinct and its own specific behaviour, while you can think ahead and visualise how to escape.

Moving as a herd: You're an animal scientist of some sort (marine biologist, zoologist, etc.) who studies herds of a certain species of animals, such as murders of crows, schools of fish, pods of dolphins, skulks of foxes, etc. While studying this animal in the wild, you come across an illegal dumping ground that contains either barrels of toxic waste, discarded rubbish, medical waste, or something else. How would your particular animal group interact with and be affected by this material? What behaviours could be exaggerated? Also decide on the closest human settlement and how the extreme animal behaviour would impact on the people and their lives.

EVIL CHILDREN

Kids, amirite? Always crying or sleeping or pooping or hungry. With their little fingers and toes, their little horn nubs, their glowing red eyes. They take and take, leaving you a husk of a person without any autonomy or ability to do anything but feed all their needs: milk, love, obedience, your very soul. And if you want to pop out to the shop, you need to hire an exorcist to come tend to the little nipper. Face it, your baby is evil….

A Short History of Evil Children

How can babies or small children be so evil in so many stories? They're brand new; they haven't had time to be corrupted by sugar or capitalism! So, what would *make* them evil? Depending on a person's faith, some children, right out of the gate, are set up to be bad (cue Original Sin), while others just turned bad due to being corrupted by their surroundings (the old "Nature vs Nurture" argument). Historical records contain stories of children being possessed by demons: for example, *A booke declaring the fearful vexation of one Alexander Nyndge* (1573) in which Alexander's older brother Edward describes the young boy's possession and Edward's work to gather the family and neighbours to pray and exorcise the demon. Additionally, early childrearing and household-advice books from the West were clearly linked to a family's or society's religious faith: *A werke for Householders and for them that have the Gydyng or Governaunce of any Company* (1530) by priest Richard Whitford; *Office of Christian Parents* (anonymous tract, 1616); *A godly forme of household government* by Robert Cleaver (published six times from 1598 to 1630); and *Mothers Blessing*, written by Dorothy Leigh to her three sons in case of her death (14 editions from 1616 to 1685), which "illustrates godly families' desire to ensure that their children had the best possible chance of salvation, and that this would be at least in part achieved through proper instruction and education."[1] The question about whether children were evil and how they became so moved from religious tracts and history to fiction, especially in the last century and a half. A classic example is Henry James's novella *The Turn of the Screw* (1898), about a governess tasked with caring for two young children in mysterious circumstances; the story raises more questions than it answers: are the ghosts encountered real? Is the governess hallucinating? Are the children evil? H.P. Lovecraft's novella *The Dunwich Horror* (1929) takes a Cosmic Horror approach and offers readers the hideous and dangerous

---

1. French, 2015, p. 30.

offspring of an extra-dimensional entity. More straightforward is Agatha Christie's *Crooked House* (1949), which depicts Josephine, a twelve-year-old killer. Richard Matheson's 'Born of Man and Woman' (1950) is about a child kept prisoner in a basement because it's some sort of a monster spider-child. William March's *The Bad Seed* (1954) offers readers a sociopathic girl whose mother discovers her murderous streak and fears that it's genetic, passed on by her own mother who was a serial killer (so, a tick on the side of nature). Meanwhile John Wyndham gives the trope a Science-Fictional edge in *The Midwich Cuckoos* (1957): after everyone in the village of Midwich is unconscious for a day, many women find themselves unexpectedly pregnant and give birth to children with very pale hair and skin who share a hive mind, grow at an alarming rate, and bring doom to the village.

As we slid into the next two decades, however, second-wave feminism influenced a variety of horror stories that depict evil babies and children as either the reason for or the result of their mothers dealing with the conflicts of motherhood and independence. The cinema classic, *Rosemary's Baby* (dir. Roman Polanski, 1968), based on Ira Levin's 1967 Gothic or Supernatural Horror novel of the same name, is one of the first films in which the child is actually Satan's. When Rosemary discovers the truth about the child (and that she was raped during a demonic ritual run by her neighbours and husband), she resists, but the sound of the baby's cries tugs at her "motherly instincts" (a recurring and not unproblematic aspect of the subgenre). Then came the iconic 1973 film *The Exorcist* (dir. William Friedkin), based on William Peter Blatty's 1971 novel, about young Regan whose mother, an actress, is raising her while divorcing Regan's father; Regan begins to act out—as we now know kids may do during a traumatic period—but the film's explanation is that the Devil is acting through her. All that said, if you ask anyone to name a story about a demonic child, it's likely they'll say Damien from *The Omen*. In director Richard Donner's film (1976; novelised by David Seltzer in the same year), a hospital chaplain convinces a father to secretly swap out his stillborn baby for another whose mother died in childbirth; unfortunately, all manner of terrible things happen around Damien, and it turns out—surprise!—he's Satan's son. That guy really gets around, huh?

A Spotter's Guide: The Kids Are (Not) All Right

- **Born evil:** Some believe that everyone is born tainted by sin and must be baptised to be free of it, and to then continue forth in life and try to sin no more. Writers have taken this idea to heart and created all manner of stories in which the kid is bad from day one. Ray Bradbury used this idea in 'The Small Assassin' (1946) about a newborn who murders his parents. In Jerome Bixby's 'It's a Good

Life' (1953) (adapted for *The Twilight Zone*) a three-year-old has god-like powers but the undeveloped mind of a small child, which puts everyone around him in danger from his moods and selfishness. In *Grace* (dir. Paul Solet, 2009) Madeline's husband and unborn child are killed in a car accident and, rather than have the foetus removed, Madeline insists on carrying to term (a slightly unscientific plan considering the fact that a dead foetus can cause sepsis in a woman's body); the baby is stillborn but then comes to life and, as it turns out, only drinks blood instead of milk.

- **Possessed:** Sometimes you're a good kid with bad luck and, *lo!*, a demon or Satan himself decides to take your body for a joy ride. *The Unborn* (dir. David S. Goyer, 2009) is a convoluted tale of a girl whose twin died in utero and who ends up fighting a dybbuk's curse on her family; the dybbuk wants revenge for losing the body it inhabited during World War II (the twin of the girl's grandmother). The girl loses her boyfriend in the film's climactic scene but then discovers that she is pregnant with twins (cue ominous music!). Meanwhile, in *The Prodigy* (dir. Nicholas McCarthy, 2019), Miles is a gifted child possessed by the ghost of a dangerous serial killer.
- **Evil twin:** Soap operas have been making much of this trope for decades, so much so that it's reached the point of parody. It is, nonetheless, a frequent plot point in Horror, too, because the idea of the evil twin or doppelgänger destabilises identity and our protagonists' notions of certainty. It raises questions about who's who (and who might only be pretending to be someone else!). The "found-footage" film *Home Movie* (dir. Christopher Denham, 2008), in which a pastor and a psychologist have twin ten-year-old kids whose creepy and dangerous behaviour increases as the film builds towards its climax, leads the viewer to wonder whether evil is spiritual or psychological.
- **Affected by illness or mysterious event:** Wrong place, wrong time? It happens, and kids, who have little autonomy at the best of times, sometimes get caught in the crosshairs. In *The Children* (dir. Max Kalmanowicz, 1980) an accident in a nearby chemical plant turns five kids on a school bus into radioactive zombies. In *The Suckling*, aka *Sewage Baby* (dir. Francis Teri, 1990), a foetus is disposed of down a toilet by the back-alley abortionist where it turns into a monster after coming into contact with toxic waste. It then goes on a killing spree in a plot line that could have been lifted right out of Conservative America's anti-abortion talking points.
- **Supernatural:** Sometimes the evil is due to a supernatural element that's not a demon possession or wonky chemicals. In *Whisper* (dir. Stewart Hendler, 2007) young David is kidnapped by an ex-felon who needs the ransom money, but soon the kidnappers discover

that David can control people via whispered commands and that his mother orchestrated the kidnapping. All kids have to grow up, and writers know that the changes of puberty can bring out pimples as well as vicious mood swings, which is one theme of *Brightburn* (dir. David Yarovesky, 2019) in which a kid from another planet turns from okay to very not-okay as he grows up in a sort of twisted take on Superman.

- **Brought back from the dead:** Horror fiction will poke at the most subversive of topics, and the death of children isn't off limits. These stories explore how grief pushes a parent to take the most outlandish action to turn back time while simultaneously punishing said parents for trying to play with nature. 'Bobby' in the made-for-television horror-anthology film *Dead of Night* (dir. Dan Curtis, 1977) is about a grieving mother who brings her drowned son back from the dead, yet the kid isn't the Bobby she knew.

- **Pesky teenagers:** Evil babies are one thing, but tweens and teens can also cause no end of havoc. One example is William Golding's *Lord of the Flies* (1954) in which a group of English public schoolboys descend into paranoia, backstabbing, mob mentality, and savagery after being stranded on a **Mysterious Island**. In the Spanish film *Who Can Kill a Child?* (dir. Narciso Ibáñez Serrador, 1976) a couple visit a small island only to discover that the kids are responsible for the disappearance of all the adults in the town. There is also the French-Romanian film *Them* (*Ils*, dir. David Moreau and Xavier Palud, 2006), in which a group of ten- to fifteen-year-old kids kill indiscriminately. It claims to be based on a true story.

Things That are Cool About Evil Children

Subverting the cultural belief that babies and small children must be protected rather than be something you must be protected from can be an easy trick to strike terror in the hearts of parents or future parents. And, for some adults, teenagers are already alien—their clothes and hair, the vocabulary they use, their weird behaviours—which can make them seem aggressive and scary, so it's natural to use them in our fiction to upset the order of how things are "supposed to be".

The Cradle Will Fall

- **Tell me about your mother:** Your subject's behaviour is important. One reason the *Jaws* sequels are so ridiculous is because nobody ever says, "Hey, sharks don't act like this!" Having some idea of actual shark behaviour to contrast with the terrifying blood lust on display would have helped ground the stories in some sort of reality, which tends to make situations a bit scarier. Writing about evil babies and children is similar; in Psychological Horror, we talk about doing some research into how sociopaths and psychopaths differ and into how human brains work. In the past couple of decades, therapy—for adults and children—has become much more common, and sensible people will want to find out *why* a kid is acting out. So, instead of just plastering *My Daddy is the Devil* on a onesie and calling it a scary story, consider a bit of research into child behaviour—and human behaviour in general—to find some nuance for your tale.

- **Little acorns into oaks:** Children are the lifeblood of cults, their minds malleable to the leaders' twisted ideas. The most famous cult story about kids is surely Stephen King's 'Children of the Corn', first published in 1974, about an unfortunate couple whose car breaks down in the Nebraska farmland only to encounter a community of kids who worship a being that lives in the fields. And did we mention there aren't any adults because, well, the kids kill them all off? This short story has been turned into eleven (11!) films including some that went direct to video or were made for television, from 1984 to 2020, proving that even a story short on words can inspire a cult following (ba-doom-cha!).
- **Filing down the serial numbers:** Evil kids have been used in various ways, but just like adding a cog to a story and calling it Steampunk isn't terribly effective, writing 666 on a young 'uns head doesn't make them the Devil. We've seen it all before, so ask yourself how you can play in the sandbox in a new way.
- **Just mean/sociopathic:** Evil children don't always have or need a supernatural explanation. Sometimes, despite having good parents, good schooling, and a good life, people just don't act right. We know now that therapy is necessary, but that doesn't always make for good Horror fiction. And while Joffrey Baratheon in *A Game of Thrones* has become a sort of sociopathic poster child, he wasn't the first. In *Mutation* by Robin Cook (1989), genetic engineering results in a super-intelligent child who kills anyone who might end up being smarter than him (like a very evil Sheldon Cooper) and performs experiments on unused embryos. And in *The Good Son* (dir. Joseph Ruben, 1993) Macaulay Culkin finally puts Kevin (from *Home Alone*) to bed with his portrayal of sociopathic Henry. So, consider how a small human could behave or act that you would find particularly creepy but that isn't supernatural (or even necessarily outright violent) to see what might prompt a new story.

- **So gross it's funny:** Horror writers and readers often find the truly outlandish or disgusting—anything that violates a norm—makes them laugh. It's a natural human response, but it can be disturbing, too. Horror stories and films can inadvertently cause laughter due to bad special effects or ridiculous story lines. So, ask yourself whether you want your readers to gasp *and* laugh, or if an involuntary laugh response to a subversive image or moment isn't what you planned.

ACTIVITIES

Parental instincts: You're babysitting for Luis and Henry, the nice couple who lives next door who haven't had a night out alone since baby came into their lives. While you're watching television the power goes out, but, before you can find some candles, everything comes back on. The show you were watching is gone and in its place is the baby-cam feed from upstairs showing the little tyke floating above the bassinet, and you feel a sudden pain stabbing through your head, making you want to do anything you can for the child. What does the baby command? Was it born evil? Is it possessed? Or are there other supernatural powers at play? Consider whether you wish to touch on issues surrounding surrogacy, implantation, or adoption for this one.

How far will you go? Your character is driving in an unfamiliar part of the country late at night and their car breaks down. Their cell phone is dead, but through the trees they see house lights, so have no choice but to go ask for help. The house is full of threatening children—from barely more than toddlers to teenagers—brandishing weapons. How do they reason with immature—and immoral—children? How far do they go before they're forced to act to protect themself? Consider whether the evil at play is nature or nurture (born evil/sociopathic, corrupted and grew to be evil, sick or otherwise infected).

ECOHORROR

The Earth will not abide our crimes much longer! It will fight back against our pollution, our habitat destruction, and our gluttonous appetite for resource extraction. Humanity will be helpless against the carnivorous plants, genetic mutations, zoonotic diseases, and geological devastation that we've brought upon ourselves. The results will be a special kind of Horror: ecohorror. Because, let's face it, it's not like the planet *actually* needs us around.

A Short History of Ecohorror

Ecohorror emerged as a distinct term in the mid-1990s, but the roots of the subgenre—its entangling, strangling, murderous roots—lie in longstanding anxieties about anthropogenic (meaning human-caused) environmental destruction. It manifests as work in which "human characters are attacked by natural forces—typically animals and plants—that have been altered or angered by humans in some way" (see also **Animals That Attack**).[1] Ecohorror stories, and especially films, depict how "nature lashes out as an aggressive force to snuff out humanity as a form of Gaia-ic vengeance".[2] They present tales in which humanity receives its comeuppance, stories in which our relationship to the Earth is drastically realigned, and "Green Panic" narratives in which the raw, malevolent side of the natural world takes its revenge. A frequent tenet is how the subgenre's protagonists must "learn to evolve with their surroundings, adapting to new rules in the face of the extraordinary"; to "refuse or otherwise fail to acknowledge and adapt to change results in annihilation".[3]

Ecohorror as an expression of ecological or environmental anxiety, as well as a retort to human hubris, has a venerable history that, in the West, dates to biblical plagues of frogs, lice, flies, locusts, and the like. Among the earliest ancestors of modern ecohorror is 'The Giant Wistaria' (1891) by Charlotte Perkins Stetson (later Charlotte Perkins Gilman of 'The Yellow Wallpaper' fame), a chilling **Ghost Story** in which the titular plant conceals a horrific secret. 'The Flowering of the Strange Orchid' by H.G. Wells (1894) riffs on Darwinian evolution and, along with Lucy Hamilton Hooper's 'Carnivorine' (1889), popularised the trope of blood-thirsty plants that still define the subgenre ('The Pavilion', 1915, by Edith *"Railway Children"* Nesbit offers another—this time feminist—take on this concept). On the animal front,

---
1. Rust and Soles, 2014, p. 510.
2. Thurston, 2019, p. 37.
3. Beard, 2011, n.p.

ecohorror advanced further with Ray Bradbury's 1951 monster tale 'The Fog Horn', which was (heavily) adapted into *The Beast from 20,000 Fathoms* (dir. Eugène Lourié, 1953). In the film version, atomic testing in the Arctic releases a dinosaur from icy hibernation and it proceeds to wreak havoc. Hot on its heels was the classic *Godzilla* (dir. Ishirō Honda, 1954) in which hydrogen-bomb tests awaken the antagonist, who kills thousands of Japanese people in a clear metaphor for the bombings of Hiroshima and Nagasaki. As one of the film's producers put it, "mankind had created the bomb, and now nature was going to take revenge on mankind".[4] The same year saw the release of *Them!* (dir. Gordon Douglas) in which fallout from atomic testing causes ants to mutate to gigantic proportions. It is characteristic of any number of giant-bug B-movies that primarily approached ecohorror as a special-effects phenomenon. More nuanced material that delved into the subgenre's psychological implications and the potential unknowability of nature would begin to emerge in the 1960s, a period during which "the revenge of nature" cemented itself as one of Horror's core motifs.[5]

The defining ecohorror of that era is probably Alfred Hitchcock's film *The Birds* (1963), adapted from a 1952 Daphne du Maurier story. The film depicts an increasingly violent series of avian attacks and, abandoning any pseudo-rational explanation, earned its Horror credentials by presenting its antagonists as "an inexplicable force of nature, whose motivations and specific origins are never made clear".[6] Far less subtle, and far more outlandish, is *Frogs* (dir. George McCowan, 1972), a seminal work of ecohorror despite its low-budget nature. This film centres on an American family whose patriarch has a long history of polluting the environment. They find themselves the target of assaults by animals including lizards, snakes, birds, and butterflies (though, oddly, rarely from the frogs, which tend to just sit around menacingly). More proactive is the shark from Steven Spielberg's iconic *Jaws* (1975; based on Peter Benchley's 1974 novel). Meanwhile, *The Nest* (1980) by Jeffrey A. Douglas (a pseudonym of Eli Cantor), offers another creature creeper in which hordes of giant mutant cockroaches devour the inhabitants of a small Cape Cod town. For the green-thumbed among you, *The Little Shop of Horrors* (dir. Frank Oz, 1986) is a further timeless example of ecohorror… and of musical comedy! Adapted from a 1982 off-Broadway version of a 1960 film by Roger Cornman (seriously, it's little shops all the way down), the film tells the story of a florist who cultivates a sentient flesh-eating plant (♪ "I've given you sunlight, I've given you rain, looks like you're not happy, 'less I open a vein" ♪). It's *delightful*!

---

4. Ryfle, 2005, pp. 44–68.
5. Wood, 1986, p. 83.
6. Soles, 2014, p. 527.

In the twenty-first century, of course, anxieties about "pollution, species extinction, or extreme weather" provide much fodder for ecohorror.[7] *The Ruins* (2006) by Scott Smith is a good example, especially in terms of vegetative, tentacular horror. It tells the story of group of tourists in the Mexican jungle who have a horrifying encounter with aggressive, sapient, parasitic vines capable of imitating human voices to lure in their victims. *The Happening* (dir. M. Night Shyamalan, 2008) depicts plant life going on the offensive against humanity, releasing a neurotoxin that causes mass suicide. The film was not well received, but the theme is core ecohorror. In *The Waste Tide* by Chen Qiufan (2013), which exists somewhere between true ecohorror and Body Horror, a "waste girl" on a heavily polluted Chinese island devoted to recycling discarded electronics is infected with a virus that generates an omniscient consciousness. She soon finds herself setting out to right the various wrongs on this so-called Silicon Isle. The novel *Annihilation* (2014) by Jeff VanderMeer is a modern classic of ecohorror and Weird Fiction more generally. In it, a four-woman expedition ventures into a long-quarantined zone known as Area X to map the terrain only to discover a landscape radically transformed and radically *transformative*. In the film version, director Alex Garland (2018) brings much of VanderMeer's disturbing imagery to life in hugely effective fashion. The Margret Atwood-inspired *Future Home of the Living God* by Louise Erdrich (2017) follows its pregnant Native American protagonist through a world where evolution itself has begun to move backwards (with predictably totalitarian results for women's reproductive rights), while South African Jaco Bouwer's film *Gaia* (2021) sees park rangers discovering a kind of survivalist fungi-cult deep in the forest. See, too, New Zealand author Octavia Cade's short fiction, which frequently touches on ecohorror themes (for example *You Are My Sunshine and Other Stories*, 2023).

A Spotter's Guide: Nasty Nature

- **Killer plants:** The most obvious incarnation of ecohorror is probably vegetative horror. Don't believe us? Go watch a timelapse video of house plants over 24 hours. They may not be mobile, but they *move*. It's unsettling. Some are carnivorous and will take over our homes and sink their tendrils into our bodies if they're given half a chance. Consider the likes of Algernon Blackwood's eerie and sublime 'The Man Whom the Trees Loved' (1912), in which a forest lures a husband away from his wife before eventually subsuming him entirely. Or John Wyndham's *The Day of the Triffids* (1951), which offers an Apocalyptic approach in which mobile plants attempt to take

---

7. Tidwell and Soles, 2021, p. 2.

over the world after a meteor shower blinds humanity. Meanwhile, comics character Swamp Thing (created by Len Wein and Bernie Wrightson in 1971 and popularised by a run of Alan Moore stories in the mid-1980s) is a humanoid mound of vegetable matter fighting for a better environment. Such a blurring of the human and the non-human isn't uncommon in the subgenre and echoes the boundary/identity collapse elsewhere in the Horror genre.

- **When elements attack:** Planet Earth isn't just its plants and animals. It's also the soil, the mountains, the air, and the water. These physical structures and mechanisms offer powerful weapons to use against us such as tremors, tornadoes, *shark*nadoes, tidal waves, landslides, and so on. Their narrative function is often to trap or otherwise corral characters in a specific location ("The road has been swept away!" or "The snow is too heavy to go out!"), but, on occasion, they allow us to imbue the abstract concept of a vengeful Earth with the true agency of an antagonist. Because events such as volcanos and earthquakes are moments "when nature refuses to stay in the background".[8] In Anna Kavan's dreamlike and difficult-to-categorise *Ice* (1967), for example, our punishment for nuclear war is an enormous ice shelf that's engulfing the world. Similarly, floods and sea-level rise are undeniably humanity's penance for environmental destruction. Even the wind, as in J.G. Ballard's *The Wind from Nowhere* (1961) can be malevolent in an author's hands.
- **Humans as villains:** Humanity fancies itself top of the food chain, with many (especially Western) cultures believing—implicitly or otherwise—that they have a divine right to harness the Earth as they see fit. Ecohorror says they could not be more wrong. Here, humanity's actions are often depicted as irresponsible or criminal: we tear down trees, we pollute the seas with oil and plastic, and we overheat the globe with our addiction to burning fossil fuels. Humans in ecohorror are shortsighted. As academic Bernice M. Murphy argues, many works in and around this subgenre see our contempt for the natural world "violently turned back upon" us.[9] Our destruction of animal habitats forms the backstory of so much **Pandemic Fiction**; our melting of the ice caps releases prehistoric horrors frozen for millennia; our bulldozing of the forests forces wild creatures into our town and cities. Yet, in ecohorror, these animals and plants are the sympathetic protagonists. In ecohorror, *we* are the monsters.

---

8. Keetly, 2021, p. 24.
9. Murphy, B.M., 2013, p. 181.

- **Kaiju:** The big daddy of early ecohorror is obviously Godzilla, but in that creature's titanic wake came a multitude of other colossal beings bringing destruction to human cities. The term "kaiju" is a Japanese word for "strange beast", and it's subsequently become its own subgenre without ever abandoning its basis in environmental unease. Alongside Godzilla, famous kaiju include the enormous flying reptile Rodan, the gigantic larva Mothra (often portrayed as a heroic character), and the three-headed, armless, winged biped King Ghidorah. Prominent modern examples include *Pacific Rim* (dir. Guillermo del Toro, 2013), in which aliens drawn to our increased pollution send kaiju to wipe us out, and John Scalzi's *The Kaiju Preservation Society* (2022) in which radiation from nuclear weapons on Earth attract kaiju from elsewhere in **The Multiverse**. Kaiju are now familiar enough that their imagery—and the associated eco-anxiety—can be played for comedy, such as in the Japanese film *What to do with the Dead Kaiju* (dir. Satoshi Miki, 2022). Though, even in that, as the trailer declares, the metaphorical meaning is clear: "Clean up the mess or humans perish!".
- **Fungoid fiction:** Fungal horror, what some call Spore Horror or "Sporror", is another approach to ecohorror that's arguably now become its own subgenre. This is unsurprising, for fungi, neither vegetable nor animal, are inherently horrific things. *They assimilate us*. They repurpose our material selves into something uncanny by reaching their fine tentacular feelers inside our bodies. Their squishy, boneless, alien shapes disrupt our rigid ways of looking at the world. Indeed, they're so strange that some people even think they *are* aliens. In both the video game *The Last of Us* (2013; adapted for television, 2023) and M.R. Carey's *The Girl With All the Gifts*, a real-life fungus called cordyceps is responsible for the Zombification of the world. Infected brains are transformed into disgusting fungal growths (note here how fungal horror is the perfect medium for grotesque descriptions!). See, too, the novella *Agents of Dreamland* (2017) by Caitlín R. Kiernan, which bridges fungal and Cosmic Horror in unnerving fashion.

Things That are Cool About Ecohorror

"We live in ecohorrific times", claim academics Christy Tidwell and Carter Soles.[10] We exist and we write in an era during which, as scholar Sarah Dillion has argued, we are transiting from cosmic horror to planetary fear.[11]

---

10. Tidwell and Soles, 2021, p. 1.
11. Dillon, 2018, p. 7.

All around us, the feigned boundaries between the domestic and the wild are crumbling. And it's one thing to describe the physical implications of that, as **Climate Fiction** does with wildfires, droughts, and floods, but quite another to capture its psychological impact. That responsibility falls squarely on Horror's shoulders. Because if we stop and think about environmental collapse with any seriousness, the magnitude—and inevitability—of it is terrifying. We *should* be afraid of the Earth's wrath, and ecohorror has emerged as a way of expressing that. Which is to say that, like nature, storytelling evolves....

Rewild Your Mind

- **Climate change:** While climate fiction is our go-to for examining the implications of rising sea levels, climbing global temperatures, and biodiversity collapse, it can sometimes be difficult for that subgenre to see the creepy, invasive, all-consuming forest for the trees. By contrast, ecohorror takes full advantage of a slightly different set of aesthetics—essentially the tropes of slasher movies, Splatterpunk, Psychological Horror, and more—to tell deeply weird and unsettling, oftentimes even shockingly intimate, stories. This subgenre cracks open cells as readily as it sheds skins. It makes immediate the gigantic, unimaginable physical and temporal scales of climate collapse and our planet's sixth great extinction by linking it to individuals' smaller worlds in moments of metaphorical crisis and even to the minute environment of our bodies. Think of the whole hurricane-ravaged globe in the close-up of a fearful, tearful eye.
- **Natural landscapes:** From the Romantic poets onwards, Western culture has sought to portray capital-N Nature in Arcadian terms. All manicured grass and butterflies perched on dogs' noses and so on. But that idea is as much aesthetic, ideological, and even political as anything else (philosopher Timothy Morton has a few things to say about this in *Ecology Without Nature*, 2007). The beautiful park you visit? That carefully tended farmland you pass on the train? They're all human artifacts, designed by human minds and cultivated by human hands. Nature, real nature, is wild and brutal and cannot be controlled. Ecohorror recognises this (as do the best eco adjacent sub-subgenres such as ecogothic and ecofeminist writing). Ecohorror's forests are filled with trees that subsume people (and sometimes keep them alive inside their trunks). In some cases, such as Neil Jordan's *The Dream of a Beast* (1983), the landscape itself mutates into a primordial world of strange blooms hostile to mere human life. Or, to put it another way, every Eden is a deadly space in ecohorror stories and all the more natural for that.

- **Decay:** A key image of ecohorror is that of decomposition. This can be rotting plant matter or even decaying meat from animal or human corpses. Yet what brings this imagery to life in all cases is vivid descriptive language that appeals to the senses. So don't just tell us what it looks like, describe the overwhelming stench of it, the moist, slimy feel of it, the sounds of insects wriggling out of it…. A good exercise is to describe a pile of rotting leaves in as unsettling a fashion as possible (or even try to describe one of the elaborately decomposed bodies from a television show such as *Bones*, 2005–'17). How far you want to take things is up to you (and the effect you wish to achieve), but the key to ecohorror is that the encounter with nature should be somewhere between disquieting and downright upsetting.
- **Promoting environmental awareness:** More visceral than mainstream climate fiction, ecohorror stories have the potential to inspire dialogue about human actions and impacts. After all, this subgenre is based on not just "fear *of* nature but also encompasses fear *for* nature".[12] If it has a message, it's that our abuse of the Earth has consequences, from monstrous creatures to catastrophic climate events. Ecohorror depicts this global agency in the most literal sense. It reminds us that we need to change or nature will change us.
- **Cryptobotany:** Think **Cryptozoology**, but for plants, as ecohorror has long had a sideline in legends about curious plants and their discovery (often the Western "discovery" of indigenous knowledge). These include unusual plants with, for instance, medicinal qualities that can spur conflict between individuals, local communities, and corporations, or even plants that have grotesque side-effects. An interesting example is the Tree of Life in *The Fountain* (dir. Darren Aronofsky, 2006), especially how it causes flowers to explode out of one character and drains the life essence of another into itself.

---

12. Tidwell and Soles, 2021, p. 14.

ACTIVITIES

Savage garden: Your protagonist and their friends are touring a so-called "Poison Garden" (such as England's Alnwick Garden), a horticultural exhibit of exotic and deadly flowers, vines, and trees. Visitors are warned *not* to stop and smell the roses here, but people will be people.... Write what happens when one of your characters gets too close to a killer bloom. Maybe they turn crazed and hunt down their friends; maybe the plant begins to transform their body into grotesque vegetable matter; maybe they find their mind linked to arboreal consciousness. This is an activity containing the seeds of many stories.

The beaches are open: There's something in the water at your nearest seaside town. It's the size of a person, but it's *not* a human being. It's being blamed for people dying in mysterious circumstances. Could these deaths be related to the nearby chemical plant? Or maybe to the raw sewage being pumped into the local rivers? In any event, people are scared, politicians are looking for scapegoats, and the truth lies in very dirty waters. Write the story of a journalist investigating the sightings. Perhaps they can find a sympathetic angle on the creature and its motivation? Perhaps they discover that not everything is as it seems.

GENDERCIDE

You've landed on a planet populated only by women. You've found yourself with a secret tribe deep in the forest where only men are to be seen. You're in the middle of a pandemic but only half of the population is dying. You might be experiencing gendercide.

A Short Note on Context

First of all, talking about this particular subgenre/trope is difficult because of the current political situation in which we find ourselves, with people in the LGBTQAI+ communities being silenced, ostracised, repressed, and physically threatened—in some cases killed—because of who they are. But it's because of the current climate, and because of what we're all learning about the various ways people can choose to present as something different from what they were assigned at birth, that your authors decided to create this section. Also note that earlier examples of stories in which all of one gender or another are missing often conflate sex (defined as biological characteristics) and gender (defined as socially constructed roles, expressions, and identifications). We've taken pains to put these stories in their historical context with as much clarity as possible.

Finally, gendercide of all kinds—including femicide (the killing of girls and women), androcide (the killing of men and boys), and the killing of third-gender people who don't fit within the binary—are not fictional storylines only; these events can be found throughout history as the result of cultural norms, wars, or other events. Depending on the author and their personal context, some strong links can be made between a story and real life, but space restrictions mean that we're limited in how detailed of an examination we can present here. It is hoped that the texts mentioned here will lead you to further discoveries.

A Short History of Gendercide

The term "gendercide" was coined by Mary Anne Warren in *Gendercide: The Implications of Sex Selection* (1985) as a twist on the word "genocide". Gendercide by definition is the elimination of a certain set of people from a population based on their sex or gender. This section explores stories about populations in which only one gender/sex goes missing or doesn't exist and, for our purposes, stories of both all-out destruction (true gendercide) and partial elimination or erasure of populations will be explored. One of the earliest examples of a single-sex society is the ancient Greek myth of the Amazons, female warriors who lived together in a society closed to men and only interacted with men to conceive, then only raised daughters, sending any boy children to be raised by their fathers. Readers will no doubt recognise it from the DC Universe comics and films featuring Wonder Woman, the daughter of Queen Hippolyta and Zeus (Wonder Woman was created by the American psychologist William Moulton Marston and artist Harry G. Peter in 1941; though Marston's wife, Elizabeth, and their life partner, Olive Byrne, had significant influence on the character).[1] Another early example is Christine de Pizan's *The Book of the City of Ladies* (1405), which the author populates with various historical and fictional women who embody virtues in opposition to the negative attitudes men had for women in the author's historical time.

Science Fiction, Fantasy, and Horror writers have often used single-sex societies to explore the politics of sex and gender, though many of the earlier stories assign gender to sex and don't investigate the differences that have come to be more recently understood. In many stories about single-sex societies, the situation has come about as the result of a disease or some sort of disaster, and the society that results is often dysfunctional, Dystopian, or, in the cases of a story in which one sex is eliminated on purpose, a type of Utopia. What's interesting to keep in mind is how the creation of these stories can very tentatively be associated with different waves of feminism that have influenced society, art, and thought for the past two centuries: the First Wave 1848–1920; the Second Wave 1963–'80s; the Third Wave in the 1990s; and the Fourth Wave in the present day.[2] An example of how these waves have affected writing and publishing—and republishing—can be found in *Herland* (1915) by Charlotte Perkins Gilman. This novel, from the first feminist wave, is about three men who, via a biplane, find a remote society of women who reproduce without men and have no knowledge of modern society, religion, or social mores. *Herland* was reprinted in 1979, during the second feminist wave, with the subtitle 'A Lost Feminist Utopian Novel'.

Of course, understanding the reason behind the popularity of stories focusing on gender and sexual politics requires an understanding of the ideas these stories allow a writer to explore. They give writers a means of examining how gender and sex, and our hang-ups and beliefs about them, affect how our societies and civilisations are built. Writing SFF/H using these ideas lets us imagine a better world according to one side of the equation. Writing Horror gives us the freedom to explore how disenfranchising and destroying a portion of the population can lead to violence from those being oppressed or even amongst those who now want to fight it out for what's left,

---

1. DC Extended Universe Wiki, n.d., n.p.
2. Pruitt, 2023, n.p.

whether it's limited resources or limited access to the (mostly eliminated) portion of the population. To put that plainly: who gets sexual access to the portion of the population that is under threat or gone, or who gets access to the ovum and sperm to rebuild society according to their "status quo"? There's also the terror of looking down the tunnel at the true end of humanity when one half of the material needed for reproduction is no longer available, something that can lay a pall over any story (see **Last Person Left Alive**).

Women-only Worlds

The "women-only" world is a utopia for some feminist writers and a nice, temporary dream for some women-identifying readers! Because so much fiction has, historically, focused on men's adventures and men's thoughts, beliefs, distractions, etc. (one of your authors researched eighty years of Apocalyptic fiction, and believe us when we say that the great majority centres manly men doing manly things!), writers can use this trope to create a world in which men and the related patriarchy, toxic masculinity, war, and issues such as the glass ceiling are eliminated. Female-centred societies in fiction are often ones in which sharing and communication are key, and the problems a society suffers—war, oppression, etc.—are believed to be a result of having men in power. Another twist to this trope is that "Some anti-feminist authors might create exactly the same kind of story to produce a dystopia, to show that women, or just feminists, are the cause of all the ills of society".[3] As ever, one person's utopia is another's dystopia! We can find many notable examples:

- ***The Female Man* by Joanna Russ (1975):** in which four versions of the same woman, each from a parallel universe, experience each other's lives and societies: one from a familiar world (the author's 1970); one in an America at the same time but in which the Great Depression never ended; a "utopian" agrarian world in which there are only females; and a "dystopian" one in which men and women are at war. This is hugely simplifying a complex, layered novel, but its political messages are clear. Reviewer Eric Lindh sums it up: "The most exciting facet is Russ' deconstruction of gender and gender roles. She builds a world without the 'poisonous binary' of gender, creating an all women utopia that is not anti-man, but pro-human. The strong negative reaction by the (male) reviewing community, who labelled it a male-hating diatribe, when it clearly is not, is a testament to the strength of Russ' arguments".[4]

---

3. TVTropes.org, n.d., n.p.
4. Lindh, 2006, n.p.

- ***Houston, Houston, Do You Read?* By James Tiptree, Jr. (Alice Bradley Sheldon, 1976):** In this Hugo-award-winning novella, male **Astronauts** accidentally Time Travel to a future in which men are wiped out, leaving only women and non-binary people in a world in which reproduction is attained via cloning. The three astronauts display negative attitudes towards women, upholding the idea of a masculinity that sees conquest as the goal. Author and active SFF convention administrator Nicholas White says of the book that "it's strongly implied that as the story ends, they [the men] are about to be killed off as a danger to humanity. It's chilling but also very subtle, and I wonder how many of those who voted for it in 1977 actually understood the full point".[5]
- **'Lithia' from *The Outer Limits* (ep. 17, season 4, dir. Helen Shaver, 1998):** A cryogenically frozen man wakes up decades after a war and a virus have killed off all the men, leaving a women-only society. The man's presence leads to aggression and jealousy (about resources and sex), and, in the end, he's refrozen as punishment.
- ***Y: The Last Man* by Brian K. Vaughan and Pia Guerra (2002–'08):** In this comic-book series, all mammals with a Y chromosome die except for one young man, Yorick (an escape artist), and his pet monkey. After teaming up with a geneticist and some other female characters (an astronaut, a sailor, a soldier, etc.), the group, which is trying to figure out why he survived, is chased across the globe by others trying to capture and even kill him. Later, after Yorick and some other men are cloned, society regains some of its former prosperity but without a population that's 50% male.
- ***The End of Men* by Christina Sweeney-Baird (2021):** In 2025, a virus sweeps through the world, killing 90% of those who have a Y chromosome. Females carry the virus, but it only affects males, with the narrative following several point-of-view characters across seven years, from outbreak to post-**Pandemic** remembrance.
- ***The Men* by Sandra Newman (2022):** Any human—foetus or born—with a Y chromosome disappears. As a result, this particular book attracted criticism and controversy for its eradication of transwomen and anyone else with a Y chromosome who doesn't identify as a cis-man.

Men-only Worlds

Men-only stories are not as common as women-only stories. Joanna Russ suggests this is "because men do not feel oppressed, and therefore imagining

---

5. Whyte, 2020, n.p.

a world free of women does not imply an increase in freedom and is not as attractive".[6] Nonetheless, they present a different set of challenges. Any writer positing a man-only world will have to be able to envision what would happen if the—grain of salt here—"softening" influence of women was absent. Moreover, many stories of men-only worlds depict the loss of women to protect and provide for as a crisis of existential meaning for heterosexual male characters. Examples illustrate these ideas:

- *Ethan of Athos* by **Lois McMaster Bujold (1986):** In this stand-alone novel from the Vorkosigan Saga, the planet Athos is a male-only settlement, originally a sort of monastery away from women who were believed to be "demonic" because of the upheaval they caused in men. Ethan is a doctor trying to solve the mystery of why a shipment of ovarian tissue necessary for reproduction on the planet has been replaced by unusable animal tissue. Reviewer Nicki Gerlach notes that the novel "showcases how good Bujold can be at introducing more serious topics in her fiction, without having the story become entirely about The Issues. In this case, the story on the surface is essentially a spy thriller, but there are deeper layers dealing with sexism, the rights of the individual vs. the society, and homophobia".[7]
- *The Knife of Never Letting Go* by **Patrick Ness (2008):** In this YA novel, young Todd's father tells him that all the women and most of the men were killed in a war with the natives of a planet his group has settled. The men can all hear others' thoughts (Noise), but later Todd discovers that women don't hear Noise; the Noise drove the men mad and they killed the women, leading to an all-male settlement that was, in fact, a group banished by the rest of the settlers. The novel won the 2008 James Tiptree Award, which recognises SFF works that expand or explore our understanding of gender.
- *The Beauty* by **Aliya Whiteley (2014):** This novella centres on a community of men after all the women die from a mysterious fungal infection. When other life forms grow out of the women's graves they're accepted by the men as stand-in women, which the resident storyteller names The Beauty: "The Beauty force the men to question their own sexual identity and, most significantly, make them consider just what they are willing to undergo to ensure the survival of the human race (in one form or another). Many of the men react in the way we would expect them to—with violence".[8]

---

6. Romaine, 1999, p. 329.
7. Gerlach, 2011, n.p.
8. Smits, n.d., n.p.

- ***Sabre Marionette* by Satoru Akahori (1995–2008):** This series, delivered via anime, audio, television, and manga, depicts a world with no women, and men make androids in the guise of girls/women to serve them.

Genderless, Sexless, or Hermaphroditic Worlds

Because gender and sexuality are fluid, it makes sense that our favourite genres would explore this aspect of life. However, because we live in a society that tends to lean towards a binary, stories that are completely genderless are still rare. Some of this has to do with how we use language; we use pronouns to describe people (he/she) with "they" being used as a gender-neutral singular pronoun causing some people to *lose their damn minds*, despite the historical precedence of its use from as far back as the 1375 mediaeval romance *William and the Werewolf*.[9]

- ***The Left Hand of Darkness* by Ursula K Le Guin (1969):** In this Hugo- and Nebula-Award-winning novel, the inhabitants of planet Gethen are ambisexual and androgynous, only becoming male or female a few days a month during a high-fertility window. Throughout, they're referred to by the pronoun "he"; Le Guin explains in an essay that the novel is a thought experiment but is quite honest that using "he" as a neutral pronoun led to problems: "that the Gethenians seem like men, instead of menwomen" and "The pronouns wouldn't matter at all if I had been cleverer at *showing* the 'female' component of the Gethenian characters in action"; she concludes by stating that this choice "is a real flaw in the book".[10]
- ***Woman on the Edge of Time* by Marge Piercy (1976):** A woman confined to a psychiatric hospital against her will in the 1970s communicates telepathically with an androgynous person from 2137, a time during which many of the issues facing people in the late twentieth century (sexism, ecological breakdown, racism, homophobia, and totalitarianism, among others) have been eradicated, with the pronoun "per" for "person" now used. Inspired by what she sees in a possible future of freedom from many social ills, the woman revolts against oppression (and a lobotomy) to help ensure that the future might be more like the one she's seen.
- **The Culture series by Iain M. Banks (1987–2012):** In Banks's utopic society, people live for several hundred years and can change sex at will, they do not need the opposite sex to procreate, and

---

9. Baron, n.d., n.p.
10. Le Guin, 1979, 'Is Gender Necessary?', p. 168.

children are often raised collectively. This set-up means that the traditional gender roles of our society aren't necessary, with Banks showing another way to live outside of cultural expectations.

Things That are Cool About Gendercide Stories

Science Fiction, Fantasy, and Horror are genres that ask, "What if?". In this regard, they're perfectly positioned for authors to examine their societies' gender expectations, sexual mores, and traditions. We have no lack of apocalyptic stories in which survivors try to rebuild the world; readers love them because they can imagine themselves as the survivors, and writers love to write them because they get to play Creator, destroying and rebuilding the world according to what they wish the world could be, or what they cynically believe the world is fated to be. Removing half the population adds a special complication to that reset and allows a writer a way to think about their own preconceived notions, possibly unrealised beliefs, and blind spots when it comes to sexual politics.

We Are More Than Our Parts

In recent years, gendercide as a subgenre has come under scrutiny because, as an older trope from the Golden Age of SFF, it feels outdated in the modern Western world where women have fought for equality in the workplace and at home, and the LGBTQAI+ community has fought for protection and recognition in the law, at work, and in the wider world. To write a story in which you just erase half of the population based on genetics reduces us to little more than XY or XX chromosomes, known as gender essentialism, a reading of life in which people are the sex they were born and so must fit into a "male" or "female" box, along with the gender expectations that match. Obviously, that's not fair to considerable numbers of people. In reality, most women want to be known as more than "walking uteruses", and men have had to deal with a new wave of very toxic masculinity that sets them up to be only "protectors" and "providers" in what's no longer their great-grandfathers' world. Non-binary, transexual and transgender, intersexual, and asexual people want to be seen for who they are and be able to participate in society.

So, consider the rules of your apocalypse: who's eradicated and why, and how are they chosen? Some of this can be handled with a thought about what you're trying to say in your story (remember theme? Yes, we are hammering on that topic again!). The SFF/H readership is, by and large, more sophisticated now than before—remember that these genres are conversations—and so, while a story about a new planet populated only by scantily clad, big-breasted women who are happy to be subservient sex slaves does have a readership, it will come across as very old hat. Feminism is in a new wave, too, so what ideas do you want to explore if you remove men from the equation? And, in general in the early twenty-first century, what do you want to say about gender?

ACTIVITIES

It's All in a Name: Your astronaut/space explorer encounters an alien population that has no pronouns at all, for people or animals or inanimate objects. Everything is referred to by name. Additionally, offspring are shed, like dandruff or skin flakes, with very little care or rearing required by the "parent". Your character has to report back to their home planet. What questions will the character have, and how can they ask when, coming from a civilisation that is so concerned with gender labels, they encounter one that doesn't seem to have any such thing? How will your astronaut character navigate this new world, and what questions will the alien population have for them?

Exaggeration: Ramp up the horror by creating a satirical gendercide in which one part of the population (you decide which!) doesn't die off or disappear but turns into some sort of monster. Consider the worst traits people are accused of having according to their sex or gender in your chosen setting (place *and* time period). Then take them to a monstrous extreme. How will the rest of humanity deal with the situation? Will they turn to violence or look for a scientific resolution to get things "back to normal"? And what about the "monsters"? Consider writing the tale from their point of view to examine how gender expectations and pressures can ultimately affect individuals.

PLACES PEOPLE SHOULDN'T GO

Sneaking a peek into an abandoned building. Skiing down a black-diamond slope. Jumping on the back of the shopping trolly and riding it through the parking lot. We all have our own approaches to adventure, but some stories take us into the dark heart of places we *really* shouldn't go. And that's where adventure trips over into Horror: when a bit of fun becomes a giant *nope*. These are places people shouldn't go....

A Short History of Places People Shouldn't Go

The notion of places people shouldn't go (PPSG) is something that's culturally determined, deriving from an ever-changing mixture of social and technological influences. On a basic level, there are places you shouldn't or can't go because you'll die or get hurt (Chernobyl or the Korean DMZ) or because of financial or technical limitations (the Outer Solar System); there are places you're not *allowed* to go for legal reasons (Area 51 or North Sentinel Island in India or even the Lascaux Caves in France); and then there places you're discouraged from going by peer groups, usually because of socio-economic inequality, racism, or a general fear of difference ("bad" parts of town, etc.). All provide compelling backdrops for writers to deploy Horror tropes on account of the built-in unease—or worse, in the case of the particularly deadly examples—that they generate in our protagonists. This is true even when our characters deliberately seek out these locations because then we can make use of hubris ("Other people have died here, but I'll be okay") to great effect as part of our artistic palette. Remember the modern adage that every frozen corpse on Mt Everest was once a highly motivated person!

Back in the day, of course, people didn't go very far from their home tribe or village. Partially this was because strangers were regarded with distrust and subject to violence—thus travel was dangerous—and partially it was because getting places took *forever* in the millennia before planes, trains, and automobiles. Not that this stopped the hardiest—or *foolhardiest*—human specimens who wanted to see the world. Even today, some people go places that they shouldn't just for the hell of it, for the bragging rights of glimpsing the wreck of the *Titanic* through a tiny porthole or seeing the curve of the planet from a billionaire's vanity spacecraft. Of course, the original bragging rights—the original social media full stop—came in the form of tall tales and half-truths about what was "out there": Vikings who struck out to the west and never returned (though archaeological evidence tells us they reached Greenland and North America); Marco Polo's adventures in the East (recorded in *The Travels of Marco Polo*, c. 1300); Arab adventurer Ibn Battuta's travels across 117,000 km of Africa, Asia, and Europe in the mid-1300s (more than any other explorer in pre-modern times); Chinese admiral Zheng He's expeditionary treasure voyages; and many more. Yet to trust in the veracity of second-, third-, or fourth-hand travellers' yarns was to take your life into your own hands. The idea of the factual guidebook, in the modern sense, came later. One of the earliest examples is *Peregrinatio in Terram Sanctam* (*A Pilgrimage to the Holy Land*, 1486), depicting a trip undertaken by Bernhard von Breydenbach in 1483–'84. In the following years, economic factors and advances in technology pushed European nations in particular ahead of their Asian and Arabic counterparts. Most (in)famously, Christopher Columbus sailed across the vast uncharted western ocean in search of a quicker passage to the rich lands of the Far East but "discovered" the Americas instead. The result was a bloody and genocidal age of colonialism and enslavement—the effects of which are still felt today on both sides of the Atlantic—with the Columbus expeditions emboldening countless European explorers, traders, and violent conquerors (oftentimes all three in one) to fan out across the world to places they shouldn't go. Among them were Amerigo Vespucci (from whom we get the name "America"), Francis Drake, Henry Hudson, Hernando Cortez, Ferdinand Magellan, James Cook, and many others. Such explorations typically had a military or extractive character, often "sponsored by governments eager for territorial expansion or by private trading firms, such as the Dutch East India Company, which traded in spices, commercial goods, curiosities and medicinal substances".[1]

This Age of Discovery—though one imagines that terminology coming as quite a surprise to the millions of people "discovered"—filled in many blank spaces on European maps of the world. This in turn inaugurated a race to reach the farthest, highest, or deepest points, the very definitions of PPSG. Enter the explorers and scientists of the late nineteenth and early twentieth centuries. Many targeted places that weren't necessarily even habitable. These expeditions got underway in the late 1800s when "international scientific consolidation took place" because these sorts of projects were "expensive, highly organised and often took place on a co-operative international basis".[2] Such voyages included that of marine biologist Charles Wyville Thomson to study the deep sea aboard the *Challenger* (1872–'76), though nobody from that ship dove deep underwater (in a **Submarine** or not)[3], and British officer Robert Falcon Scott's South Pole explorations aboard the *Discovery* (1901–'04) and the *Terra Nova* (1910–'12), during which Scott and three

---

1. Lawrence, 2015, n.p.
2. Lawrence, 2015, n.p.
3. Editors of *Encyclopaedia Britannica*, 'Sir C. Wyville Thomson', 2023, n.p.

of his crew died.[4] Both more successful—in that nobody died—and equally unsuccessful in that it failed to win the South Pole (that honour went to Norwegian explorer Roald Amundsen) was the 1914–'17 *Endurance* expedition of Irish explorer Ernest Shackelton (his leadership strategies are still taught in business schools today!). Shackelton and his crew's journey across the Southern Ocean in search of rescue is easily the most *epic* story of the so-called Heroic Age of Exploration.

Since then, people have reached the poles, scaled the highest mountains, dived to the bottom of the ocean, and fought the elements in deserts, caves, and other unfriendly PPSG. They even explored closer to home, in abandoned buildings, tunnels, and high rooftops, not to mention the selfie hunters who hang off radio towers for social-media likes. But why? One reason might be hardwired into our brains. First of all, there's dopamine, "often described as the brain's 'pleasure chemical'"; any rewarding experience can trigger the dopamine system, and it seems that "an active dopamine system can make us take more risks".[5] Furthermore, research has discovered that "people with a certain dopamine receptor are more likely to be thrill seeking".[6] So, taking a risk will give you a dopamine hit, which feels nice, which then sends you searching out another dopamine hit. The term "adrenaline junkie" makes more sense now! Naturally, not all dopamine receptors are built the same, and some people seek bigger thrills than most of the population; additionally, research shows that people with "greater brain activity in the striatum, a region involved in dopamine release" may make more risky choices because "the novelty increases dopamine release in this area of the brain, which then possibly enhances the expectation of reward".[7] This suggests that the people who climb the highest mountains, dive the deepest oceans, and go to PPSG are built a bit differently than most of us.

A Spotter's Guide: Don't Forget Your Map

Planet Earth has supplied many suitable environments for Horror settings, with or without supernatural or fantastical additions:

- **Pole to pole:** The North and South Poles are places of extreme temperatures, winds, and isolation, with myriad dangers such as storms, crevasses, frostbite, polar bears (though only at the North Pole), and a distinct lack of fuel or food. After the poles were conquered, novelists started to insert more Supernatural Horror

---

4. Lawrence, 2015, n.p.
5. Voon, 2016, n.p.
6. Voon, 2016, n.p.
7. Voon, 2016, n.p.

elements into their tales. H.P. Lovecraft's <u>Cosmic Horror</u> *At the Mountains of Madness* (1936) follows an Antarctic expedition that comes into contact with the remains of an ancient civilisation built by shoggoths that laboured for the "Elder Things". In John W. Campbell's seminal <u>Body Horror</u> *Who Goes There?* (1938), the crew on an Antarctic research base thaws out an alien's body, which begins to shapeshift and imitate them; it's been filmed several times, the most famous being John Carpenter's 1982 adaptation *The Thing*. More recently, Dan Simmons's 2007 novel *The Terror* combines a polar expedition in the 1840s and its associated horrors (bad food, extreme temperatures, ships trapped in ice) with a monster. It inspired a television adaptation (2018-'19; though only the first season follows material from the novel).

- **Mountain air:** Some people love the challenge of thin air, high altitude, and exposure. All these elements, plus a supernatural creature or two, make for an exciting read. "Found footage" films ramp up the inherent horror; for example, *Devil's Pass* (dir. Renny Harlin, 2013) combines the dangers of climbing with a mysterious bunker and creepy creatures. *The White Road* (2017) by Sarah Lotz features a protagonist who goes spelunking (more on caves below!) before reaching the dizzying heights of Mt Everest and, accompanied by a menacing spirit, investigating the dead bodies of those who've failed at both challenges along the way. *Echo* (2022) by Thomas Olde Heuvelt tells the story of a climber whose accident on the peak of a forbidden mountain has ruined his face to the point where other people go mad just by looking at him.

- **Cue the claustrophobia:** Stories about spelunking in caves don't necessarily need supernatural-horror elements to be horrifying for some people; claustrophobia can do that all by itself, thank you very much! The same goes for acrophobia (fear of heights) when the topic is mountain climbing or chinophobia when we're discussing snowy places. But caves, with their natural lack of light, tight spaces, echoes, and dripping walls can cause even the most even-keeled of us to break out in a sweat. Plus, we don't need fiction to scare us when we have the true story of a man who got stuck upside down while spelunking, died in the tiny crawl space, and was entombed there in 2009![8] 'The Beast in the Cave' by Lovecraft, first published in 1918 but written earlier when he was still a teenager, banks on our horror of the unknown in dark caves (this time Mammoth Cave in Kentucky, the longest cave system in the world that we know of ... so far!). *The Descent* (dir. Neil Marshall, 2005) brings cave exploration into the

---

8. Herbert, 2023, n.p.

present with a group of friends ending up trapped in a cave only to realise that not only are they in a previously unknown and unmapped cave—so have very little chance of being found—but there are murderous humanoid creatures they term "crawlers" in there, too. In *The Anomaly* (2018) by Michael Rutger a crew explores—and gets trapped in—a cave in the Grand Canyon where things aren't exactly normal (do you sense a theme here?). Finally, Horror and SF overlap in *The Luminous Dead* (2019) by Caitlin Starling, set on another planet with tech—such as a protection-suit/wetsuit that can be controlled from the surface—and a cave that, as usual, houses a secret.

- **But it's a dry heat:** Horror set in the desert isn't always related to the environment, as proven by the classic *The Hills Have Eyes* (dir. Wes Craven, 1977), complete with a cannibalistic family preying on anyone who accidentally crashes in the Nevada desert. Josh Malerman's *Black Mad Wheel* (2017) follows a band hired by the military to track down a malevolent sound emanating from the Namib desert in Africa. Here, too, filmmakers have taken advantage of the popularity of "found footage": *Horror in the High Desert* (dir. Dutch Marich, 2021) is a mockumentary about a hiker missing in Nevada's Great Basin Desert whose left-behind footage shows a mysterious cabin and a deformed human-like figure.

- **In too deep:** Aquatic horror often manifests as man vs fish (see **Animals That Attack**), but another thing to consider is how to raise the stakes by messing with your characters' scuba gear (sketchy regulator?), their depth (pressure and the danger of getting the bends when surfacing too quickly), and their support systems (or lack thereof when the boat leaves without them!). In *Open Water* (dir. Chris Kentis, 2003), a diving couple are stranded off the Great Barrier Reef when their boat abandons them; while nothing supernatural happens in the film, it's terrifying because it's based on a true story, with the movie speculating what might have happened. In *Rolling in the Deep* (2015), Mira Grant undermines our Little Mermaid dreams with mermaids that are nothing like Ariel. In *They Came from The Ocean* by Boris Bacic (2022), the author sends his characters to an unforgiving 11,000 feet underwater and, just for fun, adds in something stalking the stranded crew (see **Submarine Stories**).

- **Follow the breadcrumbs:** We all enjoy a hike, don't we? The smell of fresh trees, the clean air and sunshine, a random serial killer or two, and nobody to hear you scream. An early-modern Horror in this vein is Algernon Blackwood's 'The Willows' (1907), written when camping wasn't a regular family holiday so the back woods still held mystery. A malevolent force harasses two men in the European wilderness, and the way the willows seem to move of their own free will deepens the narrator's sense of terror. Nine decades later, *The Blair Witch Project* (dirs. Daniel Myrick and Eduardo Sánchez, 1999)—the most famous "found footage" Horror film—follows a trio of students who venture into the Maryland wilderness to uncover a local legend; they get lost but find a historical killer's home and then go into the basement (*definitely* a place people in Horror films shouldn't go!). Meanwhile, in Adam Neville's *The Ritual* (2011), a group of four friends dealing with their own dramas really should have stayed out of the Scandinavian backwoods, with its pagan sacrifices and violent black-metal band mates. Vaughn C. Hardacker's *Wendigo* (2017) combines the depths of the Maine wilderness with a supernatural spirit straight out of Algonquin legend (see **Cryptozoology**).

Things That are Cool About Places People Shouldn't Go

Thrill-seeking has long inspired writers, providing an opportunity to create characters who'll stop at nothing to push their limits. Dr Kenneth Kamler, an orthopaedic microsurgeon who's practiced medicine in some of the most remote and dangerous places on the planet, puts it plainly: "No animal in its right mind ever intentionally puts itself in danger by going somewhere it doesn't belong. Human beings, on the other hand, are controlled by brains whose emotional and spiritual imperatives can override the survival instinct".[9] Deep in the ocean? We have limited time with oxygen tanks. So why not ramp up the horror by adding a sea creature into the mix! High in the mountains? We have limited time with oxygen tanks (are you sensing a theme here?), so why not add a supernatural twist to make it even worse!

Waiver of Liability

- **What's scary about *that*?:** Not everyone is going to find every situation terrifying. Where one person will recoil at even the notion of spelunking, another will strap on a headlamp and say *let's go*! The challenge for writers is to highlight the dangers inherent in the activity *and* ramp up the horror element for those without claustro- or other phobias. Part of this is about raising the stakes for your character. They're scuba divers? Great. But they're scuba divers who didn't let anyone know where they were going, didn't double check

---

9. Kamler, 2004, n.p.

their tanks (well, that's just dumb), and decided that everything will be just fine if they explore the legendarily haunted shipwreck. So, consider practical ways of making things scary even before you add in any fantastical elements.

- **No trespassing:** From urban exploration that delves into abandoned and condemned buildings, rooftops, elevator shafts, and maintenance tunnels, to **Mysterious Islands** and other cultures' sacred places, if there's a *Do Not Enter* sign there's always someone ready to feed the dopamine centres of their brain and cross that threshold, sometimes to their doom. These kinds of spaces are an opportunity for you to go beyond mountain climbers, spelunkers, and deep-sea divers, and to push your characters into new PPSG to see what happens.

ACTIVITIES

Treasure under your nose: You're walking home one day when you notice that the art-deco-era apartment building that's been on the corner forever has been condemned. It's boarded up, fenced in, and covered in *Do Not Enter* signs. But … when you were a kid, you heard that the miserly old man who owned the mostly empty building was rumoured to have a deep mistrust of banks. The grown-ups around you would sometimes talk about how he stashed money in weird nooks and crannies in his building. And now is your last chance to see if that's true. How will you gear up for some urban exploration? What dangers might you face? What risks are you willing to take? And who will you take with you as back up?

Following in their footsteps: Choose an explorer and their most famous exploration and/or discovery. Do a bit of research to find out the benefits of the trip (what they gained or found) and the drawbacks (what or who they lost, and what negative effect they had on the people they encountered). Write a scene from the point of view of the people who live in the place your explorer reached, taking into consideration the customs and even folklore of the place. For inspiration, check out 'Jibaro' (dir. Alberto Mielgo, 2022), an episode of *Love, Death & Robots*, about a Spanish conquistador's encounter with a siren.

LAST PERSON LEFT ALIVE

There is something horrifying about being alone. Not alone as in your other half is out grocery shopping. Not even alone in the way that introverts crave. No, we're talking about being utterly, terrifyingly, *completely* alone: the only human on an entire planet with no possibility of ever seeing another person again. Or at least thinking that you are, because, in a lot of these stories, something even worse occurs: you're stuck with the last people you'd ever want to be alone with.

A Short History of Last Person Left Alive Stories

Deeply rooted in a cultural memory of how becoming separated from our tribe meant certain death, stories of the last person left alive (LPLA) became distinguishable as a subgenre during the nineteenth century with the emergence of "lastness" as a poetic theme. The notion of "The Last Person" (though in practice it was usually a White man) tickled the Victorian imagination from the 1820s through the 1840s. Some critics see these Apocalyptic works as—all together now—juxtaposing "the perceived menace of a wayward history and incalculable universe with the idea of the solitude and abjectness" of the human.[1] The theme was taken up by now largely forgotten poets such as Thomas Campbell and Thomas Hood, but the most prominent example is surely Mary Shelley's 1826 novel *The Last Man*. Set in the late twenty-first century, it follows the survivors of a virulent plague (and so is an early example of how LPLA stories exist at the confluence of **Pandemic Fiction** and apocalypse narratives). As Shelley's band of survivors make their way across England and continental Europe, they're eventually whittled down to just the titular last man, who decides to wander the depopulated Earth alone. A tragic work of isolation, it thus set the tone for much of what followed.

After fading for several decades, LPLA stories became prominent again, arguably more so, in the mid-twentieth century as humanity developed the technology to—and the understanding that we could—all but end the human race (think of this as applied lastness). An early example is found in Eric Frank Russell's 'Mana' (1937), an **Uplifted Animals** tale in which Earth's last human gives sentience to ants. The concept was to prove more popular on television and film screens though, especially in the 1950s during which it resonated with the cultural unease of the Atomic Age. *Five* (dir. Arch Oboler, 1951) follows a pregnant woman in the aftermath of a nuclear war

---

1. Pordzik, 2011, p. 406.

that seems to have wiped out humanity. She eventually finds four other survivors (all male), among them a White man who attempts to sexually assault her, a racist, and the African-American man whom he murders. The film is a nihilistic psychological drama filmed without much regard for Hollywood's visual conventions, but it captures the interplay of Cold War paranoia, atomic anxiety, gender politics, and racial strife in post-war America (as will, a few years later, the love triangle in the Harry Belafonte vehicle *The World, The Flesh, and The Devil*; dir. Ranald MacDougall, 1959). A defining work of the subgenre, however, arrives in 1954 with Richard Matherson's novel *I Am Legend* (another significant example of pandemic fiction), which follows the seeming sole survivor of a plague that turned the world's population into Vampires. Another famous example that still carries cachet today is *The Twilight Zone* episode 'Time Enough at Last' (dir. John Brahm, 1959), adapted by Rod Serling from a 1953 short story by Lynn Venable. The episode takes the form of a cruel joke in which a bank clerk mocked by his family and co-workers for his love of books finds himself the sole survivor of a nuclear war. Now with nothing to stop him reading, he journeys to the library only to stumble and drop his glasses, which shatter, leaving him surrounded by books he can no longer read.

The following decades brought many variations on the subgenre's existing themes and, indeed, on their key texts, with several adaptations of *I am Legend* making it to the big screen (often under different titles). *The Last Man on Earth* (dir. Ubaldo Ragona and Sidney Salkow, 1964) offers a harsh take on Matherson's original, but it's *The Omega Man* (dir. Boris Sagal, 1971) that has stood the test of time (more so than the third adaptation in 2007). Even today its scenes of a deserted—at least in daytime—Los Angeles have the power to unnerve. Elsewhere, *The Quiet Earth* (dir. Geoff Murphy, 1985), loosely based on Craig Harrison's novel of the same name (1981), follows the survivor of a scientific experiment that caused humanity to vanish. The film eventually reveals other survivors, and with them another love triangle, and is today regarded as a cult classic (it's a favourite of astrophysicist Neil deGrasse Tyson). Weightier is *Children of Men* (1992) by P.D. James, which considers demographic collapse on a societal level, and so is less LPLA and more The Last Generation of Humanity (Alfonso Cuarón's excellent 2006 film adaptation, which James has expressed her appreciation for, makes many changes to the source material,). In the novel, a fascist government has taken over an England defined by mass apathy in the face of sudden-onset global infertility. It anticipates Brexit Britain with restrictions on foreign travel for young people and with overseas workers lured into the country, exploited to do undesirable labour, and then forcibly repatriated, and this alongside how older people are deemed to be a burden on the state. The result is a philosophical, at times even theological, perspective on the notion of lastness.

Indeed, lastness has returned as a theme in the early twenty-first century as humanity faces environmental ruination and accompanying socio-political strife and collapse (all of which were stressed in Cuarón's James adaptation). The underrated *Oblivion* (dir. Joseph Kosinski, 2013) initially depicts what seems to be the last two people on Earth after aliens have ruined the planet (though the truth is somewhat more complicated). Gary Gibson's Apocalypse Trilogy—*Extinction Game* (2014), *Survival Game* (2016), and *Doomsday Game* (2019) —brings an interesting and enjoyable new spin to the LPLA subgenre for the **Multiverse** generation, following a crack team comprising the only survivors of desolate parallel Earths. Each character has already survived a violent apocalypse and is now tasked by a shadowy organisation with retrieving weapons from lifeless alternate worlds. *Z for Zachariah* (dir. Craig Zobel, 2015, loosely based on the 1974 book by Robert C. O'Brien) reheats the racially charged love-triangle trope of *The World, The Flesh, and The Devil* once again, this time with Margot Robbie, Chiwetel Ejiofor, and Chris Pine in the roles of apocalypse survivors. Sharing a name (but nothing else) with the 1964 film, the television series *The Last Man on Earth* (2015–'18) brings an unexpected—and unexpectedly watchable—comedic approach to lastness. But more thoughtful is *Good Morning, Midnight* (2016) by Lily Brooks-Dalton (later adapted into the 2020 film *The Midnight Sky* by George Clooney), which follows an elderly researcher in the Artic who may or may not be—drumroll—the last person left alive....

A Spotter's Guide: Is There Anybody Out There?

- **The last person left alive… is not alone:** In some respects, the scariest thing of all is to think you're alone but you're not. It can be deeply unsettling when you're in the house by yourself, but now imagine you're the LPLA! Who or what is out there? This can be an existentially destabilising experience for our characters, their new normal collapsing almost as soon as it's established. The late, great, and much-missed critic Mark Fisher theorised that this sensation of eeriness is "constituted by a *failure of absence* or by a *failure of presence*"; it occurs when "there is something present where there should be nothing, or is there is nothing present when there should be something".[2] In many cases, of course, the discovery of other survivors (though generally only a small number) by the LPLA is born of both the narrative necessity that almost nobody can survive by themselves and by the creative need to have someone for your protagonist to interact with (thus television's *The Last Man on Earth* introduces, as part of the joke, a whole cast of misfit survivors).

---

2. Fisher, 2016, p. 61 (his emphasis).

- **Flashbacks:** Many stories circumvent the need for interaction by integrating flashbacks into either the protagonist's life in the before times or their experiences during whatever event wiped out humanity (either case provides considerable scope here for you to flex your Horror muscles; *I Am Legend* does this to great effect). Flashbacks are this subgenre's means of fulfilling its promise to the reader while also ensuring there's some varied characterisation, dialogue, and the other expected accoutrements of fiction. More than that, it's an opportunity to reflect on what's been lost and, therefore, a chance to meditate on lastness as a limit to human life and existence. Heavy stuff: better take a break to pick through the ruins of a shopping mall!
- **A journey:** Another structural staple of LPLA stories is our protagonist travelling to a promised haven or rallying point (sometimes pre-arranged with family or friends). On many occasions they're driven by hope, following messages that suggest the presence of other survivors (such as the "Alive in Tucson" graffiti from television's *The Last Man on Earth*). Other times they may be motivated by desperation or by faith in finding somewhere better (this is pretty much the entirety of Cormac McCarthy's *The Road*, 2006). Journeys enable a vivid cross-section of how the world has been transformed. It allows for a variety of settings and threats that, in turn, ensure humanity's twilight doesn't become monotonous for readers.
- **Utilities:** While it'll take time for highway bridges to decay (especially without traffic), a lot of infrastructure will quickly cease to function without human oversight and intervention. Our LPLA will, for example, likely find themselves in a world without reliable electricity. And, with no electricity, there will be no pumps to supply clean water or, for that matter, to keep water pumped out of subway tunnels. Dams may become unstable without someone to monitor their water levels, threating huge floods. Our protagonist(s) may have to resort to travelling on foot, bicycle, or via horse-and-cart as automotive fuels spoil. They may also be faced with danger from nuclear power plants, such as in Douglas Coupland's *Girlfriend in a Coma* (1998) when reactors go into meltdown after all but seven people in the world fall asleep and fail to reawaken. Of course, modern plants have safety systems that should automatically cool the reactors in case of emergency, but where's the drama in that…?
- **Emotional arcs:** Being the LPLA (or even thinking that you are for prolonged stretches) generally takes a significant toll on our characters (and here we intersect with Psychological Horror). Euphoria at surviving—or, indeed, at finally being alone—will

often fade quickly into desperation, despair, and in many cases even substance abuse or self-harm as characters discover that solitude and loneliness are two very different things. Examples include one of the characters in *The Word, The Flesh, and The Devil* taking up with a pair of shop mannequins for company, or the protagonist of *The Quiet Earth* going mad, declaring himself—to an audience of cardboard cutouts—to be President of Earth, and eventually trying to kill himself. It can get pretty bleak, but characters typically manage to move through these psychic breaks (often upon the discovery of other survivors) and emerge with a renewed sense of purpose.

Things That are Cool About Last Person Left Alive Stories

In its purest form, lastness asks our characters—and our readers—to consider not just what it is like to be alone, but what have their—and our—civilisation accomplished? Why does any of it matter? What was it all for? Does being The LPLA come with responsibilities and, if so, to what? The past? The future? The universe? Such stories ask big questions and, consequently, this can be a melancholic subgenre that lends itself to poetic and reflective prose. On top of which, and on a more technical level, it's a useful way for novice writers to hone the skill of writing about a character by themselves.

Hello Darkness, My Old Friend

- **Not all it's cracked up to be:** Some of us might actually fantasise about being the last survivor(s) of a global disaster, but things are unlikely to be easy for our characters. Most modern individuals have, for example, little to no training in growing vegetables or in animal husbandry, let alone access to seeds or livestock. And canned foods will eventually run out. Perhaps that gives our characters long enough to find tools, learn some general skills, or gain some experience hunting (or baking or sewing), but a society of one person—or even a handful of people—doesn't have a lot of resilience. So-called "cosy catastrophe" stories downplay these hardships in favour of well-appointed sitting rooms in country cottages, but a more realistic take is likely to be tough on our protagonists.
- **Injury and illness:** Maybe your survivor is a nurse or doctor, or maybe they've had some basic training as part of their pre-disaster life, but otherwise even minor injuries will present significant problems. One of the biggest threats is infection; it's not a major issue with modern antibiotics but could readily end humanity in a story like this. So, when your characters are scavenging for food, they probably also want to pick up some medical supplies (or even a

first-aid guide or basic medical textbook). In situations where several people have survived, contraceptives and prophylactics may also need to go in the shopping trolly (though these have shelf lives!). Be aware, too, of how pre-existing medical conditions might impact the story. Treatment for illnesses such as diabetes, or other conditions that require sophisticated care or medication (such as cancer or multiple sclerosis), will be significantly affected, if not outright curtailed, by the lack of healthcare professionals and pharmaceutical supply chains. There would also be considerable challenges for anyone who uses a wheelchair or other mobility aids. Though that's no reason to avoid following such characters at the end of the world.

- **The world without us:** Humanity vanishing or dying off *en masse* is likely to lead to huge environmental repercussions. Without humanity, nature will very quickly reassert itself (see **Climate Fiction**). This is the basis of Alan Weisman's non-fiction book *The World Without Us* (2007), a thought experiment that examines how nature would rush in to fill the gap if humanity is gone. Though this won't be a silent world. Quiet, perhaps, but there will still be the noise of the wind and rain. There will, in many cases, still be the sound of animals. Thus, writing about such a lonely world will benefit from strong use of sensory language to describe this transformed environment.
- **Causes of the end of the world:** Be sure to give some thought to your backstory. *Why* exactly is your character so alone? What happened in the world? Was your protagonist involved or were they merely a bystander? You may want to consider relevant apocalypse scenarios (such as plagues, wars, scientific experiments run amuck, etc.). That said, it's of course totally legitimate to keep what occurred a mystery… at least from your character and reader, but having a sense of what happened will be beneficial to *you* as a writer in terms of worldbuilding.
- **Last person left alive… in space:** Some stories follow protagonists who are the only (or the last) human beings on a barren planet, or even aboard a spacecraft so distant in space and time that they might as well be the LPLA at the end of the universe. A classic example is Dave Lister in SF sitcom *Red Dwarf* (1988–2020), who wakes from cryosleep after three million years to find he's the last human in existence. See, too, the marooned **Astronaut** of Andy Weir's 2011 novel *The Martian*, all alone on the Red Planet. The closest thing to real-life examples that we have are probably the Command Module Pilots on the Apollo lunar missions (such as Michael Collins on Apollo 11) who, while orbiting alone around the far side of the Moon as their crewmates descended to the surface, were probably the most isolated human beings in all of history (so far!).

ACTIVITIES

Action plan: Imagine you wake up and you appear to be the only person left on Earth. What would you do? Where would you go? Do you have enough food for now and, if not, where will you find more (and how will you cook it)? Will you—*gasp!*—start re-using your teabags? And what about medicine? If you're in the city, will you head to the country, or vice versa? Perhaps you'll decamp to the nearest zoo to care for the animals? Or the local library to read to your heart's content? Or maybe you decide to stay where you are? Consider the practicalities of your choice. Once you've made your plan, use it as the basis of a story. Remember to convey how all this makes you or your character *feel*. Are you scared? Excited? Depressed?

Final testament: You are the LPLA on Earth. But you're injured. You know you don't have long left to live. Despite the fact that no one will read it, you feel compelled to write a final testament (hey, maybe Aliens will find it someday!). What does this say? Do you talk about your life and the people you loved? Do you discuss your accomplishments, or even what you think were humanity's greatest achievements? Will you express gratitude for your life or disappointment that it's ending all alone? What message do you want to leave for the universe?

CONCLUDING THOUGHTS

Finally, we would like you to remember that there's never just one way of doing things.

That probably seems like a weird thing to say that the end of a writing guide, but it's true. It obviously helps to *know* the rules and to be familiar with the histories of the fields in which we're writing—we certainly hope you've found yourself introduced to a range of both—but remember that these are just guidelines. These are just the way people have done things before. Nothing in them, nothing in *writing*, is an absolute. Show us any so-called "rule", even the fundamentals of punctuation or grammar, and we'll show someone throwing it out the airlock with gleeful abandon!

Is all this rule-breaking work amazing? Of course not! Some of it's awful!

But the same is true—arguably more so—of work that follows the rules.

Because rules, in many ways, are about maintaining the *status quo*. They're not neutral declarations. They're not apolitical absolutes. At best they're useful way-markers, at worst they're ideological stances on what is and isn't "good" literature, ones codified decades ago by dusty old writing teachers (generally straight White men in the United States and Britain). Many of these absolutes continue to be propagated today by academics and journalists who've invested whole careers in keeping things exactly as they are, straining like Thor (they'll love that!) to hold the stellar forge of Nidavellir in position.

But writing isn't about stasis.

Writing is a living thing.

Writing is about *change*.

So, if you want to write a whole story in emojis, go for it. If you want to mash subgenres together and create something new, please do. If you think to yourself, "Tiffani and Val only listed five approaches to this topic and my idea doesn't fit them", well we're here to tell you that the boxes we've sketched out aren't anything you have to fit inside. Remember that Science Fiction, Fantasy, and Horror are like the universe they reflect; they're always expanding. There is space for you!

Just think: if there were *actually* absolutes then nothing new would ever get written. And your goal is to write something new, something that's all you, something that makes editors and readers sit up and take notice.

That's the only rule worth a damn:

Make us go "*Wow!*".

SUBGENRES AND TROPES FROM VOLUME 1

CHAPTER ONE – SCIENCE FICTION
SPACESHIPS
ALIENS
BIG DUMB OBJECTS
ROBOTS, ANDROIDS,
AND ARTIFICIAL INTELLIGENCE
MILITARY SF
UTOPIA
DYSTOPIA
APOCALYPTIC FICTION
CYBERPUNK
SOLARPUNK

CHAPTER TWO – FANTASY
FOLKTALES AND FAIRY TALES
WITCHES
HIGH FANTASY
SWORD AND SORCERY
GRIMDARK
HISTORICAL FANTASY
STEAMPUNK
URBAN FANTASY
PARANORMAL ROMANCE
TIME TRAVEL

CHAPTER THREE – HORROR
GOTHIC HORROR
SUPERNATURAL HORROR
VAMPIRES
PSYCHOLOGICAL HORROR
BODY HORROR
ZOMBIES
SUBURBAN HORROR
TECHNO HORROR
SPLATTERPUNK
COSMIC HORROR

REFERENCES

@jakecasella, (2023) Twitter. Available at: https://twitter.com/jakecasella/status/1658444872112586758 (Accessed 16 May 2023).

@LibyaLiberty (2020) Twitter. Available at: https://twitter.com/LibyaLiberty/status/1312302469951545347 (Accessed 16 January 2023).

@raynayler (2023) Twitter. Available at: https://twitter.com/raynayler/status/1637625852799119360 (Accessed 20 March 2023).

Aalders, M. (2007) '"There is a Riddle Here": Uplift Fiction and the Question of the Animal', Utrecht University. Available at: https://studenttheses.uu.nl/handle/20.500.12932/26651 (Accessed 12 December 2023).

Abdullah, A.S. (2017) 'Fluids, Cages, and Boisterous Femininity: The Grotesque Transgression of Patriarchal Norms in Angela Carter's *Nights at the Circus*', *Journal of Language and Cultural Education*, 5:2, pp. 114–122.

Ahuja, N. (2009) 'Postcolonial Critique in a Multispecies World', *PMLA* Vol. 124, No. 2 (March), pp. 556–563.

Anderson, H. (2022) 'The Surprising Ancient Roots of *The Lord of the Rings*'. Available at: https://www.bbc.com/culture/article/20220824-the-ancient-roots-of-the-lord-of-the-rings (Accessed 31 January 2024).

Anonymous. (2000) '*Wild Life* by Molly Goss', *Kirkus Reviews*. Available at: https://www.kirkusreviews.com/book-reviews/molly-gloss/wild-life-2/ (Accessed 26 October 2023).

Anonymous. (2008) 'Jan. 23, 1960: Journey to the Deepest Place on Earth', *Wired*. Available at: https://www.wired.com/2008/01/dayintech-0123-2/ (Accessed 1 February 2024).

Ashley, M. (1997) 'Faerie'. in Clute, J. and Grant, J. (eds.), *The Encyclopedia of Science Fiction*. Available at: https://sf-encyclopedia.com/entry/faerie (Accessed 24 January 2024).

Atkins, A. (2017) 'What is the Origin of "Clothes Make the Man"?', *Medium*. Available at: https://alex-65670.medium.com/what-is-the-origin-of-clothes-make-the-man-7f75e070bf45 (Accessed 14 November 2023).

Ayers, Rachel. (2023) 'Competence Porn Is Comforting—Where Can I Find More of It?'. Available at: https://www.tor.com/2023/07/24/competence-porn-is-comforting-where-can-i-find-more-of-it/ (Accessed 30 July 2023).

Bachmann, S. (2012) *The Peculiar*. London: Harper Collins, Chapter 15.

Bakhtin, M. (1984) *Rabelais and His World*. Bloomington: Indiana University Press.

Baron, D. (No date) 'A Brief History of Singular "They"', *OED: Oxford English Dictionary* online. Available at: https://www.oed.com/discover/a-brief-history-of-singular-they (Accessed 7 December 2023).

BBC News. (2020) 'Cottingley Fairies: How Sherlock Holmes's creator was fooled by hoax'. Available at: https://www.bbc.com/news/uk-england-leeds-55187973 (Accessed 16 January 2024).

Beard, D. (2011) 'Eco-Horror, Defined', *Society for Cinema and Media Studies*. Available at: https://www.cmstudies.org/forums/Posts.aspx?topic=239245 (Accessed 15 October 2023).

Beaugrand, H. (1898) 'The Werewolves' [last updated: 11 January 2000] Available at: http://gaslight-lit.s3-website.ca-central-1.amazonaws.com/gaslight/werwolvs.htm (Accessed 19 January 2024).

Bekhrad, J. (2017) 'The Ancient Symbol that Spanned Millennia', *BBC Culture*. Available at: https://www.bbc.com/culture/article/20171204-the-ancient-symbol-that-spanned-millennia (Accessed 2 February 2024).

Bellamy, B.R. (2018) 'Introduction', *Science Fiction Studies*, 45:3 (November). pp. 417–419.

Blumtritt, J. (2017) 'Biopunk: Subverting Biopolitics, Part I: Sci-Fi Punk', *The New Inquiry*. Available at: https://thenewinquiry.com/biopunk-subverting-biopolitics/ (Accessed 9 January 2024).

Borges, J.L. (1964) 'The Garden of Forking Paths' in Yates, D. and Irby, J.E. (eds.), Yates, D. (trans.), *Labyrinths: Selected Stories and Other Writings*. New York: New Directions, pp. 19–29.

Bould, M. (2021) *The Anthropocene Unconscious: Climate Catastrophe Culture*. London: Verso.

Bould, M., Roberts, A. and Vint, S. (2009) 'Introduction'. in Bould, M., Roberts, A. and Vint, S. (eds.), *The Routledge Companion to Science Fiction*, New York: Routledge. pp. xix–xxii.

Bovet, R. (1684) *Pandaemonium, or, The Devil's Cloyster: Being a Further Blow to Modern Sadduceism, Proving the Existence of Witches and Spirits*. London: Printed for J. Walthoe. Available at: https://books.google.co.uk/books?id=Am5jAAAAcAAJ&vq (Accessed 19 Dec 2023).

Bozzetto, R. (1993) 'Moreau's Tragi-Farcical Island', *Science Fiction Studies*, 20: 1 (March), p. 34.

Brackett, L. (1977) 'Introduction', *The Best of Edmond Hamilton*. New York: Doubleday.

Braun, B. (2007) 'Biopolitics and the Molecularization of Life', *Cultural Geographies*, 14:1 (January). pp. 6–28.

Buell, L. (1995) *The Environmental Imagination*. Cambridge: Harvard University Press.

Burt, S. (2022) 'Is the Multiverse Where Originality Goes to Die?', *The New Yorker*. Available at https://www.newyorker.com/magazine/2022/11/07/is-the-multiverse-where-originality-goes-to-die (Accessed 4 May 2023).

Carlson, R. (2005) 'Splice it Yourself: Who Needs a Geneticist? Build Your Own DNA lab', *Wired*. Available at: https://www.wired.com/2005/05/splice-it-yourself (Accessed 6 February 2024).

Caroti, S. (2015) *Implausible, Baroque, and Surreal: The Culture Series of Iain M. Banks—A Critical Introduction*. Jefferson, NC: McFarland.

Castrodale, J. (2020) 'A "Cursed Objects" Expert Explains How Our Possessions Can Ruin Our Lives'. Available at: https://www.vice.com/en/article/k7aake/a-cursed-objects-expert-explains-how-our-possessions-can-ruin-our-lives (Accessed 29 December 2023).

Cavendish, M. (1668) *The Description of a New World, Called the Blazing-World*. London: Printed by A. Maxwell. Available at: https://digital.library.upenn.edu/women/newcastle/blazing/blazing.html (Accessed 24 January 2024).

Chunovic, L. (1994) *SeaQuest DSV: The Official Publication of the Series*. London: Boxtree.

Clarke, R. (2012) *Natural History of Ghosts: 500 Years of Hunting for Proof*. London: Penguin. [accessed via Kindle]

Cohen, Ma. (2022) *The Underwater Eye*. Princeton: Princeton University Press.

Cowlishaw, G. (1988) 'Australian Aboriginal Studies: The Anthropologists' Account'. Available at: https://core.ac.uk/download/pdf/229433308.pdf (Accessed 31 January 2024).

Craps, S. (2023) 'Ecological Mourning: Living with Loss in the Anthropocene'. in Kaplan, B.A. (ed.), *Critical Memory Studies: New Approaches*. London: Bloomsbury, pp. 69–78.

Crawford, A. (2016) 'High-Rise', *Australian Review of Books*. Available at: https://www.australianbookreview.com.au/arts-update/101-arts-update/3522-high-rise (Accessed 30 November 2023).

Csicsery-Ronay, Jr., I. (2008) *The Seven Beauties of Science Fiction*. Middletown, CT: Wesleyan University Press.

Cunsolo, A. and Ellis, N.R. (2018) 'Ecological Grief as a Mental Health Response to Climate Change-Related Loss', *Nature Climate Change*, No. 8, pp. 275–81.

DC Extended Universe Wiki (No date) 'Amazons'. Available at: https://dcextendeduniverse.fandom.com/wiki/Amazons (Accessed 5 February 2024).

Deis, R. (ed.) (2013) 'The "Killer Creature" Animal Attack Covers of MAN'S LIFE Magazine…', *Menspulpmags.com: The Men's Adventure Magazines & Books Blog*. Available at: https://www.menspulpmags.com/the-killer-creature-animal-attack-covers-of-mans-life-magazine/ (Accessed 20 August 2023).

de León, D.M. (2023) 'All at Once, the Multiverse Is Everywhere', *Yale Review*. Available at: https://yalereview.org/article/de-leon-everything-everywhere (Accessed 1 June 2023).

Denisoff, D. (2018) 'Introduction'. in Denisoff, D. (ed.), *Decadent and Occult Works by Arthur Machen*. Cambridge: The Modern Humanities Research Association. pp. 1–34

Dickey, C. (2022) 'Eight Ghost Stories in Which the Dead Won't Go Quietly', *The Atlantic*. Available at: https://www.theatlantic.com/books/archive/2022/01/ghost-stories-the-sentence-louise-erdrich/621146/ (Accessed 10 July 2023).

Di Filippo, P. (1996) *Ribofunk: The Manifesto*. Available at: https://www.streettech.com/bcp/BCPtext/Manifestos/Ribofunk.html (Accessed 10 January 2023).

Dillon, S. (2018) 'The Horror of the Anthropocene', *C21 Literature: Journal of 21st-Century Writings*, 6:1. pp. 1–25.

Dimock, W.C. (2017) '5,000 Years of Climate Fiction', *Publicbooks.org*. Available at: https://www.publicbooks.org/5000-years-of-climate-fiction/ (Accessed 19 January 2023).

Diniejko, A. (2016) 'Introduction to Victorian Spiritualism', *The Victorian Web*. Available at: https://victorianweb.org/victorian/religion/spirit.html (Accessed 14 February 2023).

Doherty, J. and Giordano, J. (2020) 'What We May Learn—and Need—from Pandemic Fiction', *Philosophy, Ethics, and Humanities in Medicine*, 15:4. Available at: https://doi.org/10.1186/s13010-020-00089-0 (Accessed 12 January 2023).

Dyson, F. (2007) 'Our Biotech Future', *New York Review*. Available at: https://www.nybooks.com/articles/2007/07/19/our-biotech-future/ (Accessed 6 February 2024).

Editors of *Britannica Kids*, The. (No date) 'Andvari', *Encyclopaedia Britannica Kids*. Available at: https://kids.britannica.com/students/article/Andvari/309845 (Accessed 15 November 2023).

Editors of *Britannica Kids*, The. (No date) 'Fortunatus', *Encyclopaedia Britannica Kids*. Available at: https://kids.britannica.com/students/article/Fortunatus/323592 (Accessed 15 November 2023).

Editors of *Encyclopaedia Britannica*, The. (2023) 'Asgard', *Encyclopaedia Britannica*. Available at: https://www.britannica.com/topic/Asgard (Accessed 24 January 2024).

Editors of *Encyclopaedia Britannica*, The. (2024) 'Cornelis Drebbel', *Encyclopaedia Britannica*. Available at: https://www.britannica.com/biography/Cornelis-Jacobszoon-Drebbel (Accessed 1 February 2024).

Editors of *Encyclopaedia Britannica*, The. (2024) 'David Bushnell', *Encyclopaedia Britannica*. Available at: https://www.britannica.com/biography/David-Bushnell (Accessed 1 February 2024).

Editors of *Encyclopaedia Britannica*, The. (2022) 'Freyja', *Encyclopaedia Britannica*. Available at: https://www.britannica.com/topic/Freyja (Accessed 15 November 2023).

Editors of *Encyclopaedia Britannica*, The. (2023) 'Hermann Ebbinghaus', *Encyclopaedia Britannica*. Available at: https://www.britannica.com/biography/Hermann-Ebbinghaus (Accessed 14 August 2023).

Editors of *Encyclopaedia Britannica*, The. (2023) 'Perseus', *Encyclopaedia Britannica*. Available at: https://www.britannica.com/topic/Perseus-Greek-mythology (Accessed 15 November 2023).

Editors of *Encyclopaedia Britannica*, The. (2023) 'Quetzalcóatl', *Encyclopaedia Britannica*. Available at: https://www.britannica.com/topic/Quetzalcoatl (Accessed 2 February 2024).

Editors of *Encyclopaedia Britannica*, The. (2023) 'Sir C. Wyville Thomson', *Encyclopaedia Britannica*. Available at: https://www.britannica.com/biography/C-Wyville-Thomson (Accessed 21 January 2024).

Editors of *Encyclopaedia Britannica*, The. (2009) 'sumptuary law', *Encyclopaedia Britannica*. Available at: https://www.britannica.com/topic/sumptuary-law (Accessed 29 October 2023).

Editors of *Encyclopaedia Britannica*, The. (2023) 'The Thousand and One Nights', *Encyclopaedia Britannica*. Available at: https://www.britannica.com/topic/The-Thousand-and-One-Nights (Accessed 31 January 2024).

Editors of *Encyclopaedia Britannica*, The. (2015) 'Triton', *Encyclopaedia Britannica*. Available at: https://www.britannica.com/topic/Triton-submarine (Accessed 1 February 2024).

Editors of *Encyclopaedia Iranica*, The. (1988) 'Babr-e Bayān', *Encyclopaedia Iranica*. Available at: https://www.iranicaonline.org/articles/babr-e-bayan-or-babr (Accessed 15 November 2023).

Elizabethan Sumptuary Statutes. (1574). Available at: https://www.elizabethan.org/sumptuary/who-wears-what.html 14 July 2001 (Accessed 29 October 2023).

Emley, B. (2017) 'How the Diving Bell Opened the Ocean's Depths', *The Atlantic*. Available at: https://www.theatlantic.com/technology/archive/2017/03/diving-bell/520536/ (Accessed 1 February 2024).

Encyclopedia of Religion. (2024) 'Annwn', *Encyclopedia.com*. Available at: https://www.encyclopedia.com/environment/encyclopedias-almanacs-transcripts-and-maps/annwn (Accessed 24 January 2024).

Evans, S. (2019) 'The Mythical Island of Hy Brasil and the Book of O'Lees', *Royal Irish Academy*. Available at: https://www.ria.ie/news/library-library-blog/mythical-island-hy-brasil-and-book-olees (Accessed 9 September 2023).

Fan, J. (2018) 'Ling Ma's "Severance" Captures the Bleak, Fatalistic Mood of 2018', *New Yorker*. Available at: https://www.newyorker.com/books/under-review/ling-ma-severance-captures-the-bleak-fatalistic-mood-of-2018 (Accessed 16 January 2023).

Fashion Institute of Technology (2016) 'Fairy Tale Fashion'. Available at: https://exhibitions.fitnyc.edu/fairy-tale-fashion/ (Accessed 14 November 2023).

Ferrarese, M. (2021) '"New Kinds of Monsters": The Rise of Southeast Asian Horror Films', *Aljazeera*. Available at: https://www.aljazeera.com/news/2021/6/2/zombie-films-breathe-new-life-into-malaysian-and-indonesia-horror (Accessed 1 August 2023).

Ficher, M. (2016) *The Weird and the Eerie*. London: Repeater Books.

Forgotten Realms Wiki. 'Magic Clothing'. Available at: https://forgottenrealms.fandom.com/wiki/Category:Magic_clothing (Accessed 15 Nov 2023).

Francke, L. (1994) *Script Girls: Women Screenwriters in Hollywood*. London: British Film Institute.

French, A. (2015) *Children of Wrath: Possession, Prophesy and the Young in Early Modern England*. Surrey: Ashgate.

Freund, A. (2020) 'Doggerland: How Did the North Sea's Atlantis Sink?', *DW News*. Available at: https://www.dw.com/en/doggerland-how-did-the-atlantis-of-the-north-sea-sink/a-55960379 (Accessed 2 February 2024).

Friedman, T.L. (2007) 'The People We Have Been Waiting For', *New York Times*. Available at: https://www.nytimes.com/2007/12/02/opinion/02friedman.html (Accessed 20 January 2024).

Genge, N.E. (1996) *The Unofficial X-Files Companion*. 1996. London: Macmillan.

Gerlach, N. (2011) 'Ethan of Athos', *SF Site*. Reviews. Available at: https://www.sfsite.com/01a/ea335.htm (Accessed 7 December 2023).

Ghosn, R. and Jazairy, E.H. (2018) 'Design Earth: Of Oil and Ice', *Science Fiction Studies*, 45:3 (November). pp. 433–439.

Gladstone, M. (2013) 'The Great Fantasy Novel Nomination: *A Wizard of Earthsea* by Ursula K. Le Guin', The Ranting Dragon. Available at: https://www.rantingdragon.com/gfn-nomination-a-wizard-of-earthsea-by-ursula-k-leguin/ (Accessed 16 January 2024).

Glassman, J. (2023) 'Instead of Arguing About This Horror Genre, Why Not Curl Up and Enjoy It?' Available at: https://www.themarysue.com/instead-of-arguing-about-this-horror-genre-why-not-curl-up-and-enjoy-it/ (Accessed 1 September 2023).

Greene, B. (2011) *In the Hidden Reality: Parallel Universes and the Deep Laws of the Cosmos*. New York: Knopf.

Harkaway, N. (2015) 'Terry Pratchett: Above All, He Was Funny', *The Guardian*. Available at: https://www.theguardian.com/books/2015/mar/20/terry-pratchett-funny-fantasy-nick-harkaway (Accessed 27 January 2024).

Harris-Fain, Darren. (2015) 'Dangerous Visions: New Wave and Post–New Wave Science Fiction'. in Link, E.C. and Canavan, G. (eds.), *The Cambridge Companion to American Science Fiction*. Cambridge: Cambridge University Press. pp. 31–43.

Hauskeller, M. (2016) *Mythologies of Transhumanism*. London: Palgrave Macmillan.

Healey, E. (2018) 'How Well Do You Know Your Irish Fairies?', *Keneth Spencer Research Library*. Available at: https://blogs.lib.ku.edu/spencer/how-well-do-you-know-your-irish-fairies/ (Accessed 18 January 2024).

Heller, S. (2014) 'Bat Boy, Hillary Clinton's Alien Baby, and a Tabloid's Glorious Legacy', *The Atlantic*. Available at: https://www.theatlantic.com/entertainment/archive/2014/10/the-ingenious-sensationalism-of-the-weekly-world-new/381525/ (Accessed 19 June 2023).

Hendrix, G. (2017) *Paperbacks from Hell: The Twisted History of '70s and '80s Horror Fiction*. Philadelphia: Quirk Books.

Herbert, C. (2023) 'Man Suffered "Worst Death Imaginable" After Being Left Upside Down in Cave'. Available at: https://www.joe.co.uk/lifestyle/man-suffered-worst-death-imaginable-after-being-left-upside-down-in-cave-405617 (Accessed 5 January 2024).

Heuvelmans, B. (1968) *In the Wake of Sea-Serpents*. New York: Hill and Wang.

Hollingham, R. (2022) 'The Record-breaking Dive Under the Arctic Ice', *BBC Futures*. Available at: https://www.bbc.com/future/article/20220503-the-record-breaking-dive-under-the-arctic-ice (Accessed 1 February 2024).

Holmes, J. (2013) 'Odds Against Tomorrow Review: The Future is Upon Us', *Rolling Stone*. Available at: https://www.rollingstone.com/culture/culture-news/odds-against-tomorrow-review-the-future-is-upon-us-172235/ (Accessed 23 May 2023).

Industrial Light & Magic. (No date) '*Valerian and the City of a Thousand Planets*'. Available at: https://www.ilm.com/vfx/valerian-and-the-city-of-a-thousand-planets/ (Accessed 19 December 2023).

Ionkov, L. and Settlemyer, B. (2021) 'DNA: The Ultimate Data-Storage Solution', *Scientific American*. Available at: https://www.scientificamerican.com/article/dna-the-ultimate-data-storage-solution/ (Accessed 6 January 2023).

Jackson, E. (2021) 'Medieval Killer Rabbits: When Bunnies Strike Back', *British Library: Medieval Manuscripts Blog*. Available at: https://blogs.bl.uk/digitisedmanuscripts/2021/06/killer-rabbits.html (Accessed 21 August 2023).

Jackson, S. (2021) 'Haunted Objects in Women's Weird Fiction', *Horrified Magazine*. Available at: https://www.horrifiedmagazine.co.uk/other/haunted-objects-in-womens-weird-fiction/ (Accessed 18 July 2023).

James, M.R. (2015) 'Some Remarks on Ghost Stories'. [Essay first published in *The Bookman*, December 1929] Available at: https://www.berfrois.com/2015/10/m-r-james-on-ghost-stories/ (Accessed 18 June 2023)

Kamler, K., M.D. (2004) 'Prologue: In Extremis', *Surviving the Extremes: A Doctor's Journeys to the Limits of Human Endurance*. Sydney: Hachette. Available at: https://www.google.co.uk/books/edition/Surviving_the_Extremes/8OvD7W1qY4kC?hl=en&gbpv=1&pg=PT6&printsec=frontcover (Accessed 21 January 2024).

Keetly, D. (2021) 'Tentacular Ecohorror and the Agency of Trees in Algernon Blackwood's "The Man Whom the Trees Loved" and Lorcan Finnegan's *Without Name*'. in Tidwell, C., and Soles, C., *Fear and Nature: Ecohorror Studies in the Anthropocene*. University Park, PA: The Pennsylvania State University Press, pp.23–41.

Kelechava, B. (2016) 'The Shifting Magnetic North Pole', *American National Standards Institute*. Available at: https://blog.ansi.org/the-shifting-magnetic-north-pole/ (Accessed 2 February 2024).

Kenny, P. (2021) 'The Ossory Werewolves'. Available at: https://kilkennycastle.ie/the-ossory-werewolves/ (Accessed 17 January 2024),

Kershner, I. (dir.) (1993) 'To Be or Not to Be'. *SeaQuest DSV*.

Keulartz, J. and van den Belt, H. (2016) 'DIY-Bio—Economic, Epistemological and Ethical Implications and Ambivalences', *Life Science, Society, and Policy*, 12:7, pp. 1–19.

Kincaid, P. (2023) 'Semi-Playful Metaphors: An Interview with Christopher Priest', *Interzone*, #294 (January), pp. 135–136.

Klein, E. (2022) 'Transcript: Ezra Klein Interviews N.K. Jemisin', *New York Times*. Available at: https://www.nytimes.com/2022/10/18/podcasts/ezra-klein-interviews-nk-jemisin.html (Accessed 6 June 2023).

Langford, D. (2022) 'Uplift'. in Clute, J. and Langford, D. (eds.), *The Encyclopedia of Science Fiction*. Available at: https://sf-encyclopedia.com/entry/uplift (Accessed 12 December 2023).

Langford, D. and Nicholls, P. (2022) 'First Contact'. in Clute, J. and Langford, D. (eds.), *The Encyclopedia of Science Fiction*. Available at: https://sf-encyclopedia.com/entry/first_contact (Accessed 3 October 2023).

Lapointe, G. (2022) 'What Happened to the Own Voices Label?' Available at: https://bookriot.com/what-happened-to-the-own-voices-label/ (Accessed 31 January 2024).

Lawrence, C. (2015) '18th- and 19th-Century European Expeditions'. in Ward, M. and Wisnicki, A.S. (eds.), *Livingstone Online*. Available at: https://livingstoneonline.org/life-and-times/18th-and-19th-century-european-expeditions (Accessed 21 January 2024).

Lawrence, M.H. (1923) 'The Mask'. Available at: https://en.wikisource.org/wiki/Page:The_Mask.pdf/1 (Accessed 6 January 2024).

Le Guin, U.K. (1979) 'The Child and the Shadow' in Wood, S. (ed.), *The Language of the Night: Essays on Science Fiction and Fantasy*. New York: Perigee, pp. 59–71.

Le Guin, U. K. (1979) 'Is Gender Necessary?'. in Wood, S. (ed.), *The Language of the Night: Essays on Fantasy and Science Fiction*. New York: Perigee, pp. 161-69.

Le Guin, U.K. (1979) 'Myth and Archetype in Science Fiction.' in Wood, S. (ed.), The Language of the Night: Essays on Science Fiction and Fantasy. New York: Perigee, pp. 73–81.

Lindh, E. (2006) 'The Female Man', *Strange Words*. Available at: https://web.archive.org/web/20061230094404/http://www.strangewords.com/archive/female.html (Accessed 5 December 2023).

Liptak, A. (2014). 'The Biography of Christopher Plover from Lev Grossman's Magicians Books'. Available at: https://gizmodo.com/the-biography-of-christopher-plover-from-lev-grossmans-1617911172 (Accessed 24 January 2024).

Liptak, A. (2015) 'Happy 100th Birthday to Leigh Brackett, the Queen of Space Opera!', *io9*. Available at: https://gizmodo.com/happy-100th-birthday-to-leigh-brackett-the-queen-of-sp-1746714014 (Accessed 16 August 2023).

Lowenthal, D. (2007) 'Islands, Lovers, and Others', *Geographical Review*. 97:2 (April), pp. 202–229.

Luckhurst, R. (2014) 'The Victorian Supernatural', *British Library: Discovering Literature: Romantics & Victorians*. Available at: https://www.bl.uk/romantics-and-victorians/articles/the-victorian-supernatural (Accessed 13 February 2023).

Lynteris, C. (2019) *Human Extinction and the Pandemic Imaginary*. London. Routledge.

Mart, T.S., and Cabre, M. (2021) *A Guide to Sky Monsters: Thunderbirds, the Jersey Devil, Mothman, and Other Flying Cryptids*. Bloomington, Indiana: Red Lightning Books.

Masters, J. (No date) 'Women's Weird: Strange Stories by Women, 1890–1940. Edited by Melissa Edmunson', *Revenant Journal*. Available at: https://www.revenantjournal.com/contents/womens-weird-strange-stories-by-women-1890-1940-edited-by-melissa-edmundson/ (Accessed 7 January 2024).

McGeown, J. (2019) 'Elizabethan Sumptuary Laws: Fashion Policing in Shakespeare's England'. Available at: https://www.shakespearesglobe.com/discover/blogs-and-features/2019/04/16/elizabethan-sumptuary-laws-fashion-policing-in-shakespeares-england/ (Accessed 29 October 2023).

McKie, R. (2022) 'Lost City of Atlantis Rises Again to Fuel a Dangerous Myth', *The Guardian*. Available at: https://www.theguardian.com/science/2022/nov/27/atlantis-lost-civilisation-fake-news-netflix-ancient-apocalypse (Accessed 2 February 2024).

McQueen, S. (2016) Deleuze and Baudrillard: From Cyberpunk to Biopunk. Edinburgh: Edinburgh University Press.

Medievalists.net. (No date) 'Wild Animals and Medieval Towns'. Available at: https://www.medievalists.net/2018/04/wild-animals-and-medieval-towns/ (Accessed 21 August 2023).

Metsvahi, M. (2015). 'Estonian Werewolf History'. in de Blécourt, W. (ed.), Werewolf Histories. Available at: https://doi.org/10.1007/978-1-137-52634-2_9 (Accessed 19 January 2024).

Milner, A. (2022) 'Viral Science Fiction: Five Types of Pandemic Fiction', *Extrapolation*, 63:1, pp. 7–20.

Morgan, G. (2021) 'New Ways: The Pandemics of Science Fiction', *Interface Focus* 11. Available at: https://doi.org/10.1098/rsfs.2021.0027 (Accessed 11 January 2023).

Morrill, J.S. (2022) 'Matthew Hopkins', *Encyclopaedia Britannica*. Available at: https://www.britannica.com/biography/Matthew-Hopkins (Accessed 1 August 2023).

Morson, G.S. and Emerson, C. (1990) *Mikhail Bakhtin: Creation of a Prosaics*. Redwood City, CA: Stanford University Press.

Morton, T. (2013) *Hyperobjects: Philosophy and Ecology after the End of the World*. Minneapolis, University of Minnesota Press.

Murphy, B.M. (2013) *The Rural Gothic in American Popular Culture: Backwoods Horror and Terror in the Wilderness*. New York: Palgrave Macmillan.

Murphy, P.D. (2018) 'SF and Anthropocentric Climate Change', *Science Fiction Studies*, 45:3 (November), pp. 425–426.

Neal, M. (2014) 'Preparing for Extraterrestrial Contact', *Risk Management*, Vol. 16, No. 2 (May), pp. 63–87.

Newman, J. (2022) 'The 6 Most Notorious Cursed Diamonds'. Available at: https://www.naturaldiamonds.com/epic-diamonds/the-6-most-notorious-cursed-diamonds/ (Accessed 6 January 2024).

Nolan, V. (2020) 'Stargates, Galaxies, and Globalisation: Science Fiction in the Information Age', *Foundation: The International Review of Science Fiction*, #135 (February), pp. 42–56.

Nolan, V. (2021) 'Science Fiction and the Pathways out of the COVID Crisis', *The Polyphony*. Available at: https://thepolyphony.org/2021/05/07/science-fiction-and-the-pathways-out-of-the-covid-crisis/ (Accessed 13 January 2023).

Nolan, V. (2023) 'A New Persistent Cough: The Coronavirus, Hyperobjects, and the Pandemic Aesthetic', *Symplokē*, 31.1-2, pp. 339–362.

Ocker, J.W. (2020) *Cursed Objects: Strange but True Stories of the World's Most Infamous Items*, Quirk Books, Philadelphia.

Ogden, D. (2021) 'Four Things You (Probably) Don't Know about the Werewolves of the Ancient World', *History News Network*. Available at: https://historynewsnetwork.org/article/four-things-you-probably-dont-know-about-the-werew (Accessed 4 April 2024).

Online Etymology Dictionary. (No date) 'folk'. Available at: https://www.etymonline.com/search?q=folk (Accessed 3 July 2023).

Ostrander, M. (2022) 'The Era of Climate Change Has Created a New Emotion', *The Atlantic*. Available at: https://www.theatlantic.com/science/archive/2022/07/climate-change-damage-displacement-solastalgia/670614/ (Accessed 15 May 2023).

Otis, A.M. (2018) 'Alien Virus Love Disaster'. Available at: https://electricliterature.com/dan-chaon-recommends-a-story-about-a-town-infected-by-progress-abbey-mei-otis/ (Accessed 16 January 2023).

Parry, W. (2012) 'Blame Hitchcock's Crazed Birds on Toxic Algae', *LiveScience*. Available at: https://www.livescience.com/17713-hitchcock-birds-movie-algae-toxin.html (Accessed 20 August 2023).

Peter Harrington: London. (No date) 'Notes: *The Blue Fairy Book*'. Available at: https://www.peterharrington.co.uk/the-blue-fairy-book-132247.html (Accessed 16 January 2024).

PIERS (Paediatric Innovation, Education and Research Network). (No date). 'Automatonophobia'. Available at: https://www.piernetwork.org/automatonophobia.html (Accessed 7 January 2024).

Pilkington, C. (2023) 'Beware the Woods: An Introduction to Folk Horror'. Available at: https://blog.scienceandmediamuseum.org.uk/beware-the-woods-an-introduction-to-folk-horror/ (Accessed 18 July 2023).

Pinet, S. (2003) 'On the Subject of Fiction: Islands and the Emergence of the Novel', *Diacritics*, 33:3/4 Autumn–Winter), pp. 173–187.

Pohl, F. (1968) 'Editorial: The Great New Inventions', *Galaxy*, 27: 5 (December). p. 6.

Pordzik, R. (2011) 'The Poetry of Lastness: Reconsidering a Neglected Motif in Early Nineteenth-Century Literature', *Anglia*, 128: 3, pp. 406–430.

Postrel, V. (2020) *The Fabric of Civilization: How Textiles Made the World*. New York: Basic Books.

Pournell, J. and Niven, L. (1976). 'A Step Farther Out: Building *The Mote in God's Eye*'. *Galaxy*, 37:01 (January), pp. 92–113. Available at: https://archive.org/details/Galaxy_v37n01_1976-01/mode/2up (Accessed 9 May 2024).

Pringle, D. (2000) 'What is this Thing Called Space Opera?'. in Westfahl, G. (ed.), *Space and Beyond: The Frontier Theme in Science Fiction*. Westport, CT: Greenwood Press. pp. 35–38.

Pruitt, S. (2023) 'What Are the Four Waves of Feminism?' Available at: https://www.history.com/news/feminism-four-waves (Accessed 25 November 2023).

Purdue, M. (No date) 'Clemence Houseman's *The Were-Wolf*: A Cautionary Tale for the Progressive New Woman'. Available at: https://www.revenantjournal.com/contents/clemence-housmans-the-were-wolf-a-cautionary-tale-for-the-progressive-new-woman/ (Accessed 19 January 2024).

Reynolds, A. (2012) 'Space Opera: This Galaxy Ain't Big Enough for the Both of Us'. in Brooke, K. (ed.), *Strange Divisions and Alien Territories: The Sub-Genres of Science Fiction*. London: Palgrave, pp. 12–25.

Rieder, J. (2015) 'American Frontiers'. in Link, E.C. and Canavan, G. (eds.), *The Cambridge Companion to American Science Fiction*. Cambridge: Cambridge University Press, pp. 167–178.

Rithdee, K. (2021) 'Into the Devil's Lair', *Bangkok Post*. Available at: https://www.bangkokpost.com/life/arts-and-entertainment/2210099/into-the-devils-lair (Accessed 1 August 2023).

Roberts, A. (2005) *Palgrave History of Science Fiction*. London: Palgrave.

Roberts, A. (2010) 'The Windup Girl by Paolo Bacigalupi—review', *The Guardian*. Available at: https://www.theguardian.com/books/2010/dec/18/windup-girl-paolo-bacigalupi-review (Accessed 23 May 2023).

Roberts, A. (2020) 'Fever Dreams: Did Author Dean Koontz Really Predict Coronavirus?', *The Guardian*. Available at: https://www.theguardian.com/books/2020/mar/05/theres-something-out-there-spread-of-disease (Accessed 3 February 2024).

Robins, D. (2021) 'The Battersea Poltergeist, *BBC*. Available at: https://www.bbc.co.uk/programmes/articles/4b8PlyxgjRft0T7b0Sjjj3B/the-story-of-the-battersea-poltergeist (Accessed 10 July 2023).

Romaine, S. (1999) *Communicating Gender*. Mahwah, NJ: Lawrence Erlbaum Associates.

Room, A. (ed.) (2001) 'Werewolf', *Brewer's Dictionary of Phrase & Fable*. London: Cassell & Co.

Rose, C. (2001) *Giants, Monsters, and Dragons: An Encyclopedia of Folklore, Legend, and Myth*. New York: W.W. Norton & Company.

Rose, N. (2007) *The Politics of Life Itself: Biomedicine, Power, and Subjectivity in the Twenty-First Century*. Princeton: Princeton University Press.

Rosens, C.M. (2020) 'Werewolf Films: 1910-1949'. Available at: https://cmrosens.com/2020/03/23/werewolf-films-1910-1950/ (Accessed 19 January 2024).

Roy-Faderman. I. (2015) 'The Alienation of Humans and Animals in Uplift Fiction', *Midwest Studies in Philosophy*, XXXIX. pp. 78–97.

Rust, S.A. and Soles, C. (2014) 'Ecohorror Special Cluster: "Living in Fear, Living in Dread, Pretty Soon We'll All Be Dead"', *Interdisciplinary Studies in Literature and Environment*, Vol.21, No. 3 (Summer), pp. 509–512.

Ryfle, S. (2005) 'Godzilla's Footprint', *Virginia Quarterly Review*, 81:1 (Winter), pp. 44–68.

Saint-Lot, M-J. A. *Vodou, a Sacred Theatre: The African Heritage in Haiti*. Pompano Beach, Florida: Educa Vision.

Sautman, B. (1977) 'Myths of Descent, Racial Nationalism and Ethnic Minorities in the People's Republic of China'. in Dikötter, F. (ed.), *The Construction of Racial Identities in China and Japan*. Hong Kong: Hong Kong University Press, pp. 76–77.

Sawyer, A. (2009) 'Space Opera'. in Bould, M., Roberts, A. and Vint, S. (eds.), *The Routledge companion to Science Fiction*. New York: Routledge, pp. 505–509.

Schmeink, L. (2016) *Biopunk Dystopias Genetic Engineering, Society, and Science Fiction*. Liverpool: Liverpool University Press.

Science (1928) 20 April Supplement, p. xiv/2.

Sconduto, L.A. (2008) *The Metamorphoses of the Werewolf: A Literary Study from Antiquity Through the Renaissance*. Jefferson, N.C.: McFarland & Company.

Scovell, A. (2017) *Folk Horror: Hours Dreadful and Things Strange*. Leighton Buzzard: Auteur Publishing.

Seidel, M.J. (2022) 'The First Climate Fiction Masterpiece: On John Wyndham's 1953 Novel *The Kraken Wakes'*, *Los Angles Review of Books*. Available at: https://lareviewofbooks.org/article/the-first-climate-fiction-masterpiece-on-john-wyndhams-1953-novel-the-kraken-wakes/ (Accessed 19 May 2023).

Sera-Shriar, E. (2022) 'Introduction', *Psychic Investigators: Anthropology, Modern Spiritualism, and Credible Witnessing in the Late Victorian Age*. Pittsburgh: University of Pittsburgh Press.

Sergeant, D. (2023) *The Near Future in 21st Century Fiction: Climate, Retreat and Revolution*. Cambridge: Cambridge University Press.

SFX. (2013) 'James Lovegrove Interview.' Available at: https://www.gamesradar.com/james-lovegrove-interview/ (Accessed 31 January 2024).

Shakespeare, W. (No date) *A Midsummer Night's Dream*, Act III, Scene 2. Folger Shakespeare Library. Available at: https://www.folger.edu/explore/shakespeares-works/a-midsummer-nights-dream/read/ (Accessed 30 November 2023).

Sikes, W. (1880) *British Goblins: Welsh Folk-lore, Fairy Mythology, Legends and Traditions*. Project Gutenberg. Available at: https://www.gutenberg.org/files/34704/34704-h/34704-h.htm (Accessed 10 December 2023).

Simons, M. (2021) 'A Philosophy of First Contact: Stanisław Lem and The Myth of Cognitive Universality', *Pro-Fil*. pp. 65–77.

Smith, L.G. (2019) *The Vine Witch*. Seattle: 47 North.

Smits, M. (No date) '*The Beauty* by Aliya Whiteley', *Shoreline of Infinity*. Available at: https://www.shorelineofinfinity.com/beauty-aliya-whiteley/ (Accessed 5 December 2023).

Soles, C. (2014) '"And No Birds Sing": Discourses of Environmental Apocalypse in *The Birds* and *Night of the Living Dead*', *ISLE: Interdisciplinary Studies in Literature and Environment*, 21: 3 (Summer), pp. 526–37.

Stueber, K. (2019) 'Empathy'. in Zalta, E.N. (ed.), *The Stanford Encyclopedia of Philosophy*. Available at: https://plato.stanford.edu/archives/fall2019/entries/empathy/ (Accessed 14 August 2023).

Su, M. (2020) 'St. Patrick and the Ossory Werewolves'. Available at: https://www.medievalists.net/2020/03/st-patrick-ossory-werewolves/ (Accessed 19 January 2024).

Suvin, D. (1972). 'On the Poetics of the Science Fiction Genre', *College English*, 34:3 (Dec., 1972), pp. 372-382.

Taylor, D. (2020) 'Strange Shakespeare: Macbeth and the Even Weirder Sisters', *Folger Shakespeare Library*. Available at: https://www.folger.edu/blogs/shakespeare-and-beyond/strange-shakespeare-macbeth-witches-even-weirder-sisters/ (Accessed 27 January 2024).

Temme, J.D.H. (1840) 'The Werewolves in Greifswald', *Die Volkssagen von Pommern und Rügen* (*The folk legends of Pomerania and Rügen*). Berlin: In der Nicolaischen Buchhandlung, no. 259, p. 308. Available at: https://sites.pitt.edu/~dash/werewolf.html#temmezarnow (Accessed 19 January 2024).

Teorey, M. (2019) 'Do You See It Too? Relationality in Pacific Northwest Sea Serpent Lore', *Mosaic: An Interdisciplinary Critical Journal*, Vol. 52, No. 4 (December), pp. 127–148.

Thurston, J.W. (2019) 'The Face of the Beast', *Human Ecology Review*, Vol. 25, No. 2, pp. 35–48.

Tidwell, C. and Soles, C. (2021) *Fear and Nature: Ecohorror Studies in the Anthropocene.* University Park, PA: The Pennsylvania State University Press.

Tolkien, J.R.R. (1936) 'Beowulf: The Monsters and the Critics', *Proceedings of the British Academy*, 22, pp. 245–295.

Tolkien, J.R.R. (1964) 'Letter to Christopher Bretherton, a Reader'. Available at: https://www.tolkienestate.com/letters/letter-to-christopher-bretherton-a-reader-16-july-1964/ (Accessed 05 September 2023).

Tolkien, J.R.R. (2008) 'On Fairy-Stories'. in Flieger, V. and Anderson, D.A. (eds.) *Tolkien on Fairy-Stories: Expanded Edition*. London: Harper Collins. pp. 27–84.

Tolkien, J.R.R. (2013a) 'Letter 154: To Naomi Mitchison 25 September 1954', in Humphrey Carpenter and Christopher Tolkien, eds. *The Letters of JRR Tolkien* (New York: Houghton Mifflin Harcourt, 2013), p. 212.

Tolkien, J.R.R. (2013b) 'Letter 227: From a letter to Mrs E. C. Ossen Drijver 5 January 1961'. in Carpenter, H. and Tolkien, C. (eds.), *The Letters of JRR Tolkien*. New York: Houghton Mifflin Harcourt, p. 322.

Trexler, A. (2013) *Anthropocene Fictions: The Novel in the Time of Climate Change.* Charlottesville: University of Virginia Pres.

Tucker, B. (9 Jan 1941) *Le Zombie* (fanzine).

TVTropes.org. (No date) 'Gendercide'. Available at: https://tvtropes.org/pmwiki/pmwiki.php/Main/Gendercide (Accessed 25 November 2023).

Vakoch, D.A. (ed.) (2012) *Psychology of Space Exploration: Contemporary Research in Historical Perspective*. Washington, DC: U.S. Government Printing Office.

Villiers, M. (2014) 'Carrying Death Away: Social Responsibility, the Environment and Comedy in Terry Pratchett's *Johnny and the Dead*', *English Academy Review*, 31, pp. 77–86.

Von Schlegell, M. (2016) 'High Peeks, Mysterious Islands', *The White Review*. Available at: https://www.thewhitereview.org/white_screen/high-peeks-mysterious-islands/ (Accessed 11 September 2023).

Voon, V. (2016) 'Why Danger is Exciting—but Only to Some People'. Available at: https://theconversation.com/why-danger-is-exciting-but-only-to-some-people-64680 (Accessed 21 January 2024).

Wall, J.E. (1983) *ISC Newsletter* (International Society Cryptozool), 10:3 (Summer).

Warner, M. (1995) 'Inside the Big Mind: Umberto Eco's Dazzling Blend of Science and Fantasy Comes Perilously Close to Pedagogy', *Los Angeles Times*. Available at: https://www.latimes.com/archives/la-xpm-1995-12-17-bk-14850-story.html (Accessed 9 September 2023).

White, E. (2016) 'In the Joints of Their Toes', *The Paris Review*. Available at: https://www.theparisreview.org/blog/2016/11/04/in-the-joints-of-their-toes/ (Accessed 15 February

2023).

Whitehead, C. (2011) *Zone One*. New York: Doubleday.

Whittet Thomson, D. (1942) 'Robert Fulton and *The Nautilus*', *Proceedings*, Vol. 68:10 (October). Available at: https://www.usni.org/magazines/proceedings/1942/october/robert-fulton-and-nautilus (Accessed 1 February 2024).

Whyte, N. (2020) '"Houston, Houston, Do You Read?" And *The Bicentennial Man*', *From the Heart of Europe*. Available at: https://nwhyte.livejournal.com/3443946.html (Accessed 7 December 2023).

Wildenberg, T. (2022) 'History's First Torpedo Strike', *Naval History Magazine*. Available at: https://www.usni.org/magazines/naval-history-magazine/2022/december/historys-first-torpedo-strike (Accessed 1 February 2024).

Wood, R. (1986) *Hollywood from Vietnam to Reagan*. New York: Columbia University Press.

Woodbury, M. (2023) 'Distinguishing Genres About Climate and Ecological Changes', *Dragonfly*. Available at: https://dragonfly.eco/distinguishing-genres-about-climate-and-ecological-changes/ (Accessed 19 May 2023).

Wright, P. (2009) 'Film and Television: 1960-1980'. in Bould, M., Roberts, A. and Vint, S. (eds.), *The Routledge Companion to Science Fiction*. New York: Routledge, pp. 90–101.

Xu, C.X. (2015) 'Science or Science Fiction? Uplifting Animals', *Yale Scientific*. Available at: https://www.yalescientific.org/2015/05/science-or-science-fiction-uplifting-animals/ (Accessed 8 December 2023).

Yaszek, L.(2009) 'Cultural History'. in Bould, M., Roberts, A. and Vint, S. (eds.), *The Routledge Companion to Science Fiction*. New York: Routledge, pp. 194–203.

Yeats, W.B. (2015) 'Irish Faries', [from 1890] Reprinted in *The Irish Times*. Available at: https://www.irishtimes.com/culture/books/wb-yeats-on-fairies-at-howth-a-great-colony-of-otherworld-creatures-travel-nightly-1.2263062> (Accessed 18 January 2024).

Young, J. (2008) 'Interview: Terry Pratchett on the Origins of Discworld, his Order of the British Empire and Everything in Between', *Scifi.com.* [archived from the original on 15 January 2008] Available at: https://web.archive.org/web/20080115061550/http://www.scifi.com/sfw/issue449/interview.html (Accessed 27 January 2024).

Zak Bagan's The Haunted Museum (2020) 'Why are guests required to sign a waiver before entering?' FAQ: General. Available at: https://thehauntedmuseum.com/faq/ (Accessed 6 January 2024).

Živković, Z. (2018) *First Contact and Time Travel: Selected Essays and Short Stories*. New York: Springer.

AUTHORS' BIOGRAPHIES

Tiffani Angus holds a PhD in creative writing and spent over a decade teaching writing and publishing at universities in the US and UK with a special emphasis on SFF/H writing. She is the co-author of *Spec Fic for Newbies* Volume 1 (Luna Press Publishing, 2023). Her debut novel, *Threading the Labyrinth*, was a finalist for the British Science Fiction Association and British Fantasy Society awards for Best Novel. A Clarion 2009 graduate, she's published Fantasy, Science Fiction, Horror, and even erotica short stories in a variety of anthologies and writes 'Subgenre Deep Dive' guest columns for the British Fantasy Society. Currently a freelance writer, editor, and proofreader, she lives in Bury St Edmunds with her partner. You can find her at www.tiffani-angus.com.

Val Nolan is a Science Fiction author and academic who holds a PhD in contemporary literature and has taught university level literature and creative practice for fifteen years. He is the author of *Neil Jordan: Works for the Page* (UCC Press, 2022) and co-author of *Spec Fic for Newbies* Volume 1 (Luna Press Publishing, 2023). He is also the author of academic articles in *Science Fiction Studies, Foundation, Journal of Graphic Novels and Comic Books, Irish University Review, Irish Studies Review, symplokē*, and *Dictionary of Literary Biography*. A Clarion graduate (2009), his fiction has appeared in *Year's Best Science Fiction, Best of British Science Fiction, Unidentified Funny Objects, Opulent Syntax*, the 'Futures' page of *Nature, Andromeda Spaceways*, and *Interzone* (for which he also writes the 'Folded Spaces' column about the history of Science Fiction criticism). He has been shortlisted for the Theodore Sturgeon Award (for his story 'The Irish Astronaut') and twice been a finalist for the BSFA Awards. He is currently a research fellow at Aberystwyth University in Wales where he was awarded Lecturer of the Year in 2022.

www.ingramcontent.com/pod-product-compliance
Lightning Source LLC
Chambersburg PA
CBHW070650120526
44590CB00013BA/895